DATE DUE			
Dec 18 '74			
Feb 25 '75			
Mar 11 '75			
Nov 8 79			

THE FALL OF
YUGOSLAVIA

ILIJA JUKIĆ
THE FALL OF YUGOSLAVIA

Translated by Dorian Cooke

HARCOURT BRACE JOVANOVICH

NEW YORK AND LONDON

940.53497

J93f

90901

nov.1974

Printed in the United States of America

Library of Congress Cataloging in Publication Data

Jukić, Ilija, 1901–
The fall of Yugoslavia.

1. World War, 1939–1945—Yugoslavia. 2. Yugoslavia
—Foreign relations—1918–1945. 3. World War, 1939–
1945—Diplomatic history. I. Title.
D754.Y9J8413   940.53'497   73–16431
ISBN 0–15–130100–X

First edition
B C D E

THE FALL OF
YUGOSLAVIA

INTRODUCTION

The appalling conditions throughout Yugoslavia following Hitler's blitzkrieg in 1941 froze the blood of all who lived there, and of their friends and foes as well. There was a general feeling that hell had been let loose, and that any return to normal standards was impossible. It was as though the Four Horsemen of the Apocalypse had swept through the land, sowing the seeds of strife, carnage, death, famine, and pestilence.

Under the full fury of their afflictions, the people of Yugoslavia began to call to mind another prophecy, one peculiar to themselves and their country. Before the war, it had been possible for people to speak of it only in whispers, because it foreshadowed the doom of their government leaders as well as their own doom. A complete version appeared in print for the first time during the war, when it was the subject of great public interest and there were no obstacles to its being published. It was known as the Kremna prophecy, and it was made in the last century by Mato, a clairvoyant who lived in Kremna, a little village near Užice, in western Serbia.

On June 11, 1868, the day Prince Michael of Serbia was assassinated, Mato of Kremna went to the weekly market in Užice. About midday, he suddenly became very agitated. He started to run, faster and faster, shouting to all in the market place that he had seen a vision of four men killing Prince Michael, that he could see them fleeing in different directions. The local police were quick to take him into custody. Three hours later, news came that the Prince had been assassinated in an ambush in Košutnjak Park, near his palace outside Belgrade. The question was: How could Mato of Kremna have known about the murder at the very instant that it was taking place? This has remained a mystery to the present day.

In a calm manner, Mato of Kremna then told the police interrogators about his vision of the future of the Serbian people from that day to the end of World War II. Mato declared that Serbia would one day become a kingdom, that the king of the ruling dynasty would be murdered, and that another dynasty would succeed to the throne. He prophesied further that Serbia would be involved in a great war from which she would emerge victorious and unite with other territories to become a new, large state. He foretold the violent death of one of the rulers of the new country and said that his successor would not remain long on the throne.

Those familiar with the history of Serbia will have no difficulty in unraveling the threads of this prophecy: the gruesome fate of King Alexander Obrenović, assassinated early in the morning on June 11, 1903; World War I; the murder of King Alexander Karadjordjević in Marseilles on October 9, 1934; the short reign of Peter II.

In March, 1941, when Yugoslavia was in a precarious position and being subjected to the rival pressures of Germany and Britain, Prince Paul, the regent, had a conversation with the vice-premier, Vladko Maček, under whom I worked at that time. He seemed resigned to the situation. "There's nothing to be done about it," he said. "Things are going to be bad for us in this war. That's what the Kremna prophecy said." Maček had never heard of the prophecy, and he asked me about it. At the end of my story, I made a special point of mentioning that the prophecy also foresaw that after the war Yugoslavia would be re-established, larger than before and with "a man of the people" in the seat of power.

The most interesting part of the prophecy is the part dealing with the frightful conditions in Yugoslavia during World War II. The horrors throughout the land, it said, would be such that the living would "envy the dead" and would visit the graves of their dear ones, lamenting that they were not there beside them and thus free from the ghastly torments of their lives. This particular part of the prophecy gave a striking description of these hardships, foretelling the horrible massacres of the innocent

4

Serbian population in Croatia by the Ustashi, the Croatian disciples of racist Nazism, and the Chetnik slaughter of innocent Croats. The Communist Partisans conducted an internecine war against the Ustashi, and later against the Chetniks as well. Their attacks on German and Italian occupation troops and their acts of sabotage resulted in punitive expeditions and bestial reprisals, the burning down of houses and villages and the shooting of hostages, often a thousand or more in a single operation. Of all people, the civilian population suffered most in this hell. People perished in huge numbers. Some were hanged; some were shot; some had their throats cut; some were thrown alive into pits or over precipices; some were tortured and mutilated in jails and camps; some were crushed to death by tanks; some were burned alive. The list of ways is endless. General Glaise-Horstenau, German army representative in Croatia, wrote to a friend in 1943: "For some time now the railways in Slavonia have been decorated with men hanging from posts along the track." The tragic fate of refugees from the battle areas moved even the stony heart of Gestapo head Heinrich Himmler's representative; in January, 1944, he wrote to Himmler telling him that during recent battles some 230,000 men, women, and children had fled from Bosnia: "No words can describe all the tragedies taking place among this great multitude of people." Even the great Dante would have been incapable of describing all the horrors and atrocities that afflicted the unhappy people of Yugoslavia during the last war.

There are many passages in the war diary of Vladimir Dedijer that describe these terrible events and the reactions of people who had survived them or witnessed them. They could be extracts from the prophecy of Mato of Kremna. One such, which he reprinted in his memoirs, *The Beloved Land,* records Milovan Djilas's shattering impressions of a massacre that he discovered in July, 1942, in the western Bosnian village of Urija: "First, beside the road, under the broad branches of a huge pear tree, I came upon two peasants. . . . They had been shot in the back of the head. . . . Nearby were six more peasants, murdered. . . . We went on our way a little distance . . . and suddenly, in the middle of the road . . . ten or twelve corpses. I think there were two middle-aged men—the remainder were women, girls, chil-

5

dren, babies. Three or four paces from this heap of blood and flesh, was an empty cradle . . . the child was lying in the heap of corpses, but its head was completely smashed. . . . The remaining corpses too were disfigured. . . . Among them were two mothers with their infants. . . . I entered a house. . . . In one room were two dead sons and an old woman . . . dead. . . . In another house . . . beside the hearth a peasant woman, her throat cut. . . . Thus, house after house. There had been no living to bury the dead. . . . In all truth, there is one thing only in my brain and my heart, in my whole being, and no doubt in all of us: life is not worth living in this world while there are men who commit such inhumanities. There is no other solution: we, or they. . . ."

On January 30, 1943, Dedijer made this diary entry: "We found a long procession of refugees . . . barefoot, hungry, ill-clad. . . . One woman—middle-aged—with four small children, comes along . . . all barefoot, ragged; the mother's bare belly shows through her rags. She goes up to some of our men. 'Brother,' she says, 'put an end to these children's misery, kill them. I have not the strength to do it.' Two men take off their own shirts and clothe the little ones . . . give the last scraps of their food. . . . Where are these 40,000 souls to go? Liberated territory is not unlimited, and starvation is ravaging."

The following month he wrote describing how one night he came to a house and, on entering, heard the sound of a death rattle. He found a mother throttling her own child. "She was sickened with it all. Whine, whine, the child begging for food. She was weary and hungry, her back breaking from carrying the youngest, her arms dropping off from pulling the other two along. If I had arrived on the scene a moment later, there would have been a corpse for us to find in the morning. She meant what she said when I met her on the road this evening: 'Death would be a blessing to us. . . .' The mind boggles. The heart stops, petrified. Has anyone ever suffered so much as our people are suffering?"

In *Closing the Ring*, Winston Churchill called the ghastly state of affairs in Yugoslavia "a tragedy within a tragedy." The truth is that it was far, far more complex than that. One tragedy was the occupation of Yugoslavia—the punitive expeditions and

6

bloody reprisals of the occupation forces. A second tragedy was to be found in the Ustashi massacres of the Serbian population and their battles against the Chetniks, which were followed by Chetnik reprisals against Croats. A third tragedy was the internecine conflict between the Ustashi and the Communists. A fourth was the conflict between the Communists and the Chetniks and other anti-Communist military units relying on the German and Italian armies for support. All these tragedies combined to create one immeasurable tragedy, surely one of the greatest within a nation in modern history. The extent of this tragedy can best be gauged from certain statistics submitted to the 1948 Inter-Allied Reparations Conference in Paris by eighteen of the warring nations. According to these statistics, Yugoslav casualties amounted to 1,706,000 dead—11 per cent of her population— and 425,000 disabled; 1,610,000 citizens had endured prison, concentration camp, or slavery; there were 525,000 orphaned children. The number of Yugoslav casualties was one-third the total number for all the other Allies with the exception of the Soviet Union. The proportion of disabled Yugoslavs in relation to the population was eleven times the average proportion for the other Allied countries.

From this, two cardinal questions impose themselves: How did a tragedy of such magnitude come about? Could Yugoslavia have averted it? These are questions that have tormented me from the beginning until the present day. From a position of considerable importance in the Yugoslav government, first in Belgrade and later in exile in London, I was able to witness the tragedy's origins and keep abreast of its development. During and after the war, I questioned a host of people who had survived it or had knowledge of it through their official duties. I read nearly everything that appeared in print about it during and after the war. This book is the result of my researches and endeavors.

I have read many discourses on the nature of history and how political events, armed conflicts, and the catastrophes of war in the development of the human race should be interpreted. Of all the ideas I have come across, two in particular appeal to me. The first was enunciated by Lord Brand: "Error is still a greater evil in human affairs than sheer badness . . . it is the greatest curse on the human race." The other comes from Hugh Trevor-Roper:

"Nothing in history is inevitable: the doctrine of inevitability is simply an easy device whereby historians avoid the responsibility of historical thought."

I shall take due regard of both of these maxims. They will serve as the warp and woof of my book.

CHAPTER 1

A brief glimpse into the history of the people of Yugoslavia is essential for a clear understanding of the tragedy that befell them in World War II.

The fall of the Austro-Hungarian monarchy had led, by the end of 1918, to the formal establishment of the Kingdom of the Serbs, Croats, and Slovenes, a name changed in September, 1931, to Yugoslavia. This was a unification of the Kingdom of Serbia, which had included Macedonia since 1912, with all the provinces of southern Austria-Hungary inhabited by Slovenes, Croats, and Serbs. At the same time, the Kingdom of Montenegro was incorporated into the new state. Croatia and Montenegro were not enthusiastic about this development, feeling that they were losing their previous national status.

Croatia had been an independent kingdom from the early ninth century until 1102, when she united with Hungary to frustrate persistent assaults from Venice on the Adriatic coast. Later, under the Habsburgs, Croatia and Hungary fought to ward off penetrations by the Ottoman Empire and to recapture areas conquered by the Turks between the fifteenth and seventeenth centuries.

The Ottoman thrust through Serbia and into the heart of Croatia and Hungary left deep furrows. One portion of the Serbian population was driven northward and settled in areas captured from Croatia and Hungary by the Turks, leaving certain lands in the south to the Albanians and to Turkish settlers. Croats, too, were driven northward. As Catholics, they were regarded as enemies of the Ottoman Empire and were subjected to brutal persecution. The new Moslem masters installed

9

Orthodox Serbs in the abandoned homes of fugitive Catholics in Bosnia and Herzegovina and in the conquered areas of Croatia, which explains the extraordinary religious and ethnic mixture in the population of Bosnia-Herzegovina and in the parts of Croatia that came under Turkish rule. As the Christian armies under Habsburg leadership drove the Turks out in the seventeenth and eighteenth centuries, new population migrations took place.

Some of the Catholic and Orthodox peoples (particularly the members of the Patarine sect then living in Bosnia and Herzegovina) had embraced Islam during the long period of Ottoman rule, and some of the Catholic population had gone over to the Orthodox church. The differences between Christians of the Western and Eastern rites in these regions in this period were not acute because both were persecuted by Islam, but these differences became more severe with the revival of nationalism in Europe in the nineteenth century.

Croatian nationalism had envisaged a state including Bosnia and Herzegovina, Dalmatia, Istria, and part of Vojvodina, with the capital at Zagreb. Serbia, with her capital at Belgrade, had aspired to acquire Bosnia and Herzegovina, part of Dalmatia, Vojvodina, and part of Croatia, on the grounds that a considerable number of Serbs lived in these areas. Bitter disputes raged between extremists on both sides. But there were also moderate elements who argued that the opposing aspirations could best be reconciled by a union of all Croats and Serbs in a single state. Their artless optimism prevented them, however, from taking into account the differences in the religious, cultural, and political background of these peoples. The ruling classes in Austria-Hungary did everything in their power to inflame antagonisms and hatred between Croats and Serbs, to make the task of keeping them under control easier.

Had the Serbo-Croatian union been founded on a federal basis at the beginning, rather than on a crude centralism, many of the upheavals between 1919 and 1939 would have been avoided. A Yugoslav federal system would also have satisfied the aspirations of the Montenegrins and of the Bosnian-Herzegovinian Moslems. Moreover, such a system would have been particularly suitable for the Slovenes, the most advanced nation in Yugoslavia. Their independent state, dating back to the seventh century, had succumbed to German expansionism in early times. The most eloquent testimony to their cohesiveness and national vitality is to be found in the fact that they preserved their identity for thirteen centuries in fighting against the pressures of the powerful German world. It was a heavy blow for them when, in 1919, a quarter of their population was thrust under Italian rule. And it was an equally heavy blow for the Croats when Italy took over Istria, Rijeka, Zadar, and some of the islands along the Croatian Adriatic coast.

The Macedonians, too, would have welcomed a federalist system. Though the majority are of the Orthodox faith, they are of exceedingly diverse ethnic origins. In addition, they have suffered as the Serbs and the Bulgarians fought two wars in this century, each to insure its own dominance over the population.

At the time of its establishment, the Kingdom of Yugoslavia had a population of about 12 million. This figure included 4,800,000 Serbs; 3,200,000 Croats; 1,100,000 Slovenes; 850,000 Slav Moslems; 500,000 Macedonians; 500,000 Albanians; 376,000 Hungarians; 316,000 Germans; 120,000 Turks; 120,000 Rumanians and Aromani (descendants of ancient Roman colonists); 20,000 Italians; and 150,000 people of other ethnic origins. In terms of religion, the population was divided approximately as follows: 46 per cent Orthodox, 39 per cent Catholic, 12 per cent Moslem, 2.3 per cent Protestant, .7 per cent Jewish. Of the total population, approximately 10,500,000 were Slavs and 1,600,000 non-Slavs.

The elections for the first Constituent Assembly, which took place on November 28, 1920, revealed the patchwork composition of the kingdom. More serious aspects were also revealed: the closing of Croatia's nationalist ranks against Belgrade's centralist plans, and the large number of votes polled by Communist party candidates. Stjepan Radić, the popular leader of the Croatian Peasant party, received three-quarters of the Croatian vote. The Communists gained an enormous number of votes in Montenegro and Macedonia, and in the former two party members who supported federalism were elected. Supporters of federalism won a majority in Slovenia, also; and the Moslems were federalists almost to a man.

The Croats elected sixteen representatives who, like Radić, sought the establishment of the new state on federal lines. They went to Belgrade, though without Radić, to try to get their program moving in the Constituent Assembly. There, however, the main Serbian parties, with the help of a few Croatian and some Slovenian deputies, voted for a strongly centralist constitution. The Croatian federalists then withdrew, and a boycott of Belgrade by 85 per cent of the Croats brought the Croatian question into the full light of day.

Radić, who at each election increased his vote, finally went to Belgrade to attempt to get the constitution changed to meet some of the demands of his people. There he ran into the obstacle of King Alexander's secret plans to proclaim himself dictator. On June 20, 1928, during a debate in the Assembly, Radić was shot; he died forty-nine days later. The other deputies from his party immediately boycotted this "Bloody Assembly." Thereupon, instead of dissolving the Assembly and announcing new elections, Alexander proclaimed a dictatorial regime.

This caused some of the young people in Croatia who had been brought up in the radical tradition of Croatian nationalism to seek different methods of fighting Serb hegemony. Their leader was Ante Pavelić, who, in 1927, had been elected deputy for the city of Zagreb. Ten days after Alexander's proclamation, he fled the country, first to Vienna, then to Sofia, where he entered into an alliance with Ivan Mihajlov, the leader of the Macedonian revolutionary organization in Bulgaria, to plot the downfall of Yugoslavia and the assassination of the King. He next went to Italy, where he enjoyed Mussolini's hospitality until the collapse of Yugoslavia.

Alexander dominated both domestic and foreign policy from the formation of the Yugoslav state. Shortly before his death, in 1934, he freely admitted to his intimate friends that he had made a mistake in proclaiming a dictatorship and that he would shed this burden upon his return from a state visit to France. He sent word to Vladko Maček, Radić's successor, who was in prison, that he would be released as soon as he got home from France, in order that they might try to reach a settlement of the Croatian question.

The reason for this radical change in policy can be found in the sphere of foreign affairs. Alexander was well aware that his young kingdom would be in mortal danger if Mussolini created a hostile bloc made up of Austria, Hungary, Bulgaria, and Albania. To avoid such a political encirclement, he and his premier, Nikola Pašić, decided to seek friendship with Mussolini. They even refused alliance with France to insure the Italian's signature on the Italo-Yugoslav Friendship Pact. Alexander, who hoped to dominate the Balkans, was also prepared to sign a military treaty with Italy as a safeguard against German expansion, for, with a German-Austrian *Anschluss*, Germany would be a next-door neighbor.

The King's policy was doomed to failure, however, because Mussolini's plans for Yugoslavia were quite different. First, the Italian leader signed a treaty in 1926 with Albania and turned that country against Yugoslavia. Next he lured Austria and Hungary to his side. These moves caused Alexander to sign a friendship pact with France on November 11, 1927. In response, Mussolini stepped up subversive activities in areas where Yugoslavia was weakest.

Fully aware of these dangers, Alexander secretly entered into negotiations with Mussolini in an attempt to get him to change his policy. These talks went on for two years—1930–1932—but to no purpose. During this time, Mussolini urged Pavelić and his followers, known as Ustashi (insurgents), to step up their sabotage in Yugoslavia. He also persuaded the Hungarians to permit Ustashi activities from their territory. Alexander's response was twofold: he strengthened his ties with Czechoslovakia, which provided some support for the defense of his eastern flank against Hungary, and he established a Balkan alliance for protection in case of war with Italy and Bulgaria.

On December 16, 1933, King Alexander went to Zagreb to celebrate his forty-fifth birthday. Pavelić dispatched an assassin from Italy. This man, Petar Oreb, could not bring himself to act because of the crowds of children lining the King's route. He decided to make an attempt on the following day, when Alexander was due to attend a solemn mass in the Catholic cathedral, but he was arrested early that morning. The realization that he was in deadly peril made an overwhelming impression on the King; he cut his visit short, went to his palace at Lake Bled, in Slovenia, and wrote his will, naming his nephew Prince Paul first regent should anything happen to him before his son Peter came of age.

Alexander's resentment against Mussolini now reached boiling point. He held him responsible for the dispatch of the terrorist to Zagreb and was determined to get revenge. He was convinced that, given the right conditions, the Yugoslav army was capable of defeating the Italian army. Great Britain's envoy extraordinary in Belgrade, Nevile Henderson, who was in the King's close confidence, has told in his memoirs how eager Alexander was to show him his military plans for this operation. Having learned of Mussolini's preparations for the conquest of Ethiopia, the King hoped to take him unawares, when the main body of his troops had been sent overseas. A vital prerequisite for the success of this venture was an agreement with Maček and an assurance of solidarity between Croats and Serbs.

Germany, too, was a factor not neglected. Hitler was anxious to exploit the tense relations between Alexander and Mussolini in his bid to incorporate Austria into the German Reich, which Mussolini bitterly opposed. He made it known that he was willing to conclude an agreement with the King, and even to allow Yugoslavia to unite with Bulgaria. When I was in Sofia in mid-June, 1939, I was told that if Maček came to terms with the Serbs on behalf of Croatia, the Bulgarians would enter the Yugoslav federation thus formed. The real basis for agreement between Alexander and Hitler was their common interest both in preventing the return of the Habsburgs to Austria and in opposing Mussolini.

Jean Louis Barthou had become French foreign minister in February of 1934. He turned his country's foreign policy energetically toward the establishment of an anti-Hitler defense ring, to be achieved by what was known as the Eastern Pact, binding the Soviet Union, Poland, and the Little Entente (Czechoslovakia, Yugoslavia, and Rumania) to France in a defense grouping against Germany's territorial expansion. Some sort of "Danube Pact" was also envisaged for the defense of Austrian independence. Large roles were assigned to Italy and Yugoslavia, but first France had to bring about a reconciliation between Mussolini and Alexander.

Barthou went to Belgrade at the end of June for introductory talks, and it was agreed that Alexander should pay a two-week state visit to France starting on October 9 to lay the groundwork for the reconciliation between the King and Mussolini. With the encouragement of Paris, Mussolini extended the hand of friendship to Yugoslavia in a speech in Milan on October 5. Yet at that very moment, terrorists who had arrived in France were making their final plans for killing the King. Had they been sent with Mussolini's knowledge? Italian historians who have investigated the problem conclude that it was not in Mussolini's interest for Alexander to die at that time. There are strong indications, however, that the Italian Military Intelligence Service (SIM) was involved in the plot.

The tragic death of King Alexander ten minutes after his arrival at Marseilles, and of Barthou an hour later, put an end to all their plans. It is hard to say whether Barthou could have succeeded in reconciling Alexander and Mussolini. Yet his successor, Pierre Laval, concluded an agreement with Mussolini three months later, and the King's successors were party to the Franco-Italian military convention for the defense of Austria signed in May, 1935. This convention collapsed only a few months later, however, as a result of Mussolini's Ethiopian campaign and the League of Nations sanctions against Italy. Yugoslavia then made a secret offer to Britain of the use of all her naval bases in the event of an Anglo-Italian conflict. Had Alexander been alive, Paris would have had a hard task trying to prevent him from going further and seeking a military solution of his country's differences with Italy.

Soon Hitler's position was considerably strengthened when France and Britain failed to compel him to evacuate the Rhineland, which he had occupied on March 7, 1936. From that moment on, everyone in a responsible position in southeastern Europe nervously wondered whether the Western powers would (and if so, how) offer them protection against Hitler's and Mussolini's ambitions.

Yugoslavia's regent, Prince Paul, had been educated in England before World War I. There he had become acquainted with members of the upper class who were to play an important part in British political life in the 1930s. He therefore realized at an early stage the direction that British policy was going to take. He was also on friendly terms with members of the Astors' Cliveden set, which supported appeasement of Hitler. One of the most convinced advocates of this group's doctrines was Nevile Henderson, who was sent to Berlin as ambassador in mid-1937.

He had been in Belgrade from 1931 to 1935 and had worked actively for a *rapprochement* between King Alexander and Mussolini. Paris sent a protest note to Belgrade, declaring that Yugoslavia must come to no agreement with Italy without French approval. In Belgrade, Henderson openly voiced his opposition to excessively close Franco-Yugoslav ties, and minimized the importance of the part France would play in the defense of Yugoslavia. He also brought up the possibility of an Anglo-German *rapprochement* and agreement, and he spoke of a possible Axis comprising London, Berlin, and Belgrade.

Paul was well aware of the advances Hitler had been making to Alexander from 1933 on, and, like his predecessor, he regarded Mussolini as Yugoslavia's deadly foe. He therefore thought it beneficial to have an anti-Mussolini counterbalance on Hitler's side. His first secret meeting with Hitler took place in the summer of 1935; a second followed on October 8, 1936. Twelve days later, however, the first links were forged in Berlin of the Rome-Berlin axis. Count Ciano, then the Italian minister of foreign affairs, has related that Hitler told him in Berlin that Germany had come to friendly terms with Yugoslavia and that he wished Italy to do the same. He was also urged to advise Hungary to discontinue her revisionist policy toward Yugoslavia. (The same advice was tendered to Bulgaria.) Hitler's aim was to frustrate the plans of French diplomacy to include Yugoslavia in a Franco-Czechoslovak alliance against Germany and to extend the obligations of the Little Entente to meet a German attack against any one of its member nations. As it was, the members of the Little Entente were pledged to come to each other's assistance only in case of a Hungarian attack.

Why did Prince Paul reject the French plan, which was also rejected by King Alexander and Nikola Pašić in 1924? I discussed this question several times with Alexander Cincar-Marković, the Yugoslav minister in Berlin at the time Berlin and Belgrade were beginning to draw closer together. Cincar-Marković became foreign minister early in February, 1939, when Milan Stojadinović, premier and foreign minister, was removed from office by Paul. I became Cincar-Marković's assistant in March, 1940. He told me that Hitler, in return for Yugoslavia's refusal to join an anti-German alliance, had undertaken to guarantee that Italy and Bulgaria would conduct themselves in a manner of genuine friendship toward Yugoslavia. Paul explained to me on several occasions that his principal concern was to frustrate a Hitler-Mussolini line-up against Yugoslavia, and to prevent Yugoslavia from being the first country to be attacked. He also told me he did not believe that France and Britain would come to Yugoslavia's aid in such an event. The fate of Austria and Czechoslovakia seemed to confirm the Prince's view. A firm stand against Hitler was taken by Britain only after he had torn up the Munich agreement. By then, Paul was prepared to align himself with Britain and France.

King Alexander had intended, as already mentioned, to come to terms with Maček, the leader of the Croatian Peasant party, in order to build a strong home front for a military confrontation with Mussolini. Prince Paul followed through with this idea. His premier, Dragiša Cvetković, signed an agreement with Maček on August 26, 1939. The Croatian leader then came to Belgrade, after an eleven-year boycott of the city by the Croats, to take up the post of vice-premier in a new government. The agreement re-established Croatia as a territorial unit, with the historical status of "banovina" and a large measure of internal self-government.

When Mussolini announced his country's nonbelligerent status during the German-Polish fighting, the Yugoslav government declared its neutrality. Nevertheless, it decreed partial mobilization. The Prince's designs were at variance, however, with the British decision to show Mussolini every indulgence and to keep Italy neutral. He proposed to London and Paris that Mussolini should give concrete guarantees to stay neutral during the war or to accept war. The guarantee for Yugoslavia would be withdrawal of Italian troops from Albania and the occupation of Salonika by French and British troops. This proposal had been rejected. In addition, British efforts in Belgrade prevented, in early September, the overthrow of King Boris and the proclamation of the union between Yugoslavia and Bulgaria.

After the signing of the Hitler-Mussolini alliance in May, 1939, the basic plan for a war against Britain and France was laid down. Item 7 of Mussolini's war directives, dated May 30, stated that Germany and Italy were to occupy the whole of the Balkans and the Danube basin. But Hitler opposed this plan. He wanted to keep both areas out of the war, so that he might have the full benefit of sorely needed raw materials and foodstuffs. On the eve of war he made a departure from this position, though only to a limited extent, when, on August 12, he urged Ciano to launch the Italian army against Yugoslavia. He was extremely anxious to have Mussolini on his side when Germany invaded Poland. But Mussolini refused, and Hitler returned to his original idea.

British policy saved Yugoslavia from war in 1939. The Foreign Office took the view that Italian neutrality was beneficial to Britain and France, and for that reason no moves should be made in the Balkans that might prompt Italy to change this policy. French army chiefs, on the other hand, strongly favored the opening of a Balkan front in order to compel Hitler to withdraw a substantial number of divisions from the western front. At a conference of the chiefs of staff of French and British forces held on December 11, 1939, agreement was reached that no moves should be made that might provoke Italy.

The Rumanian government sent Mihai Antonescu to Rome at this time to sound out Mussolini's mood. Ciano informed him on December 26 that, in the event of a Soviet attack, he was prepared to render assistance to Rumania similar to that given to Franco in Spain. The Italian leaders then attempted to find out whether Maček would permit their troops to pass through Croatian territory to assist Hungary in the event of an attack— by Germany or the Soviet Union—or in case of an attack on Rumania. Maček replied that he would consent only if Italian troops were accompanied by French and British troops.

Maček at this time summoned me to Belgrade to be his *chef de cabinet*. We often spoke of the difficult position we would be in if Mussolini entered the war on Hitler's side. Accordingly, he accepted my suggestion that I pay a call on the French minister in Belgrade, Raymond Brugère, to discuss our position. We felt that at any moment we would be compelled, either by circumstances or by our own decision, to enter the war on the Franco-British side, and that our difficult situation would be greatly relieved if Italy were on the same side. Paris and London, we felt, should try to win Italy over. Brugère received my proposal with a large measure of skepticism, pointing to Mussolini's deadly hostility to the democracies. Maček was satisfied with this reply.

On December 24, 1940, Ciano expressed his agreement with the French ambassador on the desirability of a Balkan bloc.

Giuseppe Bastianini, the Italian ambassador in London, had informed Ciano a day earlier that Chamberlain was ready to give Italy "a free hand in the Balkans." I was approached a week later by a French and a British emissary about the possibility of a reorganization of the Danubian region. Two years later, I was informed by the British ambassador, G. W. Rendel, that London and Paris had at that time toyed with the idea of returning Croatia and Slovenia to a Danubian federation under Italian influence, and uniting Serbia and Bulgaria under the Karadjordjević dynasty. Berlin had somehow gotten wind of these highly secret negotiations. Ribbentrop's reaction to them was extremely sharp. Mussolini himself was moved to write to Hitler: "We have never contemplated, and do not now contemplate, fostering the creation of 'that bloc,' which has been suspect to us from the moment it became sponsored by the great democracies." In accord with this, on January 9, 1941, Ciano replied to the British ambassador that Mussolini was not yet willing to discuss the Balkans. Ciano was urging Mussolini to seek agreement with London and Paris, but Mussolini resisted this right up to the fall of the Maginot line, which finally put an end to his pipe dreams and drew him into Hitler's camp.

Hitler had told Mussolini several times that he recognized the Adriatic and the Mediterranean as an Italian sphere of influence. But when Mussolini failed to enter the war, Hitler would not permit him to carry out his Mediterranean policy. An attack on Yugoslavia could have started a war in the Balkans and given an opening for the Western powers, and even Russia, to spring in. At their Brenner meeting in March, 1940, Hitler tactfully urged Mussolini to drop his plan. On April 11, Mussolini promised Hitler he would leave the Balkans in peace. Two days earlier, he had told Ciano that it was essential to make a quick move toward Croatia; if he took advantage of the confusion in Europe, "France and Britain will not attack." In his history of World War II, Churchill admits that he was aware of Mussolini's desire to attack Yugoslavia at that time and that he was opposed to war with Italy if the Italian attack was limited to "taking some naval bases in the Adriatic." But when he realized that Mussolini wanted war with Britain and France regardless of Yugoslavia, he advised Secretary of State for War Anthony Eden to inquire how

Yugoslavia could be won over to their side. France, too, was making great efforts to secure this move.

Although Mussolini had given his pledge to Hitler, he could not keep his eyes off Croatia. At the end of April, he told Marshal Rodolfo Graziani: "We must bring Yugoslavia to her knees. We need her raw materials." However, on May 13, impressed by Hitler's breakthrough on the western front, Mussolini decided to strike against England and France, not against Yugoslavia. Ciano recorded in his diary that Mussolini told him a campaign against Yugoslavia would be "a humiliating expedient."

I took office as assistant foreign minister on March 15, 1940, in an atmosphere of sickening disquiet caused by reports that Mussolini was preparing a military campaign against Yugoslavia. We consulted with our Balkan Pact allies—Rumania, Greece, and Turkey—but the talks produced meager results and were discontinued.

The news of Mussolini's preparations for an attack on us led to a decision to re-establish diplomatic relations with the Soviet Union. Mussolini was aware that this move was directed against him and, immediately after the fall of France, he instructed Ciano to explain to Hitler that it was "necessary to break up Yugoslavia." At a meeting in Salzburg on July 7, Hitler rejected the plan, saying that all their forces were needed to deal with Britain and that they should not complicate the situation in the Balkans, where matters could easily be settled to Italy's satisfaction after the war.

Soon after the Salzburg meeting, it was brought to our attention by various German agents that Hitler was not permitting Mussolini to attack Yugoslavia. These consoling reports were accompanied by the discreet suggestion that Yugoslav neutrality was no longer sufficient, and that Yugoslavia now had to align her policies with those of the Axis. We received these reports with a great deal of skepticism, although they were, in fact, accurate. They were confirmed after the war by, among others, Count Ciano, who noted in his diary that Ribbentrop had told the Italian ambassador, Dino Alfieri, on August 16 that "it is necessary to abandon any plan for an attack on Yugoslavia."

Mussolini was exceedingly disgruntled with Hitler, both because he had stopped him from attacking Yugoslavia and because he had sent him instructions not to come to any agreement with Russia. Russia had declared herself ready to recognize Italian hegemony in the Mediterranean, and Mussolini now wanted to emulate Hitler, who a year before had signed the infamous Nazi-Soviet Pact. Mussolini was enthusiastic about a plan whereby he and Stalin would carve up the Balkans into spheres of interest in the same way that Hitler and Stalin had agreed on spheres of interest in eastern Europe. But this was not at all to Hitler's liking. His plans for the invasion of Russia had now been hammered out. First, however, he had to get control of Hungary and Rumania. As a first step, he persuaded them to accept German-Italian arbitration in their dispute over Transylvania. This took place in Vienna on August 30. There, Hitler offered German protection to Rumania, and the first German army units were sent into Rumania at the beginning of October. This displeased both Stalin and Mussolini. Stalin restricted himself to protests; Mussolini decided to attack Greece in order to pay Hitler back in kind.

Mussolini was anxious for Bulgaria's support in this military venture, and he expected King Boris to welcome the opportunity to fulfill one of Bulgaria's cherished ambitions—the conquest of Greek Thrace. Boris consulted Berlin and turned down Mussolini's invitation to join him against Greece.

Hitler's plans against Stalin were still in their infancy. Furthermore, winter, that great guardian angel of Russia and the Balkans, was approaching. Thus, driven by the imperatives of his grand strategy, Hitler was working for a limitation of martial conflagration in the Balkans, and this was what kept Yugoslavia out of the war for the fourth time in 1940. And the brave resistance of the Greek army against the Fascist invaders, who began their advance into Greece on October 28, saved Yugoslavia from war for a fifth time.

The Italian invasion placed Yugoslavia in mortal danger. Many influential Yugoslavs regarded it as a prelude to an attack on their country. After the fall of France, the atmosphere in Yugoslavia was one of grim depression. The question on everyone's lips was which way the powerful German war machine would turn next. The feeling was that Mussolini would take advantage of Hitler's victories to get his own hostile plans against Yugoslavia moving as quickly as possible. We were unaware then that

Hitler, for the time being at least, was frustrating Mussolini's plans.

Everywhere in Yugoslavia there was deep regret for the swift defeat of France, particularly in Serbia, with her close ties to France. The Serbian and French armies, together with a few British troops, had fought shoulder to shoulder on the Salonika front during World War I, and together they had broken through and liberated Serbia. From this grew a legend of Salonika as the bedrock of Yugoslavia's defense. It was thought that in any future war Salonika would again be the focal point where Yugoslav and Franco-British armies would meet. It would be the last refuge for a Yugoslav army in retreat before Nazi or Fascist invaders, and the place where Franco-British support would arrive. The French also assigned this role to Salonika: special units of the French army would be transferred from Syria to Salonika; from there they would aid Yugoslavia and her Balkan allies in their resistance.

In Salonika, Yugoslavia had her own customs-free zone, which offered great privileges. Moreover, though Belgrade military circles regarded the Adriatic as a closed sea, they looked upon the Aegean as safe and open. Mussolini's occupation of Albania in 1939, however, made it possible for Italy to block Yugoslavia's gateway to the Mediterranean at the Strait of Otranto. The gateway to the Aegean via Salonika could also be completely closed if Greece remained neutral. Before the outbreak of the war, the Greek statesman Eleutherios Venizelos declared that in the event of war between Italy and Yugoslavia, Greece would not allow arms for Yugoslavia to be unloaded in Salonika. It was a cause of deep concern to the Belgrade government in the prewar years, and some thought was given to a radical solution to the Salonika problem.

Ciano notes in his diary that in January, 1939, he and Mussolini were trying to break the solidarity between Yugoslavia and Greece by putting pressure on Premier Stojadinović and driving him toward Salonika. Hitler encouraged this as a means of breaking up the Little Entente and the Balkan Alliance. Stojadinović accepted the Hitler-Mussolini proposals with enthusiasm. But two weeks after his talks with Ciano, Prince Paul dismissed him from the government. When Mussolini occupied Albania, Yugoslavia did not receive a single square inch of Albanian territory, because Paul did not wish to be associated with Mussolini in this squalid affair.

After that, the situation in Europe, including that in the Balkans, went from bad to worse. Salonika became a burning issue when Mussolini invaded Greece. After consultation with his closest Serbian associates, Paul decided to draw Hitler's immediate attention to Yugoslavia's interest in the Salonika question. The Germans replied that in this matter the Yugoslav government must approach the Italian government. Yugoslavia made this diplomatic move in Berlin because Germany had been involved in the earlier Italo-Yugoslav talks on Salonika, had approved them, and had actually urged Yugoslavia to move into Salonika. Prince Paul calculated that an Italo-Yugoslav dispute would not be in Germany's interest, and therefore Hitler would make the sort of suggestions to Mussolini that Belgrade wanted. It was decided that unofficial emissaries should be sent to Rome and Berlin to draw attention to the importance Yugoslavia attached to Salonika. The emissary to Rome was a Belgrade lawyer, Vladimir Stakić. The emissary to Berlin was Danilo Gregorić, managing director of the newspaper *Vreme*. Stakić saw Ciano on November 11; Gregorić saw Ribbentrop on November 23 and 24.

No record of the talks between Gregorić and Ribbentrop has been found, but their substance can be established from what Gregorić told Viktor von Heeren, the German minister in Belgrade, when he asked him on November 3 to arrange for Ribbentrop to see him in Berlin. Gregorić gave Heeren the feeling that his aim was to explain the enormous importance of Salonika for Yugoslavia, that Salonika in Italian hands would be "a chain around Yugoslavia's neck." He explained that his country was prepared to make certain concessions to Italy: a frontier revision and the demilitarization of the Adriatic coast. In a telegram of November 14, Heeren said that the Italo-Greek war "reawakened in Serbian circles and especially in the army the old Serbian desire for a free outlet to the Aegean through Salonika." The Serbian people had tolerated the possession of Salonika by their Balkan ally, Greece, he went on, but the possibility that Italy might gain possession of it meant military encirclement and a direct threat to southern Serbia, the very part of the country where the "historical shrines of the Serbian people are located."

They would, he wrote, take up arms to prevent Salonika falling into Italian or Bulgarian hands if they could be sure that this would not bring Germany into the conflict against them. They would think twice about demanding or seizing Salonika as long as it remained in Greek hands. They would certainly become completely uninterested in the fate of Greece if they knew that the Axis powers would recognize Yugoslavia's hereditary claim to Salonika. An assurance in this respect could be a decisive step along the road to a lasting peace in relations between the Serbian people and their Italian and Bulgarian neighbors.

Stakić told Ciano that if Italian policy still set any store by the friendship pact signed by Ciano and Stojadinović, official circles in Belgrade desired fervently to strengthen it into a real alliance. Yugoslavia might consent to the demilitarization of her Adriatic coast as a token of good will. Ciano immediately informed Mussolini, who readily accepted the proposal. Ciano himself was enraptured, and he wrote in his diary that same day that it was better for Italy "to create a solid basis of understanding between Italy and Yugoslavia" than "to gather for ourselves a mass of uneasy and untrustworthy Croats." He added: "This would be useful, whether the morrow brings us anti-Russian or anti-German policy."

CHAPTER 2

Hitler's answer to Mussolini's attack on Greece was in accord with his grandiose scheme for inducing Britain to make peace. As a preliminary step, he decided to force Stalin into political capitulation—with or without war. The old anti-Comintern pact of 1936 binding Germany, Japan, and Italy together had lost its *raison d'être* with the Nazi-Soviet Pact of August 23, 1939. Hitler now came up with the Tripartite Pact, which was signed by Germany, Italy, and Japan on September 27, 1940.

The Soviet foreign minister, Vyacheslav Molotov, was invited to Berlin for talks with Hitler and Ribbentrop on November 12 to 14, 1940. Molotov did not reject in principle a cardinal point of the Tripartite Pact: that Russia's sphere of influence should be in the direction of the Persian Gulf and the Indian Ocean. But he insisted that Germany should first abandon her agreement with Finland regarding the passage of German troops to Norway and that Bulgaria and the Dardanelles should come into the Soviet security zone. Hitler rejected both of these demands. Molotov received no information about Axis intentions concerning Yugoslavia and Greece. Immediately after these talks, Hitler and Stalin began to go their separate ways.

At Hitler's bidding, Hungary, Rumania, and Slovakia (which had been made an independent state the previous year) acceded to the Tripartite Pact. King Boris, of Bulgaria, at a meeting with Hitler on November 18, consented to Bulgaria's adherence to the pact, with the understanding that the formalities be completed later. He also consented to the entry of German troops into Bulgaria at a later date. Upon learning that Boris had been to see Hitler, Molotov summoned the Bulgarian minister in Moscow and proposed that Bulgaria conclude a treaty of mutual assistance with Russia. He promised that Russia would back Bulgarian national aspirations at the expense of Turkey, Yugoslavia, and Greece.

The Greeks swiftly repulsed the first Italian advances into their country. Their military successes were responsible for Hitler's order to his army commander in chief to "make preparations . . . in case of necessity, to occupy the Greek mainland . . . entering from Bulgaria," and to continue "all preparations for the east" without regard to what might result from discussions undertaken to clarify Russia's conduct in the near future.

Mussolini, quick to realize that only Hitler could extricate him, sent Ciano to see Hitler on November 18. Hitler pointed out that the British had taken advantage of the attack to get themselves installed on Crete and other islands, and would do the same in Thrace and around Salonika. He stressed that the Italian defeats had encouraged Russia to step up her demands in the Balkans, and had set back the chances of bringing Turkey closer to the Axis. Yugoslavia's reaction had so far been impossible to determine. The psychological consequences of the reverses on the Greek front, he said, should under no circumstances be allowed to lead to an extension of the war into the Balkans. There were three routes running from north to south through Bulgaria into Greece, and one of them skirted the Yugoslav frontier for ten kilometers, which meant that movement of transport was dependent upon Yugoslavia's good will. Hitler added that Yugoslavia would have to be offered a guarantee of her territory and a promise of Salonika. In return, she would have to agree to the demilitarization of the Dalmatian coast. Hitler proposed this demilitarization on the basis of the talks between Heeren and Gregorić.

On November 20, Ciano informed Hitler that Mussolini had expressed his unqualified agreement with the Führer's proposals concerning Yugoslavia. He also said that Prince Paul was firmly behind the plan and was ready to co-operate. Hitler's comment was that Paul would go down in history as a great statesman if he succeeded in gaining possession of Salonika during his regency, and he suggested that if Paul wanted the throne of Yugoslavia, it would be advisable to support him.

On the same day, Hitler dispatched a letter to Mussolini reprimanding him for having undertaken the Greek venture without prior consultation. Although the Rumanian oil fields had previously been "completely inaccessible to English bombers, their planes have now approached to within less than five hundred kilometers." He went on to say that "Yugoslavia must . . . if possible collaborate with us . . . in the settlement of the Greek question. Without an assurance from Yugoslavia the chance of a successful operation in the Balkans cannot be taken. I must point out, however, that it is impossible to conduct a war in the Balkans before March. Any threatening pressure on Yugoslavia now would therefore be useless. . . . Yugoslavia must be won over by other means."

In his November 22 reply, Mussolini said that he was "ready to guarantee the present boundaries of Yugoslavia and to recognize Yugoslavia's right to Salonika, on the following conditions: (1) that Yugoslavia adhere to the Tripartite Pact; (2) that she demilitarize the Adriatic; (3) that her military intervention be agreed on, in other words, that it occur only after Greece has received an initial blow from Italy." On November 29, after the Germans questioned him on the demilitarization, Mussolini withdrew his second stipulation.

This letter from Mussolini opened the way for Hitler to begin talks with Yugoslavia. Cincar-Marković had a conversation with Hitler on November 28. The Führer opened the talk by expounding his plan for a world coalition from Yokohama to Spain. He said that countries like Yugoslavia were essentially within the sphere of Italy, since they were Mediterranean countries. Germany had no territorial claims in the Balkans, but he would make certain that any agreements Italy and Germany made with Yugoslavia were faithfully upheld. He was now in a position to persuade Mussolini to adopt the policy toward Yugoslavia he had always urged but had never been able to force upon him. A unique situation had arisen, and his views on the consolidation of the Balkans would prevail. He was not asking permission for his troops to pass through Yugoslavia, he said; he wanted to get the situation in the Balkans settled only because of Russia. He pointed out that Russia had promised Bulgaria assistance in obtaining possession of certain areas of Yugoslav, Greek, and Turkish territory. He believed that Yugoslavia's relations with Germany and Italy could be put on a satisfactory basis by a nonaggression pact. Since Yugoslavia was going to get Salonika, she could make a nice gesture and consent to the demilitarization of the Dalmatian coast, which amounted to little more than a courtesy.

On December 5, Hitler informed Mussolini of his conversation with Cincar-Marković without mentioning the German guarantee that Italy would honor the provisions of any agreement reached. He did report his proposal for a nonaggression pact, which, he stressed, would be psychologically easier to explain to Hungary and Bulgaria.

The same day, Prince Paul held a conference with the three chief members of his government—Dragiša Cvetković, the premier, Vladko Maček, the vice-premier, and Anton Korošec, the minister of education—to inform them of the conversation between Cincar-Marković and Hitler. Maček told me that they all agreed that Paul should keep the dialogue going so that Yugoslavia could avoid having to be in either of the belligerent camps. In its reply to Hitler, sent on December 7, the Yugoslav government declared itself ready to open talks on a nonaggression pact with Berlin and Rome on the basis of the existing Italo-Yugoslav Friendship Pact. Special emphasis was laid on Yugoslavia's gratitude to Germany for her role in improving relations with Italy, Bulgaria, and Hungary.

Hitler had the Yugoslav note in his hands on December 8 when he talked with Italian Ambassador Dino Alfieri, who had just arrived from Rome with an urgent message from Mussolini. According to Alfieri, Mussolini had been panic-stricken on the fourth when he received crushing news about the Italian army on the Albanian front, and he was now thinking of asking Hitler to act as mediator to arrange an armistice with Greece. Apparently enraged by this, Hitler cut Alfieri short and launched immediately into a wild attack on the Italian decision to invade Greece; he asked for a meeting with Mussolini within two days. Mussolini delayed sending a formal reply for a fortnight. It was only after Alfieri pointed out the dangers of procrastination that a meeting was arranged for January 19, 1941. Mussolini's description of his terror at meeting Hitler, as Alfieri reported later, gives an accurate picture of the man: "I haven't enough blood in my veins to be able to blush before Hitler."

Alfieri conveyed to Ribbentrop Mussolini's regret at not having been able to meet Hitler within two days and told him that the Duce would welcome any action on the part of Germany that would hasten Yugoslavia's accession to the Tripartite Pact. Mussolini, in his November 22 letter to Hitler, had given his consent to the nonaggression pact. Why did Mussolini now start declaring contradictory attitudes on the same issue, one to Belgrade, the other to Berlin?

There are two possible interpretations of the game that Mussolini was playing. Both reveal his fervent desire to secure either Yugoslavia's accession to the Tripartite Pact or an enlargement of the Italo-Yugoslav Friendship Pact. He exulted in the thought that Yugoslavia's accession to the Tripartite Pact might result in her entry into the war against Greece, or at least in some aid to Italy against Greece, provided that the scope of the pact could be enlarged. He ought to have known that Yugoslavia was helping Greece by sending munitions and food and had refused to permit the passage through Yugoslav territory of one thousand trucks from Germany bound for Albania. Permission was refused even after Berlin had intervened at Rome's request. Subsequently, under pressure from Italy, a consignment of German aircraft parts for Yugoslavia was stopped as a penalty for the Yugoslav refusal. Hitler and Ribbentrop attributed the Yugoslav defiance to the Italian reverses in Albania.

Hungary, which had a good number of her nationals in Yugoslavia, played a complex and subtle game. At that time, she was not raising the question of a revision of the frontier with Yugoslavia. In fact, on December 12 she signed a treaty of perpetual friendship with Yugoslavia. This was in accord with Hitler's policy of allaying Yugoslav fears of possible Hungarian territorial demands. In addition, the Germans now had a ready retort to the Hungarian excuse that fear of Yugoslavia prevented her from allowing large numbers of German troops bound for Rumania to be transported on Hungarian railways.

Indications of the cordial relations between Yugoslavia and Hungary had become evident in the summer and autumn before the actual signing of the pact. Delegations from the two countries visited back and forth, which created a favorable atmosphere for *rapprochement*. This would have been insufficient, though, had not Yugoslavia and Hungary been ruled by two men who were looking far ahead and making long-term plans—Prince Paul and Admiral Horthy.

Admiral Miklós Horthy, Count István Bethlen, and Count Paul Teleki had headed the Szegedin Committee, which had overthrown Béla Kun's Communist regime in 1919. With France as intermediary, they had received from the Yugoslav government six thousand rifles and Hungarian prisoners of war. In gratitude, this triumvirate, which controlled Hungary between the two world wars, had kept its revisionist claims on Yugoslavia to a minimum. Horthy had wanted to establish friendly relations with Yugoslavia as early as the spring of 1926. Acting on the calculated assumption that Yugoslavia could be persuaded to weaken or abandon altogether her alliances with Czechoslovakia and Rumania, he had offered King Alexander a genuine alliance, seeking in return some minor revision of their common frontier, which he called "symbolic." Everything had been arranged for a meeting between them after the King's return from France. But Alexander's assassination put an end to Horthy's plans.

The triumvirate, anxious about Hungary's future, looked for an opportunity to relieve the heavy pressure of Hitler's hand. It kept its eyes on Rome, the chief safeguard against German hegemony. Mussolini's entry into the war was a sharp blow, particularly when, as a result of his defeats, he increasingly became a satellite of Hitler. Then the eyes of Hungary turned toward Yugoslavia, through whom some sort of gateway to the west still remained open. As a former admiral, Horthy admired the British navy and had great respect for Britain. He was well aware that Prince Paul had close connections with high circles in Britain and enjoyed great esteem among them. This impressed him deeply.

In the winter of 1939, the triumvirate sent its closest confidant, Tibor Eckardt, to Belgrade to discuss a Yugoslav-Hungarian alliance. Paul had kept up the contacts that Alexander had established with Horthy; moreover, he and Horthy had a number of traits in common. They were both staunch anti-Communists. Neither was a devotee of the democratic tradition. Autocratic regimes, tempered with the principles of constitutional government, were most to their liking. They were both men of the past rather than of the present. They delighted in political ideals that were difficult to reconcile with modern political thought. Horthy had grown up in the shadow of Franz Joseph, emperor of the union of Austria and Hungary; Paul's ideal was Charles V, ruler of the Holy Roman Empire in the sixteenth century.

In November, 1940, Paul mentioned the possibility of a Yugoslav-Hungarian union to Slobodan Jovanović, who was to become Yugoslav premier in London. According to the archives of the Foreign Office, Horthy declared at that time that he and Alexander "would have made of the two countries a single allied force" had Alexander not been assassinated. Paul also mentioned that only Boris stood in the way of a union between Yugoslavia and Bulgaria. On two occasions he told me that he had worked on a plan for the unification of Yugoslavia and Bulgaria, but he had been unable to carry it out because there was a lot of opposition among the Serbs. He was fascinated with the idea that his family, the Karadjordjevićs, might gain the thrones of some of the neighboring countries, as the Habsburgs had once succeeded in doing. The idea of a Yugoslav-Hungarian union may have been a dream, but the harsh realities of 1940 made it obvious that if the two countries were closely associated, they would both be better able to withstand Hitler's oppressive demands. On December 17, the British minister in Budapest informed the Foreign Office that an influential member of the government had told him: "Trying to make friends with your friends, Yugoslavia and Turkey, we shall hope to find a channel for friendship with London and Washington."

As the fateful year of 1941 drew nearer, the ring of diplomatic pressures around Yugoslavia tightened. Hitler declared that he would not enter Greece if Greece ended the war with Italy and insisted on the removal of all British bases.

However, on December 20, he issued a directive setting up Operation Marita—the campaign against Greece—to be launched possibly as early as March. The transportation of major units to Rumania, where the troops were to be trained, immediately got under way. At the same time, pressure on Yugoslavia was stepped up. On December 21, Ribbentrop informed Cincar-Marković that the Führer had read the Yugoslav note of December 7, but that this still left open "the important question of

Yugoslavia's accession to the Tripartite Pact." These words could have meant only that Germany and Italy were not prepared to promise Yugoslavia Salonika unless she acceded to the Tripartite Pact. This came as something of a surprise to Cincar-Marković, since the original idea of a nonaggression pact had come from the Führer himself.

On December 31, Hitler informed Mussolini that Yugoslavia was not prepared to join the Tripartite Pact and that nothing could be done until the psychological climate had been improved by military successes in the field. Mussolini replied that Yugoslavia would follow Bulgaria's example in the matter of accession to the pact, "for she had no other choice, if only because of her geographic position with respect to Bulgaria, Hungary, Rumania . . . and as a neighbor of Greece whose fate was sealed."

Winston Churchill has described Soviet policy as a "riddle wrapped in a mystery inside an enigma." This is a perfect description of Russia's policy toward Yugoslavia at that time. When, at the end of June, 1940, I heard that Mussolini wanted to negotiate a treaty with Moscow, I at once thought it would be similar to the treaty that democratic Italy had signed with Czarist Russia in 1909. That secret treaty was aimed at restraining Austro-Hungarian expansion in the Balkans. Obviously Mussolini was alarmed at the rapid and large-scale German victories in the west and was now going to attempt, with Soviet assistance, to prevent Hitler from obtaining complete domination over the Danube basin and the Balkans. In this case, I reasoned, Mussolini would maintain a friendly policy toward Yugoslavia. But shortly afterward, I heard that Mussolini wanted to attack Yugoslavia, and I was beset by gloomy thoughts.

I remembered being told by Petkov Stajnov the previous year, in Sofia, that Molotov's assistant, Vladimir Potemkim, had told him that "Yugoslavia will be smashed by the Fascist powers and carved up between them." On June 25, 1940, Molotov raised the subject of Russia's interest in Hungary, Bulgaria, and part of Rumania with the Italian ambassador to Moscow and made some vague mention of Turkey and the area south of Batum. He also declared Russia's willingness to recognize Italy's hegemony in the Mediterranean area provided Italy recognized Russia's hegemony in the Black Sea. He proposed immediate talks on the subject with Italy and Germany. The urgency arose from the Soviet decision to demand Bessarabia, which she did within the next three days. Molotov did not make a single reference to Yugoslavia. Apparently Russia was ready to abandon Yugoslavia to the Axis powers if her demands with respect to Rumania, Bulgaria, and Turkey were met. On July 17, the American ambassador in Rome learned that the Soviet government had granted recognition to the rights of Italy in the Mediterranean in return for Italian recognition of Russian rights in the Black Sea.

Ciano delayed his reply to Molotov because basically he opposed the idea of drawing closer to Russia. But when the Italian ambassador to Moscow warned him that without a preliminary political settlement there would be no settlement of the question of deliveries of oil from the Soviet Union, vital for the Italian navy, he finally consented to additional secret political negotiations. On August 16, however, Ribbentrop informed Rome that it was not an opportune moment for starting negotiations with Moscow, because pressure was then being exerted on Rumania to have talks with the Hungarians and Bulgarians about revising her frontiers in their favor.

The second phase of the secret Italo-Russian negotiations came after the Hitler-Molotov talks in Berlin. Hitler told Molotov he would have to consult with Italy about his demand for bases in the Dardanelles. So Moscow began to make friendly gestures toward Italy, playing down Italian reverses on the Greek-Albanian front, though the Germans in Greece were delighted at the Italian defeats. Molotov and Deputy Premier Anastas Mikoyan lunched at the Italian embassy on December 13; it was a lively get-together. Germany welcomed the improvement in Italo-Soviet relations, because it was in her interests as well. But once the Italo-Russian negotiations had assumed a concrete shape and it was learned, on January 6, 1941, that Italy would "respect Russian interests in the Balkans and Asia," Ribbentrop pointed out to Italy that Russian interests had to stop short of the Balkans. No treaty could be signed, he said, "that might lead to a break with Turkey." Germany did not want Russia to get into the Balkans again by the roundabout way of an agreement with Italy when she herself had just been ushered out through the door, so to speak.

As relations with Mussolini improved, Stalin's interest in Yugoslavia began to dwindle. The first Yugoslav minister to Moscow after the resumption of diplomatic relations, Milan Gavrilović, arrived to take up his post at the beginning of August. Two months later, Božin Simić, a retired colonel, joined him. His duty was to make contact with Russian military circles and find out whether Yugoslavia could buy arms from Russia, since it was impossible to get them anywhere else. It seemed that everything was going to run smoothly.

Relations between the Russian minister in Belgrade, V. A. Plotnikov, and the Yugoslav foreign ministry had been somewhat marred by the arrest of a Russian journalist on the legation staff. Plotnikov was immediately summoned to Moscow, and he left Belgrade early in 1941 in a bad mood. But he did not refuse to take with him the list of arms that Yugoslavia wished to buy from Russia.

Plotnikov never returned to Belgrade, and the list disappeared. The official explanation was that the Soviet government had taken offense at the Russian journalist's arrest and at the fact that members of its legation were being followed by the Yugoslav secret police. This was an evasion. The real reason could be traced to the secret negotiations with Mussolini, in which the Russians were willing to recognize Yugoslavia as an Italian sphere of interest in return for Italy's recognition of Bulgaria and the Dardanelles as a Soviet sphere of interest.

The Yugoslav ambassador in Bucharest informed us at the beginning of January that the Soviet minister there had declared that Germany's route to the Balkans ran through Yugoslavia, not Bulgaria, and that this was the route the Germans would take. In the light of such information, the failure of Plotnikov to return to Belgrade began to look sinister. On February 3, Cincar-Marković instructed Gavrilović to "assure the Soviet leaders of the identity of our interests and theirs in Bulgaria in view of the critical situation in the Balkans." The only person he was able to reach was the deputy commissar for foreign affairs, Andrei Vyshinsky, who, on February 8, replied evasively that the Soviet attitude toward Bulgaria would depend on how the situation developed. Gavrilović made his own comment on this: "As she does not want war with Germany, and as her own territories are not affected, Soviet Russia will maintain her present attitude and policy in a slightly modified form of nonbelligerency. This means that Russia will quietly allow German troops to enter Bulgaria, if it should come to that. . . . She will leave the countries directly involved to defend themselves or not, according to how they interpret their own interests."

Gavrilović asked our foreign minister to authorize him to propose a military alliance to the Soviet Union. If we failed, we would be able to say to our many Russophiles, "It is not our fault." I discussed this delicate issue with Cincar-Marković, who said: "I dare not make such a proposal to the Soviet government, because so far they have not proved discreet and trustworthy negotiators. They are capable both of rejecting our offer and of telling the Germans about it. What sort of a situation would we be in then?" (I later realized how right Cincar-Marković had been. After the war I learned that Molotov, on Stalin's instructions, had given the German ambassador in Moscow a detailed account of Stalin's conversation with British Ambassador Stafford Cripps on July 13, 1940. In that conversation, Cripps had submitted Churchill's proposal that the Soviet Union play a leading role in the Balkans.) Moscow declined Yugoslavia's offer of talks to establish a joint approach to Bulgaria, although in Berlin three weeks earlier, on January 17, 1941, the Russians had repeatedly declared that they had a major interest in Bulgaria. The Soviet ambassador had said: "The Soviet Government stated repeatedly to the German Government that it considers the territory of Bulgaria and of the Straits as the security zone of the USSR. . . . The Soviet Government regards it as its duty to give warning that it will consider the appearance of any armed forces on the territory of Bulgaria and of the Straits as a violation of the security interests of the USSR."

On the same day, Molotov conveyed the identical message to the German ambassador in Moscow. He expressed his surprise that Germany had not yet replied to the Soviet government's proposals of November 25, 1940. He said in addition that he was delivering the same note to the Italian ambassador. Obviously Stalin hoped Mussolini would induce Hitler to yield on the question of Bulgaria and the Dardanelles. Mussolini hoped to get Moscow's recognition of Yugoslavia as an Italian sphere of interest. That was why Molotov ignored the Yugoslav proposal on Bulgaria.

Two days later, Hitler met Mussolini and told him that he attached tremendous importance to Yugoslavia. Yugoslavia could be a dangerous adversary, because even Bulgaria would refuse the passage of troops across her territory unless Yugoslavia remained peaceful. That is why she had been promised Salonika.

On October 28, 1940, immediately following Mussolini's attack on Greece, the Greek premier, John Metaxas, asked for British naval and air support for the protection of Corfu and Athens. The British chiefs of staff said that aid to Greece would have to be limited and that Crete would have to be kept out of enemy hands so that it could be used as a refueling base by the British. The magnificent Greek resistance to Mussolini's attack fired Churchill's imagination, and he now threw himself into the task of building up a major front in the Balkans that might induce Stalin to make a stand against Nazi penetration in that direction. With this in mind, he wrote to the British foreign secretary on November 26: "We should like Turkey and Yugoslavia now to consult together so as, if possible, to have a joint warning ready to offer Bulgaria and Germany at the first sign of a German movement toward Bulgaria."

The arrival early in 1941 of a large number of German troops in Rumania alarmed the Greeks. They raised with the Yugoslav government the question of its attitude in the event of a German attempt to attack Greece through Bulgaria or Yugoslavia. A conference was called to discuss the subject with Prince Paul. On January 10, Paul informed the Greek premier that Yugoslavia would not under any circumstances permit an attack on Greece from her territory or the transport of arms through it. In mid-January, the British government sent the commander-in-chief of its army in Egypt, Major-General Archibald Wavell, to Athens to discuss the question of British military assistance. He offered to send Greece some aircraft, tank units, and artillery. The Greeks declined the offer on the grounds that such small units could be of little assistance but could be a provocation to the Germans to launch their attack. After Metaxas died, on January 29, the new premier, Alexandros Koryzis, confirmed his predecessor's declaration that Greece would seek British assistance if German troops moved in from Bulgaria. He repeated the view that "the premature despatch of an insufficient force could only have disastrous results."

The Turkish government, on the advice of, and with some prompting by, the British government, raised with the Yugoslav ambassador in Ankara, Ilija Šumenković, a whole range of questions connected with the presence of German troops in Rumania. Šumenković was instructed to open discreet negotiations.

Churchill was not thrown off his course by the failure of these first attempts to secure Turkish and Yugoslav agreement to a joint stand against the passage of German troops through Bulgaria and to a joint defense of Salonika. He never lost sight of the possibility that if a really powerful front could be opened in the Balkans, he would manage to turn Stalin against Hitler. Accordingly, he sent Anthony Eden and General John Dill, chief of the Imperial General Staff, on a tour of Cairo, Athens, and Ankara, to see if they could speed up the creation of a Greek-Yugoslav-Turkish bloc. They left for Cairo on February 12, 1941.

On March 7, Eden repeated to Churchill a view he had expressed before, that, as he later wrote, "If we withdrew from the operation now, we would have lost the last chance of bringing Yugoslavia into the war." Their observations show clearly that Churchill and Eden were defending the decision to assist Greece primarily on political grounds, and foremost among these was their fervent desire to turn Yugoslavia against Hitler.

While the British cabinet was deliberating what policy to follow, General Wavell was conducting a successful offensive, launched on December 9, 1940, against the Italian army in Libya. Churchill had notified Wavell that his task was "to maul the Italian army and rip them off the African shore." "I felt strongly," wrote Major-General John Kennedy, director of military operations for the British General Staff, "that we ought to push ahead as far as possible in Libya—even to Tunisia, if the Italians broke." He pointed out that it might be possible to rout the Italians along the entire African coast and thus be in a position to offer fighter protection to shipping convoys. "We had not enough troops," he wrote further, "for intervention in Greece. We had calculated that at least twenty divisions, plus a considerable air force, would be needed to hold Salonika alone." He added that the Germans could easily occupy Greece, and from there inflict heavy damage on British shipping, while the British would be in a position to "afford almost complete protection to that same shipping if we could win the control of most of the African coast-line. . . . And we stood to gain more by winning the African coast for ourselves than by denying Greece to the Germans. On this issue, we should resist political pressure for all we were worth."

Kennedy went on to relate how pleased both Wavell and the military people in London were that the Greeks and Turks were still declining offers of assistance. This gave them cause to believe that plans for a Greek expedition would be shelved. But no sooner had British troops reached the outskirts of Tobruk, and Wavell had reported that there were opportunities for a further advance into Tripoli, than Churchill began to urge that his main effort be directed to Greece and the Balkans. On February 11, at a war cabinet meeting, when Dill declared that "all the troops in the Middle East are fully employed and . . . none are available for Greece," Churchill became exceedingly angry.

"It seemed," wrote Kennedy, ". . . that the British Government was now trying to force an unsound policy down Wavell's throat, and down the throats of the Greeks and Turks. We felt that it would be playing into the hands of the Germans to send our forces to the European side of the Mediterranean at this stage of the war, and that, if they were sent, they were certain to be annihilated or driven out again."

Interestingly enough, Churchill listened calmly to Kennedy's frank arguments against a front in the Balkans during the weekend the two spent together on February 15 and 16. Kennedy wrote that Churchill was then uncertain about the correct approach to Greece. This is apparent in the telegram Churchill sent to Eden in Cairo on February 20: "Do not consider yourselves obligated to a Greek enterprise if in your hearts you feel it will only be another Norwegian fiasco. . . . But of course you know how valuable success would be."

In the meantime, however, something happened that Kennedy had not at all expected: Dill and Wavell changed their minds. They now reported that an expedition to Greece had a fair chance of success. On the basis of this, the chiefs of staff drafted a memorandum recommending implementation of the plan. Kennedy's view was that it was quite wrong that the war cabinet, before making its final decision, failed to seek an opinion based on purely military considerations, either from the chiefs of staff or from Wavell. "All the service advice given on the problem," he wrote, "had been coloured by political considerations—a very dangerous procedure."

On February 24, the war cabinet unanimously adopted Churchill's plan for an expedition to Greece. Eden was anxious that Greece accept British aid, because he felt certain that the arrival of British troops in Greece would draw Turkey and Yugoslavia into the war. And so, at the Athens conference with the Greek premier, the chief army leaders, and the King, Eden deliberately exaggerated the scale of British assistance. Major-General Francis de Guingand, who had been given the task of reshaping plans in order to uphold Eden's assertions, described the process as "bordering on dishonesty." And when he saw the wounded in a Greek military hospital, he wondered "whether we were going to be instrumental in helping to make these poor, brave people to suffer more than their legitimate share." He condemned Eden for exaggerating the possibilities of British aid and said that the British commitment to assist Greece would have been creditable if Greece had asked for assistance. As it was, "we misled her as to our ability to help."

At the conference it was agreed that, in view of the uncertainty about Yugoslav and Turkish attitudes, the bulk of the Greek army should withdraw to an established defense line on the Aliakmon River, which would be reinforced by British troops. Eden was to try to get a definite reply from Paul on whether Yugoslavia was going to defend Salonika. He received this reply in Ankara on February 27. Yugoslavia's difficult geographical position and the impossibility of obtaining any appreciable help from potential allies were dictating a policy of accommodation with Germany, the message said. However, Yugoslavia would defend herself if attacked and would not permit the passage of foreign troops through her territory.

Eden found the Turkish reply equally unsatisfactory. He recalls in his memoirs that the Turkish ministers "pleaded that their country was so weak in armoured vehicles and in the air that it could not intervene if the Germans moved against Greece." The Turks approved the British landing in Greece and said they would defend themselves if attacked.

Earlier, the Turkish ambassador in Washington had informed the U.S. State Department that Turkey was not prepared to prevent the entry of German troops into Bulgaria, because of the danger of the collapse of the chief bastion of British defense in that area, leaving the whole of the Near East and Asia in danger. And Prince Paul told Bliss Lane, the American minister in Belgrade, that "he cannot attack Bulgaria in the event that German troops enter Bulgaria as this would put Yugoslavia in the wrong before the world. . . . General [Pešić] explained . . . [the] great difficulty of resisting with a million men against united German and Italian, and perhaps Bulgarian and Hungarian armies. . . . Even if the United States helped him, Yugoslavia would be finished before our assistance arrived."

These two communications, sent to American officials within a space of two days, explain why the Eden mission to create a joint Turko-Yugoslav front against Bulgaria was a complete fiasco. German troops began to cross into Bulgaria from Rumania on March 2, 1941. The Turkish foreign minister, Sükrü Saraçoğlu, told the Yugoslav ambassador on March 3 that with the German entry into Bulgaria it was too late to consider joint Turko-Yugoslav action. But Eden continued to have thoughts about it. "I could not stop thinking of Yugoslavia. This was the country with the best and largest army in the Balkans and with an air force which, though made up from many makes of aircraft, far exceeded in total the strength of any other Balkan country, and indeed our own in that theatre of war." Ronald Campbell, British minister in Belgrade, returned to his post on March 5 with a letter for Paul from Eden; Eden promised a frontier revision in Istria to Yugoslavia's advantage if Yugoslavia joined Britain. But even this failed to shake Paul's determination to avoid war with Germany over the impending invasion of Greece. Furthermore, the whole question of British help to Greece was in the balance, because the commander in chief of the Greek army, General Alexandros Papagos, had not withdrawn his troops to the Aliakmon line, nor had Eden succeeded in creating a joint

Turko-Yugoslav front. Churchill now began to have doubts about the wisdom of his Greek plan. And the chiefs of staff came to the conclusion that the plan appeared to be much more of a gamble than it had seemed at first. On March 5, Eden informed Churchill from Athens that, on returning from Ankara, he found a completely changed situation: a dispirited commander in chief of the Greek army and nonfulfillment of the agreement to withdraw Greek troops to the Aliakmon line.

That evening, Churchill replied to Eden that the war cabinet found it hard to believe that "we now have any power to avert [the] fate of Greece unless Turkey and/or Yugoslavia come in. . . . We must liberate [the] Greeks from feeling bound to reject a German ultimatum. If on their own they resolve to fight, we must to some extent share their ordeal." The following day, Eden reported from Cairo that the people there had again examined the problem thoroughly and the decision made at Athens had been right. On March 7, the war cabinet confirmed its earlier decision to land British troops in Greece, accepting "the fullest responsibility" for the action.

Churchill now began to strain every nerve to get Yugoslavia to co-operate. He called on President Franklin D. Roosevelt himself for help on March 10: "*At this juncture the action of Yugoslavia is cardinal. No country ever had such a military chance. If they will fall on the Italian rear in Albania there is no measuring what might happen in a few weeks.* The whole situation might be transformed, and the action of Turkey also decided in our favour. . . . I need scarcely say that concerted influence of your Ambassadors in Turkey, Russia, and above all in Yugoslavia, would be of enormous value at the moment, and indeed might possibly turn the scales."

In a telegram to Eden on March 14, he forecast the possibility of a *Putsch* in Yugoslavia, saying, "The attitude of Yugoslavia is still by no means hopeless, and a situation may at any moment arise which would enable you to go there."

In his letter to Paul, Eden had expressed the desirability of a visit to Belgrade. Paul had politely rejected the proposal. In the meantime, Eden had made a last attempt to get the Turks to promise to help Yugoslavia. At a meeting on March 19 between Eden and Saraçoğlu, a watered-down message was agreed upon, which, in the end, Saraçoğlu failed to send. Eden obviously did not know at the time about Hitler's letter of March 4 to the Turkish president informing him that German troops would not come near the Turkish frontier, or of the Turkish president's reply that, for their part, the Turks would not initiate any military action against Germany.

CHAPTER 3

By late February of 1941, Hitler had eliminated all diplomatic obstacles in the path of his military expedition to Greece—except Yugoslavia. As a reward for co-operation with Germany, Bulgaria had been promised an outlet to the Aegean through Greek Thrace. Secret negotiations between the German and Bulgarian general staffs had ended with a protocol, signed on February 2. For reasons of military security, formal accession to the Tripartite Pact was not announced until just before the entry of German troops into Bulgaria. Also for reasons of security, the Bulgarian government had proposed to try to "tranquilize Turkey and Yugoslavia and thus to reduce the probability of their intervening." On February 17, the Turks had signed a joint nonaggression declaration with the Bulgarians.

Throughout January and early February, we in the foreign ministry were aware of a strange lull in relations with Germany. Prince Paul had taken all the threads into his own hands. Cincar-Marković was the only person in the foreign ministry who knew that Stakić and Gregorić, our intermediaries who had visited Rome and Berlin in November, visited them again on February 4. According to Stakić, Mussolini proposed an Italo-Yugoslav alliance instead of Yugoslavia's accession to the Tripartite Pact. He also offered a population exchange: Croats and Slovenes living in Italy would be moved to Yugoslavia, and Albanians in Kosovo would go to Albania. Yugoslavia would remain outside the war and gain possession of Salonika. Rome immediately informed Berlin of the Mussolini-Stakić talks. The communication said that Stakić had offered negotiations for broadening the Friendship Pact with Italy, which would facilitate Yugoslavia's accession to the Tripartite Pact. The basis for the negotiations was to be the demilitarization of the Yugoslav coast and the acquisition of Salonika. The Duce was favorably disposed toward the offer, with the proviso that German approval was obtained.

Meanwhile, Gregorić requested a Cvetković-Ribbentrop meeting and, if possible, a Cvetković-Hitler meeting. While the initial preparations for the arrival of the Yugoslav representatives were taking place, Hitler decided on the beginning of April for the attack on Greece.

Cvetković and Cincar-Marković arrived in Salzburg on February 14 for talks with Ribbentrop. Cvetković stated that Yugoslavia did not wish the war to spread to the Balkans, that she was fighting against Bolshevism, and that she could play a useful role in preventing British penetration into the Balkans. Ribbentrop said that since Hitler had come to power Germany had consistently upheld a policy of friendship toward Yugoslavia. Germany had practically won the war, and the time had come for all countries to determine their attitude toward the new order. He said that Roosevelt's policy would compel Japan to strike at Britain in the Far East. And even Stalin would not move against Germany. Ribbentrop, obviously trying to induce a mood of compliance, assured Cvetković that by acceding to the Tripartite Pact, Yugoslavia would be joining no anti-British alliance. Cvetković raised the matter of his own plan for joint action with Turkey to put an end to the Italo-Greek war and prevent the establishment of a British front in the Balkans. In view of the concentration of German troops in Rumania, pressure could be brought to bear, with the help of Hungary and Bulgaria, on Turkey to take part in the plan. One condition, however, was that Germany herself must not move into the Balkans.

The meeting with Hitler took place the same day. Hitler declared that Germany was moving not against Greece but against Britain, which was getting a foothold there. Cvetković unfolded his plan for a Balkan bloc to preserve the peace; Hitler replied that any decisions regarding the termination of the Italo-Greek war must be made by Mussolini. Cvetković said that if Germany feared attacks on the Rumanian oil fields from British bases in Greece, the Balkan states could issue a formal declaration banning flights over their territories. Hitler replied that

Britain would not allow such a declaration to curtail her freedom of action. He added that Germany would not permit Bolshevism to enter the Balkans, whereas Britain would give Russia a free hand in the area. He disclosed that the Russians had offered Bulgaria a large part of Macedonia if she signed a treaty with them and allowed Russian troops into Bulgaria.

Finally Hitler came to his most important objective: Yugoslavia's membership in the Tripartite Pact. He called it "a unique historic opportunity . . . to fix her place in Europe definitely for all time," and added that Germany and Italy were ready to conclude the treaties. The matter of the demilitarization of the Adriatic had been raised, but Mussolini no longer insisted on this. As soon as Yugoslavia acceded to the pact, she would be able to construct a naval base at Salonika under a German-Italian guarantee.

This short summary is taken from the notes of the official German stenographer present at the meeting. Certain important remarks made by Hitler about Mussolini were omitted, but Cincar-Marković gave his version of them when he returned to Yugoslavia. Cvetković, he said, had made a sharp attack on Mussolini's policy in the Balkans. They noticed that Hitler's tone was malicious when he spoke of Mussolini's weak position. He exclaimed several times: "There's nothing you need to give to Mussolini. *Nichts. Gar nichts!*" He said he understood Yugoslavia's reluctance to grant German troops passage through her territory; if Germany obtained this right for her troops, Mussolini would be sure to demand the same for Italian troops. So he would make no such request. Moreover, the German army already had a route to Greece through Bulgaria. Finally, he said he would welcome an early visit from Paul to clarify all these issues.

On February 15, Cvetković and Cincar-Marković submitted a rosy report of their conversation with Hitler to a conference of the top ministers. On the following day an optimistic communiqué was issued.

President Roosevelt had complied with Churchill's request in January to send a man to the Balkans and the Middle East in support of the British efforts to create a front against Hitler. William J. Donovan had been chosen. He saw Prince Paul,

Cvetković, Maček, and Cincar-Marković in Belgrade on January 22 to 25. He also had a meeting with General Dušan Simović, commander in chief of the air force.

On January 25, Bliss Lane reported to Secretary of State Cordell Hull on the Donovan talks. "From remarks made by Prince Paul, Cvetković, and Maček," he wrote, ". . . it is clear that [the] Yugoslav Government is . . . determined to protect its territory against attack."

The British ambassador in Washington, Lord Halifax, sent a note to Hull on February 5 requesting support for the Yugoslav-Greek talks on joint action against the threat posed by the concentration of German troops in Rumania. Four days later, Hull advised the Yugoslav government of the United States government's position as recently expressed by Roosevelt.

Lane came to see me the following day. We knew each other very well, and we were able to speak frankly. Reminding him of the Maček-Donovan talks, I pointed out that he was wrong in suggesting that Maček was in favor of appeasing Hitler. He then gave me a complete account of the Hitler-Molotov talks, emphasizing the need to resist Hitler. I described the truly desperate position of Yugoslavia. Hitler was at the height of his power. German troops were passing through Hungary into Rumania, keeping Yugoslavia hemmed in from the north and the east. In the southeast, Yugoslavia faced Bulgaria, a country that would probably be receiving German troops very soon. On the northwest and west, we had Mussolini, who had always been ill-disposed toward us. Soviet policy was a complete enigma. Turkey was unwilling to take a definite stand against Hitler. We could expect little help from Britain. "We could easily take a strong stand against Hitler," I told him, "if the Americans were already in the war. Co-operation between Yugoslavia and Turkey could be arranged, if only you Americans were to send a few hundred bombers to bases in Turkey for use against the Germany army."

"We don't have hundreds of aircraft to send anywhere," Lane cut in. "We hardly have enough to satisfy Britain's minimal needs."

"But Yugoslavia is already halfway to being gulped down the Nazi monster's gorge," I exploded. "It has only to snap its jaws—and that's the end of Yugoslavia. Why are you pushing us toward its jaws?"

"But we are not pushing you into the war," Lane said with embarrassment. "Others are doing that. You propose that we send bombers to the Turks. I wonder if that is wise. At one time they told us that foreign troops in Bulgaria would be a *casus belli* for them, whereas now they won't even think about going to war for Greece. They make everything depend on Yugoslavia."

I told him we had the same information from our ambassador in Turkey. Finally, I asked his pardon for having allowed my outspokenness to get the better of diplomatic courtesy; I hoped he would understand how strongly I felt, faced with the overwhelming catastrophe that would overtake my country if the mighty German war machine started rolling over it.

Hull received a report from Donovan saying that Britain could defeat the German armies in the Balkans, provided they had the co-operation of the Balkan states. Two days later, under the influence of Donovan's optimism, Hull did something that had never before been done in the history of diplomacy. He stopped personally at our minister's residence in Washington with a message from President Roosevelt. The message said that a vote would soon be taken on the Lend-Lease Act, which would permit the President to supply arms to "nations that are now the victims of aggression or which might be threatened with aggression." Cvetković and Cincar-Marković were with Hitler at that very moment.

On February 18, Lane was received by Prince Paul. Paul confessed that Hitler had demanded Yugoslavia's accession to the Tripartite Pact, but he assured Lane that Yugoslavia had refused. At the same time, Hull received a report from the American ambassador in Ankara saying that the Turkish premier was not prepared to make any commitments.

Roosevelt then sent the following message to Paul: "I am addressing this message to Your Royal Highness with a view to emphasizing the interest of the United States in the outcome of the war. . . . I wish to convey to you my feeling that the world in general regards with very real sympathy any nation which resists attack, both military or diplomatic, by the predatory powers." Lane delivered the message on the evening of February 23. The Prince told him that he would resist an attack and refuse to sign any political treaty with Germany that would encroach on Yugoslavia's sovereignty. Accordingly, Lane informed the

President that Yugoslavia would not sign the Tripartite Pact under any circumstances. The Germans, Lane continued, were aware that Yugoslavia would resist and had therefore resorted to the route through Bulgaria rather than take the easier and more logical route through Yugoslavia.

The British diplomatic offensive on Prince Paul was equally persistent. Ronald Campbell saw Paul on the day that Cvetković and Cincar-Marković had their talk with Hitler. Paul asked whether British troops would fight on in the Balkans for an indefinite period if the Balkan states were compelled to defend their freedom. If the British commitment was only for a few weeks, then those countries, with their entire war potential, would be destroyed.

The British government's reply of February 20 was not at all encouraging. It said that Yugoslavia should make an agreement with Turkey to take simultaneous, co-ordinated action against the Germans in the event that they marched into Bulgaria. The British government, for its part, would do everything in its power to render them assistance. It did not believe that in such circumstances the Balkan countries would be destroyed and their war potential disappear. The note also stated that Britain was delivering considerable quantities of war materials to Greece and Turkey, and that these quantities would be increased as soon as the Americans stepped up their supply of arms to Britain.

Naturally, Berlin was not idle during this period. On February 16, Ribbentrop instructed the German minister in Belgrade to hasten Yugoslavia's accession to the Tripartite Pact and Paul's meeting with the Führer. At the same time, we received a detailed report from our minister in Moscow, Gavrilović, informing us that Hitler was preparing a military campaign against Russia in the next couple of months. Gavrilović had received his information from the Swedish minister in Moscow. In his report, Gavrilović stated that Göring had done his best to get Hitler to change his mind about attacking Russia, but without success. (This was to be confirmed at Göring's trial at Nuremberg.) Gavrilović's report gave the earliest possible date for the attack as May 22, 1941, and the latest as June 22.

Maček and I had often said in our conversations that Hitler would have to start his war against Russia by 1941, since he had been unable to conquer Britain in 1940. The conclusion we had come to was that Hitler would not undertake an invasion of Britain while leaving an intact Russia at his back, because he would be in a hopeless position if the invasion failed. Gavrilović's report confirmed our conclusions and raised Maček's spirits considerably. He kept saying that now we would have to take care that Hitler did not attack Yugoslavia before turning on Russia; once he had gone in that direction, he would have his hands full and would leave us in peace. The deeper Hitler got bogged down in Russian mud, the more easily and freely Yugoslavia would breathe.

Prince Paul could not postpone his meeting with Hitler for long, because the hour for hammer blows in the Balkans was rapidly approaching. His only remaining hope was that at the meeting, set for March 4, he could succeed in deflecting the German army from Yugoslav soil.

On February 24, Mussolini saw Stakić for the second and last time. Stakić informed him that Paul had decided on an agreement with Italy broadening the existing Friendship Pact. Once again, the matter of Yugoslavia's wishes regarding Salonika was raised. Paul considered the improvement of the political climate essential; otherwise Yugoslav public opinion, which was under strong British influence, might respond sharply. He suggested that Mussolini make a suitable public announcement. Two days later, Ribbentrop instructed Rome to allow no broadening of talks with Yugoslavia until Germany received a reply from them; he wanted Rome and Berlin to take an identical stand. The Italo-Russian talks had not yet been broken off at this point. Mussolini had informed Berlin on February 15 that he was already overdue in replying to Moscow on the question of the Dardanelles. The next day, Mussolini's reply to Molotov, which camouflaged Hitler's real objectives toward Russia, was approved by Germany. The Mussolini-Stalin negotiations ended in complete failure, because Hitler would not permit Mussolini to enter into any kind of agreement that might run counter to his own plans for the Balkans.

Mussolini, extremely anxious to conclude a new agreement with Yugoslavia, sent Berlin an account of his first conversation with Stakić. A close examination of his comments makes it clear that he was harboring a secret desire that Hitler keep out of

Greece. His treaty with Yugoslavia, he said, would "cause the moral and military collapse of Greece . . . the intervention of German armed forces in Greece would become superfluous."

The Duce was pleased with Hitler's position in his talks with Cvetković and Cincar-Marković; but his disappointment with their attitude, and more particularly with Paul's, was unmistakable. Expecting so much to come of his talks with Stakić, he was obviously disappointed that Paul did not jump straight into his arms. He complained about this to Stakić when he saw him on February 24. By that time he realized that he had lost Yugoslavia as a pawn in his game; five days later, Ciano told Hitler and Ribbentrop that the Duce considered a bilateral treaty with Yugoslavia less interesting now that Bulgaria had acceded to the Tripartite Pact. Clearly, Mussolini had expected that a treaty with Yugoslavia would have prevented German troops from moving into Greece and Bulgaria.

Cincar-Marković and I were in Budapest from February 27 to March 1 for the exchange of the instruments of ratification of the recently concluded Pact of Perpetual Friendship with Hungary. A special courier brought us the information that German troops would move into Bulgaria on March 1, when Bulgaria signed the Tripartite Pact. It was immediately clear to me that there was no longer any question of our resisting Hitler's swoop down into Greece, and that weightier talks had taken place with Berlin than was known in our ministry.

We returned to Belgrade on March 2. Cincar-Marković asked me to investigate as many nonaggression treaties as possible, and to let him know which one was best suited to Yugoslav relations with Germany. The next day he told me, in the strictest confidence, that Paul was going to visit Hitler the following evening, taking with him the draft of a treaty as a proposal for stabilizing Yugoslav-German relations.

Paul's talks with Hitler on March 4 lasted from 5:00 P.M. to 9:30 P.M. According to Ribbentrop, Hitler repeated the assertion that Britain had already lost the war, and that Yugoslavia had a unique opportunity to establish and insure her position in the Europe of the future. By acceding to the Tripartite Pact, Yugoslavia could secure for herself a German guarantee of her territorial integrity and an outlet to the Aegean. If Yugoslavia failed to secure Salonika in time, she would be incurring the risk that some third party would get it. Germany did not expect Yugoslavia to take part in the war, but she would see to it that Salonika was in Yugoslav hands when the war ended.

Paul was impressed by Hitler's arguments, but he expressed apprehensions about possible internal disorder. He feared he would not be in his present position in six months' time if he accepted this arrangement, and he reserved his decision on the matter.

The German account failed to mention that Paul spoke up very sharply against Mussolini at this meeting as the murderer of King Alexander, and that Hitler warned the Prince that all of Yugoslavia's neighbors were demanding parts of her territory. Paul told me on September 27, 1955, that Hitler had explained to him that he wished to spare Yugoslavia *"aus eigenen egoistichen Gründen"* ("for his own selfish reasons"). The Prince interpreted this to mean that Hitler knew he would have to share Yugoslavia with Italy if she were drawn into the war; whereas he wanted Yugoslavia all for himself, without war, as a supplier of valuable raw materials and foodstuffs.

On his return to Belgrade on March 5, Paul called a meeting of the Crown Council for the next day. Prior to the meeting, I saw Maček. As usual, I gave him my report of all new developments. I especially drew his attention to the fact that, when I had informed Cincar-Marković on March 1 that the Germans had started moving into Bulgaria, he had taken it very calmly. I raised again the matter of the report submitted by Cincar-Marković to a special meeting of the most important Serbian ministers and army respresentatives—to which neither he (Maček) nor Fran Kulovec, who had entered the government after the death of the Slovenian leader Anton Korošec, had been invited. By chance, a copy of the report passed through my hands. The report envisaged the accession of Yugoslavia to the Tripartite Pact if Hitler refused a bilateral pact with us. It underlined the expectation that the Allies would not victimize Yugoslavia after the war in order to reward Italy, Hungary, and Bulgaria, countries that were already guilty of greater offenses than Yugoslavia would ever be. Maček then told me that Kulovec had just reported to him the result of his discussion with General Petar Pešić, minister of war, and the chief of the general staff, General Petar Kosić. They both opposed entering the war. In a war with Germany, Kosić maintained, the Yugoslav army might lose its hard-earned reputation, because the German war machine was devastating. In view of all this, I guessed that Maček would hear two points of view at the forthcoming meeting: one from Cvetković, who, by virtue of his office, would most probably favor an energetic line; and the other from Cincar-Marković and Pešić, who would defend a policy of appeasing Hitler, and would probaby echo Paul's personal sentiments. Maček agreed with me, and a few hours later he told me our prediction had been correct.

The various reports coming in on Hitler's preparations for an attack on Stalin had a tremendous influence on the participants at the first Crown Council. News from Slovakia gave us details of strategic roads being built by the Germans to facilitate the invasion. Signposts in Slovakia and occupied Poland were being changed to give better directions to the troops bound for the Russian frontier. But the most important information was the report from our minister in Moscow that Hitler was planning to attack Russia by June 22 at the latest. Since we were also receiving reports about Ukrainians and White Russians being trained by the Germans for various duties, no doubts were left in our minds that Hitler was very soon going to repeat Napoleon's blunder. A single thought dominated the minds of all as they made their way to the Prince's palace at Dedinje: adopt any possible diplomatic maneuvers to spare Yugoslavia the horrors of war, if only until Hitler's main forces came to grips with Stalin's.

At 10:00 A.M. the meeting opened, under Paul's chairmanship, and it lasted for three hours. The council was composed of the other two regents, Radenko Stanković and Ivan Perović; Premier Cvetković; Vice-Premier Maček; Minister of State Kulovec; Foreign Minister Marković; Armed Forces Minister Pešić; and Royal Court Minister Milan Antić.

Paul reported that he had seen Hitler two days earlier, and that he had failed to prevail upon him to accept a nonaggression treaty. Hitler adhered to his demand that Yugoslavia accede to the Tripartite Pact. He said that Hitler had repeated his offer to obtain not only Mussolini's approval of the German commitment to respect Yugoslavia's frontiers, but also his actual countersignature on the same document. Hitler said he understood the Yugoslav position perfectly and was willing to exempt Yugoslavia from the obligation of military assistance and from having to accept the passage of foreign troops across her territory. But, Paul said, he told Hitler he was not able to give his consent to the pact. He concluded, "I am not clear in my own mind whether Hitler will attack us if we fail to accede to the Tripartite Pact, or whether he is going to leave us in peace, despite our not being bound to Germany either by a bilateral treaty or within the framework of the Tripartite Pact."

Cvetković then spoke out vigorously against permitting the Germans or Italians to occupy Salonika, because that would mean Yugoslavia's complete encirclement and would lead to further demands, which, if accepted, would result in Yugoslavia's complete capitulation. He recommended the defense of Salonika and insistence on a bilateral treaty with Germany.

Pešić pointed out that Yugoslavia's military situation would become critical if there was a conflict with Germany. Yugoslavia was already virtually surrounded, and a line of retreat could scarcely be said to exist. We would not be able to resist for more than two months. There were no prospects of effective help from Turkey, Britain, Greece, or Russia. He advised a policy of appeasement in order to avoid war.

The next speaker, Stanković, accepted all of Cvetković's arguments but proposed a different strategic approach in order to meet the objections raised by Pešić. His idea was that the Yugoslav army in the south ought to find itself a De Gaulle and join the Greek and British troops, using the fighting in the north as a smoke screen. However, Pešić said he could not under any circumstances accept the idea that government orders should be disobeyed by one section of the army; this was what active fighting in the south, and only token fighting elsewhere, would imply.

Maček asked Cincar-Marković: "Can we obtain from Germany the necessary guarantees for our future security by acceding to the Tripartite Pact without making any commitment to furnish military assistance to the German-Italian camp? And what faith can we place in German promises and guarantees?" Cincar-Marković answered that Germany was offering a guarantee of Yugoslavia's territorial integrity and had induced Italy to give the same guarantee; she was not requesting any assistance in the war from Yugoslavia. Germany was prepared to ratify these promises in the most solemn form, provided that Yugoslavia accede to the Tripartite Pact. He declared that failure to accede to the pact would provoke German distrust and open the door wide to Italian-German-Hungarian plots. He added that Germany was offering Yugoslavia Salonika in the future territorial rearrangement of the Balkans, and he urged speed lest Hitler step up his demands.

Kulovec came out strongly in favor of a peace-preserving policy, even within the framework of the Tripartite Pact, provided, of course, that Germany accept the Yugoslav conditions of nonparticipation in the war, no passage for foreign troops, and no transport of war materials through Yugoslav territory. "If our accession to the Tripartite Pact postpones our entry into the war . . . even for a single month, I am all in favor of it. The argument that we shall be completely encircled if the Germans or Italians seize Salonika does not impress me very much. I am of the opinion that we are already completely encircled. We shall have ample opportunity to fight if Germany fails to keep her promises." He concluded with a Latin tag: *"Qui habet tempus, habet vitam"* ("He who has time has life").

With the exception of Paul, who did not vote, all the participants voted in favor of accession to the Tripartite Pact under the conditions mentioned. Cincar-Marković saw Heeren, the German minister in Belgrade, the next morning and told him the council's decision. He named Yugoslavia's conditions in the following order: (1) no obligation to furnish military assistance in the war either now or in the future; (2) no passage of troops, and no transport of war materials, through Yugoslav territory; (3) German and Italian guarantees to respect Yugoslavia's territorial integrity; (4) permission to make all this public; (5) reservation of Salonika for Yugoslavia in the new Balkan reorganization.

The German government accepted all the Yugoslav conditions on March 9. However, on the following morning, Heeren handed Cincar-Marković an amended reply. The German government requested that the words "unless Yugoslavia should express her wish for that" be included in the clause releasing Yugoslavia from the obligation to furnish military assistance to the members of the Tripartite Pact. Hitler did not consent, according to the amended reply, to a public statement that Yugoslavia was not obliged to furnish aid in any contingency regardless of any extension of the war.

The second Crown Council met on Monday, March 10. It was decided to inform the German government that Yugoslavia abided by the original conditions.

The German reply to this arrived on the afternoon of Wednesday, March 12. The German government adhered to its previous reply, justifying it on the grounds that if the facts were known, other states acceding to the pact might insist on the same exemptions, and Germany was not willing to make the same concessions to them. In informing Ribbentrop of Cincar-Marković's immediate reaction, Heeren strongly recommended that Germany comply with Yugoslavia's request to make public her exemption from furnishing military aid to the Axis. In his reply of March 14, Ribbentrop rejected this appeal.

The third Crown Council met that same day and approved the German demands. It was left to Cincar-Marković to work out with Heeren all the necessary details and to submit them to the Council of Ministers for final approval. At this meeting Milan Antić proposed that Yugoslavia also request a corridor from the Yugoslav frontier to Salonika. The proposal was rejected following the intervention of Cvetković and Maček. They argued that it was odious to accept even the promise of Salonika at a time when the gallant Greeks were fighting, and that the promise had been accepted by Yugoslavia only to prevent some other state from gaining possession of the city. Yugoslavia should not go beyond that. The demand for a corridor, however, had already been put to Heeren two days earlier.

The people who mattered politically in Yugoslavia began to wonder what had prompted the German demand for an amendment to the exemption clause. Paul concluded that the Germans were planning to bring Stojadinović back to power in Yugoslavia; for that reason, he was handed over to the British in Greece on March 19.

On March 5, Lane obtained Secretary Hull's authorization to inform the Yugoslav government of Roosevelt's February 22 message to Paul. I acted as interpreter between Maček and Lane, who saw Paul on March 7. The Prince confessed he was "waver-

ing" over a decision on what to do about the German encirclement of Yugoslavia. To attack Germany would be "suicidal" for
Yugoslavia and would cost "two or three hundred thousand lives
and [result in the] devastation of the country . . . until the
end of the war and partition . . . between Germany, Italy,
Hungary and Bulgaria." Despite this, Yugoslavia would not
allow the Germans to pass through her territory. "We will not
capitulate," he asserted. "We will never be on our knees." Lane
informed Hull that the Prince was the man who would "make
[the] ultimate decision," and that he (Lane) and the British
minister "are doing all we can to strengthen his attitude."

Paul accepted only one of the many suggestions made by Eden
in a letter of March 3: he sent an emissary of the Yugoslav
general staff to Athens to make contact with Greek and British
army representatives. The emissary, Lieutenant Colonel Milisav
Perišić, had talks with them on March 8 and 9. He inquired
about the strength of the Anglo-Greek forces allocated for the
front against the German onslaught, the defense of Salonika, the
flow of arms, and what aid the Yugoslav army could expect from
Britain. Lieutenant-General Henry Maitland Wilson, commander
of the British forces in Greece, noticed at once that the Yugoslav
military did not understand modern methods of warfare. "It was
evident that the effect of bombing on an inadequately protected
port had not been appreciated and conditions similar to 1916–18
were visualized."

Since Wilson received no communication from Belgrade following his talks with Perišić, Eden asked the Yugoslav government to approve a visit from him or from Dill. On March 15, this
request was rejected. When Campbell informed him that Yugoslavia's resistance was weakening, Eden gave him authority to say
that any pact "must include a German promise not to attack
Salonika." On March 19, Eden sent to Belgrade a mutual friend
of his and Paul's, Terence Shone, minister of the legation in
Cairo, with another suggestion that someone come to Belgrade.
Eden commented later: "The Prince Regent's reply, after his talk
with Shone, though very friendly, showed a continuing repug-
nance towards any meeting."

There was displeasure in Washington when the Yugoslav
National Bank requested that its gold, deposited for safekeeping
with the U.S. Treasury, and amounting to $22 million, be con-

verted to dollars and half of it transferred to the Bank of Brazil. In this connection, Lane went to see Paul and the Premier on March 16. Paul told him that "Yugoslavia would not sign [a] pact with [a] military clause permitting occupation of the country. Yugoslavia will fight rather than accept such conditions." In addition, he said, an attack on Germany "would be folly." Lane also reported to Hull that Cvetković, like Paul, had indicated that "Yugoslavia would not consider occupation of Salonika a *casus belli*." In conclusion, Lane said that "Yugoslavia may feel obliged to sign [a] pact with Germany without military clauses." On March 19, Lane sent a personal message to Under Secretary of State Sumner Welles saying that Paul would be dining with him privately on the following evening and that he would do his best to "strengthen his resistance then, even though it may be too late."

At this dinner, Lane pressed the Prince not to accept the Tripartite Pact, but Paul told him that the pact, without any military clauses, was soon to be signed. Lane pressed on, until the Prince exclaimed, "You big nations are hard, you talk of our honor, but you are far away." Two days later, Lane tried to convert Cvetković to his point of view. Finally, on March 23, Lane reported that he had learned from the highest sources that the decision had been made for Yugoslavia to sign the Tripartite Pact.

Eden tried to get Moscow to intervene with Belgrade against Yugoslavia's accession to the pact. On March 22, Cripps went to see Vyshinsky, who told him sharply that the Soviet government saw no basis for discussing with London problems "extraneous" to Soviet-British relations. On the same day, Churchill sent an appeal to Cvetković and, later, a message to Paul suggesting that Yugoslavia attack the Italians in Albania.

On March 23, the Prince told Lane that he had given his earlier promise not to accede to the pact because at that time he had had no intention of doing so. He said that the Croats and the Slovenes, the other two regents, and the opposition party of General Petar Živković had "urged him to sign." Lane reported that he had "never seen the Prince so upset . . . almost without self control. . . . He ranted about Bulgarian perfidy, British stupidity and opposition of Croats but he refused to consider possibility of not signing pact and capitulating to Germany."

. . .

The formal elaboration of the agreements connected with Yugoslavia's accession to the Tripartite Pact was completed by March 19. A meeting of the Crown Council was held on March 20, and the relevant documents were adopted. The Council of Ministers was convened at nine o'clock that evening, for the same purpose. During the day, I went to the British embassy to meet Terence Shone, who, being on a secret mission, could not come to my office. He asked me to inform Maček that the British were asking Yugoslavia not to sign anything with Germany. While at the embassy, I asked to see the British minister. Campbell received me immediately, and told me he was very anxious about Paul's fate, because he was not popular with the Serbs, and public opinion was agitated by the rumors that we were acceding to the Tripartite Pact. He feared a possible *coup d'état* that might sweep away the Serbo-Croatian agreement along with Prince Paul. I informed him of the general terms we had laid down in our negotiations with Germany. Later, I gave an account to Maček of this conversation. I then left for Zagreb, where I had some urgent business. I came back to Belgrade on the eve of the March 27 *Putsch* and witnessed its first moves without realizing what they were. As a precautionary measure against the demonstrations called for the following day, a cordon of troops was put around the old court palace.

During my absence from Belgrade, a crisis had arisen over the resignation, on March 21, of three ministers who had refused to accept the Tripartite Pact. General Simović had nearly provoked another government crisis, on the evening of March 23, when he informed Paul that, if the pact was signed, air force headquarters, general staff headquarters, and the Prince's palace might be bombed by junior air force officers. Some of the council members proposed Simović's immediate arrest. A ministerial conference was called instantly. Simović's arrest was ruled out by Paul, who sent him to General Pešić. Pešić, in turn, sent him back to Paul, and said: "Take my resignation with you. What is left for me to do, if he is seeing you behind my back?"

Meanwhile, the country lived under the German ultimatum, delivered on the morning of March 22, demanding a definite answer within thirty-six hours. Heeren waited for his answer in

Cvetković's office, and just before midnight on March 23, he was informed that our delegates would be in Vienna on March 25.

The protocol of Yugoslavia's accession to the Tripartite Pact was signed by Cvetković and Cincar-Marković, in Hitler's presence, on March 25. Ribbentrop and Ciano signed for Germany and Italy. Immediately afterward, the Yugoslav delegates received all the agreed notes, addressed to the Premier and signed separately by Ribbentrop and Ciano. The first note promised respect for Yugoslavia's territorial integrity; the second promised that the Axis powers would not seek transport of troops or war material through Yugoslav territory; the third confirmed that the Axis powers would not seek military assistance from Yugoslavia unless Yugoslavia herself should desire to furnish it; the fourth promised Yugoslavia Salonika, and a Yugoslav corridor, in the reorganization of the Balkans. Cvetković gave a written guarantee that Yugoslavia would not reveal the third and fourth notes without the agreement of the Axis powers.

After the signing ceremony, Cvetković and Cincar-Marković were received by Hitler, who expressed his satisfaction at Yugoslavia's accession to the pact. This, he said, gave Yugoslavia the moral right to play a part in the forthcoming reorganization of southeastern Europe. He assured Cvetković that, should Yugoslavia ever find herself in a precarious situation, "she would always find in the Führer an honest, loyal mediator, broker, and friend."

Those involved in organizing the *Putsch* were having their difficulties. On March 24 and 25, one section of the leadership was hesitant about proceeding with it. Simović favored demonstrations to bring about the fall of the Cvetković government and hasten his own rise to power. Another difficulty arose over the timing. It was finally agreed that the *Putsch* should be carried out after Cvetković and Cincar-Marković returned from Vienna. General Bora Mirković, deputy commander in chief of the air force, and actual leader of the *Putsch,* persuaded Simović to take over the premiership after the *Putsch,* and thus assume ostensible responsibility for it. He was hesitant, however, in the final hours, to carry out the *Putsch* at the agreed time.

The British realized that something was brewing, and they

even knew who the ringleaders were. The British agent responsible for the infiltration of the Yugoslav army told me after the war that they had, in the president of Narodna Odbrana (National Defense), Ilija Birčanin, the most ideal tool. General Donovan had informed the British Middle East command that Simović had told him the army would not tolerate Yugoslavia's accession to the Tripartite Pact. After the *Putsch*, and Donovan's departure, we discovered that Simović had also met an American army general staff representative in Planica, Slovenia. Immediately following the resignation of the three ministers from the Cvetković government, Campbell asked Eden for authorization to threaten severance of diplomatic relations if Belgrade acceded to the Tripartite Pact, in order to "encourage the opposition to overthrow the Government and annul their signature." Eden rejected the proposal. "I agree that . . . suggested *coup* would have to be staged at the moment of reaction caused by signature and this may be very soon." The next day, Eden sent Campbell authorization to act on his own if he had no time to consult him. On March 24, when it finally became clear that the Yugoslav ministers were going to sign the pact the next day, Eden sent Campbell a telegram: ". . . You have my full authority for any measures that you may think it right to take to further change of Government or regime, even by *coup d'état*." Eden has frankly admitted that before sending this telegram to Campbell the British "had for some time been supporting one of the Serb parties, which had a Minister in the Government. He had taken the lead in resigning over the Pact." On March 26, Churchill sent a telegram to Campbell: "Do not let any gap grow up between you and Prince Paul or Ministers. Continue to pester, nag, and bite. Demand audiences. Don't take *NO* for an answer. . . . At the same time, do not neglect any alternative to which we may have to resort if we find present Government have gone beyond recall. Greatly admire all you have done so far. Keep it up by every means that occur to you."

The Serbian party mentioned by Eden was the Agrarian party. Its leader was Milan Gavrilović, then Yugoslav minister in Moscow. His deputy, Miloš Tupanjanin, who was very active on behalf of the British intelligence service, managed to influence some of the *Putsch* leaders without their knowing that they were being indirectly manipulated. At about 2:00 P.M. on March 26, he planted the seeds of a rumor that Generals Simović, Mirković, and Bogoljub Ilić were about to be placed on the retired list. Mirković, who made all the arrangements for the *Putsch,* confessed to me that he came to his final decision soon after 2:00 P.M. on March 26. He tried to get in touch with Simović, but found he was having his siesta. When Simović came to air force headquarters at 5:00 P.M., Mirković informed him of his final decision. Simović made another plea for postponement, but when he realized that Mirković was adamant, he said he would stay at home during the night in order to defend the conspirators should the coup miscarry. Mirković replied, "There will be no need for defense. It's either success for us or the firing squad."

The mobilization of many classes, and orders to the army to maintain a state of readiness, made it easier to carry out the *Putsch.* Although demonstrations were expected, the internal situation was sufficiently calm to permit Paul to leave Belgrade on the evening of March 26 for a few days' rest in Slovenia. Mirković concluded that Paul had heard rumors of the preparations for the coup and was going north to organize a counter-coup. He decided to stop the Prince at all costs. An army unit was sent to blow up the railway line at Batajnica, some twenty kilometers north of Belgrade. Soon thereafter, Mirković was told that Paul's family was going to remain in Belgrade. Realizing now that the Prince's journey held no danger, he immediately countermanded the order. The Belgrade chief of police was told to delay the departure of the Prince's train, because the line was mined. The train finally left the Topčider railroad station at 10:00 P.M., after a delay of more than an hour. Paul was awakened at about 4:00 A.M. and told of the *Putsch* in Belgrade. His train was directed to Zagreb, where Maček met him at the station and drove with him to the governor's palace. Simović telephoned Paul and asked him to appeal to Maček to come to Belgrade and join the new government. Maček told Simović that Paul would be returning to Belgrade later in the day and demanded that the Prince and his family be allowed to leave the country unmolested. He made this a condition for any further talks with Simović.

Paul arrived in Belgrade at about 7:00 P.M. and persuaded King Peter to accept the *Putsch* and the new government, which was acting in the King's name but had no authority from him.

Peter's proclamation to the people about ascending the throne and forming a new government was read by a young officer impersonating the King. Prince Paul and his family left Belgrade for Greece at eleven o'clock on the night of March 27.

If the Prince had been in Belgrade at the time of the *Putsch,* it probably would have failed, because the conspirators had very small forces behind them. The other two regents had tried to stage a countercoup, but they had insufficient authority. When Maček had suggested staging a countercoup in Zagreb, Paul declared that he could not accept responsibility for the civil war that might ensue. Furthermore, the Prince's family in Belgrade was surrounded by military units under the command of the conspirators. This, more than anything else, decided him against a countercoup.

The new government of General Simović, composed of representatives from all the main political parties, found itself faced with the gravest imaginable problems. Churchill praised the *Putsch* enthusiastically, exclaiming that Yugoslavia had "found her soul" early that morning. After the first day of delirium among the public and some wild outbreaks of anti-German and anti-Italian feeling, a more serious mood set in. The senior members of the cabinet, prompted by Maček's message from Zagreb, realized that Hitler and Mussolini had to be placated. After examining the documents in the top-secret files connected with the previous government's accession to the Tripartite Pact, they found that the treaties were not so bad after all. Vice-Premier Slobodan Jovanović, a respected legal authority, said that the pact was valid unless abrogated. The first explanations given by Simović and Foreign Minister Momčilo Ninčić to the German and Italian ministers in Belgrade were that the *Putsch* had been directed against the internal regime, not against their countries, and that the new government recognized the validity of Yugoslavia's accession to the Tripartite Pact. They emphasized that, in order to safeguard her interests, Yugoslavia would look to its strict implementation. On March 27, the deputy chief of the general staff, General Milan Nikolić, told the Italian military attaché that in the event of a German attack on Yugoslavia the Italian troops in Albania would become hostages of the Yugoslav army. On March 31, Simović repeated this threat, precipitating a grave crisis with Italy. Simović thus showed his capacity for acting thoughtlessly in delicate situations, and upsetting the mood of political conciliation that the majority of his government desired.

Ninčić asked me to get in contact with the German minister in order to create a favorable climate for new talks with Germany. On March 28, I informed Ninčić that Maček had asked me to do the same, instructing me to appeal to Heeren to do everything possible to preserve the peace between Germany and Yugoslavia. Ninčić told me to let Heeren know that if the Germans needed Salonika for their military operations, Yugoslavia would be satisfied with Valona instead. I pointed out to Ninčić that this was a very delicate move, and suggested we use the German news agency correspondent, Walter Gruber, to send the first feelers out to Heeren. Gruber readily agreed, and also promised to pass the information on to Berlin.

Heeren met me in my office that afternoon. After I conveyed Maček's appeal to him, we moved on to the proposal Gruber had already put before him. He referred to the years of effort and negotiation that had been necessary to get Salonika for Yugoslavia, and to Berlin's recognition that the Serbo-Bulgarian dispute over Macedonia and Salonika must be ended once and for all. Therefore, he did not see how anything could be changed now. He was exceedingly sorry that there was now danger of a conflict between Germany and Yugoslavia. He realized that the war, if it came, would be a harsh one, because both the Germans and the Yugoslavs were brave soldiers. I repeated that a great and powerful nation like Germany should be prepared to put aside past grievances, particularly now that both Maček and Ninčić had given their assurance that the new government would honor all the old pledges. Heeren then lodged a complaint about certain incidents and disturbances directed against him and members of his staff that morning. I reported this to Ninčić's office immediately, and was instructed by Ninčić to express to Heeren our government's regret over the incident and also to request an audience with him for Milan Grol, leader of the Democratic party.

In the course of my second audience with Heeren that day, we touched briefly on the main topic of our concern. As I was leaving, he said, with a sigh, "If it were up to us to decide on war or peace, it would be peace, but as things are . . . " Outside, after we had shaken hands, he made a final comment: "Whatever happens, you Croats have no cause to fear the horrors of war, because you are correct in your behavior toward the Reich." After his first contact with Ninčić and me, through Gruber, Heeren had sent this message to his government: "The composition of the new Cabinet . . . is a guarantee that it will find strong support also in Serbian circles. It would have the strength to adhere to a foreign policy line even if it should be unpopular. An understanding with this Cabinet would therefore establish a clear situation. The person of the Foreign Minister and the cooperation of the Croatian wing is a guarantee of a basic tendency to avoid a conflict with the Axis."

Ninčić knew Mussolini well from the time of the signing of the Italo-Yugoslav Friendship Pact. This acquaintance was expected to stand us in good stead—that was why he had been appointed foreign minister. He now succeeded in ironing out the bad impression made by Simović's threats to the Italian minister. Talks were resumed with him in hopes of getting Mussolini to persuade Hitler to accept the new government's assurances. This was the gist of a declaration sent by Ninčić to the German and Italian ministers on the afternoon of March 30. It also contained a codicil affirming the Yugoslav government's determination that implementation of the pact would not infringe on Yugoslavia's vital interests. The Italian minister proposed that this codicil be deleted. There were further negotiations on this and on a visit to Rome to arrange matters with Mussolini.

Then the invitation to our ministers to come to Rome was canceled on March 31. That was a bad sign. Simović sent a telegram that day to Göring, expressing the hope that good relations would be established between the new government and Germany. Ninčić informed the Germans that he would like to go to Berlin to discuss ways of preventing a disaster. Maček, who had talked with German emissaries in Zagreb, also expressed willingness to go to Berlin. At that moment, Germany wanted to set Maček at odds with Belgrade. Ante Pavelić's followers in Zagreb told the Germans that they were unable to raise a revolt in Croatia without the German army, and that it was essential to win Maček's support for the Croatian separatist cause. Aware of the German aim, Maček stated that in this extreme crisis his solidarity with the Serbian people remained unshaken. He arrived in Belgrade on April 4 and assumed the office of vice-premier. On the eve of his departure from Zagreb, he had delivered a historic speech in the cause of peace and Serbo-Croatian solidarity. After an enthusiastic welcome from the people of Belgrade, he made another speech along the same lines.

All the efforts of diplomacy, both Yugoslav and Italian, had failed to placate Hitler's rage. Mussolini had been overjoyed when asked by the Yugoslav government to act as intermediary for a German-Yugoslav *rapprochement*. But as soon as he heard that Hitler would not accept his mediation, he immediately adopted Hitler's position. Hitler adhered obstinately to the decision he had communicated to his army leaders on March 27, "to smash Yugoslavia militarily and as a state. . . . Politically, it is especially important that the blow against Yugoslavia be carried out with inexorable severity and that the military destruction be carried out in a lightning-like operation. In this way, Turkey [also] would presumably be sufficiently deterred."

Eden, informed of the *Putsch* on his way back to England, interrupted his journey at Malta and returned to Cairo. He offered to come to Belgrade, but was politely turned down by the new regime. In his place, Dill flew to Belgrade on March 31. He met Simović, but the two failed to work out a plan of action. Simović later indicated that he had refused to sign a military agreement with Dill when he realized how small was the military aid being offered. The same night, Simović and Ninčić saw the Soviet chargé d'affaires, who proposed an immediate dispatch of Yugoslav delegates to Moscow to conclude a treaty of alliance. Molotov's message said that "every hour counts." That same day a mission was sent to Moscow. The Yugoslav minister in Moscow was surprised, for he had had no inkling that the Soviet government was ready for such a move. He was skeptical, as were some of us in Belgrade. We proved to be right. Stalin thought it desirable to encourage Yugoslav resistance to Hitler, and he offered a treaty of alliance; in the end, all we received from him was a treaty of friendship and neutrality in the event of an attack on Yugoslavia. This treaty was signed on April 5.

Another mission was sent to Ankara; it fared no better. General Miloje Janković went to Greece on April 3 to meet General Papagos and General Wilson. According to Wilson's account, the discussions revealed that Yugoslavia's military leaders had an entirely exaggerated idea of the strength of the British forces in Greece, and that they had made no real preparations to meet a German attack. "Thus closed the most unusual and at the same time the most unsatisfactory conference I have ever attended," he wrote.

On April 2, the Yugoslav military attaché in Berlin reported to Belgrade that the Germans would attack Yugoslavia on April 6. Twice on April 5 the British sent warnings that the German attack would come the next morning. Simović dismissed the information as nonsense. Thus no preparations were made to meet the Germans, which explains the great panic in Belgrade when the attack came.

Churchill summed up the situation correctly: "The mistakes of years cannot be remedied in hours. When the general excitement had subsided, everyone in Belgrade realised that disaster and death approached them and that there was little they could do to avert their fate."

CHAPTER 4

Hitler was completely taken aback by the news of the *Putsch* in Belgrade. At first he thought it was a joke. But when Heeren's report arrived, with news of the anti-German demonstrations, Hitler flew into a rage. He later confessed that he had never in his life been so indignant. He immediately called an emergency meeting of his military leaders to inform them of his decision to destroy Yugoslavia. He left the conference hall twice, to tell the Hungarian and Bulgarian ministers that their countries would soon obtain satisfaction of their territorial demands against Yugoslavia. He also sent a telegram to Mussolini, which said: "From the beginning I have regarded Yugoslavia as the most dangerous factor in the conflict with Greece. . . . For this reason I did everything and honestly tried to include Yugoslavia in our community of interests."

General Wilson has said in his memoirs that Hitler launched his campaign against Yugoslavia and Greece with stronger forces than were needed: twenty-seven excellently equipped divisions, seven of which were Panzer divisions. In the south two elite regiments, the Grossdeutschland and the Leibstandarte, were hurled into battle in order to achieve a lightning breakthrough on that front and make contact with the Italians as quickly as possible. The remaining German forces consisted of infantry and motorized and mountain divisions. On March 29, German and Italian general staff representatives agreed on a demarcation of operational zones for their armies.

At the same time, negotiations were under way between the German and Hungarian general staffs. The Hungarian military chiefs were prepared to submit to German demands, but the Hungarian premier, Count Paul Teleki, was not. While he was talking to Zoltan Tildy, leader of the Smallholders party, about his hopeless struggle against Hitler's demands, he was informed that German troops had crossed into Hungary. Teleki had been very upset by British threats against Hungary should she yield to Hitler. Also, he felt it dishonorable to renege on the Perpetual Friendship Pact with Yugoslavia, signed only four months earlier. All this severe psychological strain drove him to suicide in the predawn hours of April 3. He left the following note for Regent Horthy: "We have broken our solemn word out of cowardice. We have gone against the spirit of the Treaty of Eternal Friendship. . . . The nation is aware of this: we have squandered its honour. We have sided with gangsters. . . . We are going to loot corpses; we shall be the most infamous among all nations. I failed to hold you back. I am guilty."

Horthy reported the event to Hitler the same day. At the Ministerial Council meeting on April 1, at which he had presided, it was argued that Hungary should try to save face by counting on the breakaway of Croatia, which would annul Hungarian obligations to Yugoslavia. Hitler finally consented to the postponement of Hungarian operations against Yugoslavia until April 14. These operations were to come under the command of the German army, which had permission to conduct any actions it wished from Hungarian territory. On April 5, Hitler proposed to Mussolini that the Italian army be placed under German command in the campaign against Yugoslavia; Hitler would keep Mussolini personally informed about "the general considerations necessary for joint operations," and these would be known to them alone. The Duce accepted the proposal the following day. He was delighted, he said, that it had been put to him in "so extremely delicate a manner."

In addition to the gallantry of Teleki, the well-meaning conduct of Heeren during these tragic days also stands out. He was recalled on March 30. On his arrival in Berlin he was summoned to a meeting of military experts to discuss plans for the terror-bombing of Belgrade. He spoke out against it. When he realized that he could change nothing, he left the meeting and burst into tears. I heard the story after the war, from Heeren's Italian colleague. Heeren also wrote a moving appeal to Ribbentrop on April 3 not to take "punitive action against

Belgrade." At that time German radio stations were broadcasting fabricated news about attacks on German citizens and ill-treatment of the German national minority in Yugoslavia. On April 3, the German consul general in Zagreb warned Berlin about the damage caused by such false propaganda. All these appeals were in vain, however, because Hitler had decided to wreak his monstrous vengeance on Belgrade, on the whole of Yugoslavia, and on the Serbian people in particular.

Meanwhile, at the top level in Belgrade, there were still expectations of help from Moscow. The Soviet chargé d'affaires informed my ministry that Molotov had made a move in Berlin in the cause of preserving peace between Germany and Yugoslavia. Molotov's probable motive was to induce Hitler to open the negotiations on the Balkans that Stalin so desperately wanted.

Hitler's proclamation that the German army had started operations against Yugoslavia and Greece was issued on April 6. At 6:40 that morning, the sirens started their ghastly wailing in Belgrade, followed by the roar of German bombers and the thunder of antiaircraft guns. The air was saturated with explosions. Bombs began to fall near the quarter where I lived, rattling windows and causing houses to rock and tremble as if they were about to collapse. The diabolical drone of the aircraft, the deafening thunder of unremitting explosions, the whistle of falling bombs, the cries for help of the wounded, and the shrieks of the terrified sounded to many people like the Last Trumpet.

I remained in the cellar during the first three waves of bombing. At 8:15 there was a lull, and I went up to my apartment on the fifth floor. Right inside my front door was a heap of broken glass from my windows. The house across the street had been completely razed, and thick smoke poured from the house next to it. A bomb had fallen down the stairwell and into the cellar, killing eleven people and setting fire to several neighboring stores.

I dressed hurriedly. The telephone was out of order, but my driver came to pick me up as usual, and we set out for the ministry. Our trip was a difficult and painful one, for the route was obstructed by overturned streetcars, wrecked automobiles, and heaps of bodies. Shops and stores were gaping holes, their windows shattered and their doors wrenched off. At 10:00 A.M. the fourth wave of bombers came.

Chaos reigned. We were unable to get in touch with our minister or with Premier Simović. I sent my secretary to the Hotel Bristol, where Maček and the Croatian ministers were staying. They were not there, and no one knew what had happened to them. A colleague and I agreed that I should take one section of the staff to Vrnjačka Banja, the emergency evacuation center previously allotted to the foreign ministry, while he tried to hang on for a few more hours. I left Belgrade with my party at midday. Every few yards on our way out of the city we saw bodies. At Mount Avala, about seventeen kilometers from Belgrade, we came upon a military detachment. An officer I knew told me that Maček had passed by half an hour before. Sadly, we looked at the billowing columns of smoke rising from many fires burning in the capital. The soldiers around us seemed in superb fighting form but their faces showed deep distress over their impotence.

We arrived at Vrnjačka Banja at 5:00 P.M. The British minister and his staff were already there. Ninčić had gone to Sevojna, near Užice, which had been reserved for the cabinet. He telephoned at six o'clock to ask if telegrams could be sent out. Since the British minister had a portable transmitter we could use, Ninčić instructed me to send a telegram to our ambassador in Ankara authorizing him to sign an agreement with Turkey forthwith for joint action against Germany. Then I talked to Maček, who expressed joy in learning that I had come through the morning's horrors in one piece. He told me that on the following day he was going to take his leave of the Premier, because he had decided to return to Zagreb to share the ills of the war with his own people. In his place he would send the chief secretary of his party, Juraj Krnjević, who had spent ten years in exile and knew the Western world well.

The question of Turkey's declaration of war against Germany had been raised repeatedly by our ambassador in Ankara. Initially he had received backing from the British representatives there, but the German blitzkrieg soon convinced the British that it was not in their interests for Turkey to enter the war against Germany at that time.

On the day of the invasion, Cordell Hull made a speech sharply condemning Germany's barbarous attack on Yugoslavia, and promising immediate dispatch of assistance. Also, the Yugoslav army command had sent an urgent appeal to the British high command in Greece requesting as many British bombing attacks as possible on the invading German columns along the Yugoslav southern front.

I arrived at the cabinet's headquarters on April 7. We were all anxious because none of us, including the Minister of the Armed Forces, knew anything of what was happening on the various fronts. We still believed that our resistance would be stabilized in the mountainous regions of Bosnia, the Sandžak, Herzegovina, and Montenegro, and we therefore transferred the government headquarters to Pale, near Sarajevo, on April 10. The Premier, who had taken charge of operations, told the cabinet meeting on April 13 that the front would be stabilized farther to the north. The same day, however, he went to the army high command to hand over command to General Danilo Kalafatović and authorize him to surrender. We were then informed that the government seat had been transferred to Nikšić, in Montenegro, and that we must move early the following morning. I had seen signs of a general disintegration on the previous day. A train full of air force technicians had been standing on the same spot on the Pale-Sarajevo line for three days. The men had received no food and were threatening to go out looting. Warned by the inhabitants of this danger, we explained the situation to the military authorities, but nothing had been done about it by the time we left. One of the officers, a friend of mine, told me that the men in his battalion had been unable to get any equipment, even rifles.

Everything I had heard, seen, and personally experienced up to then had led me to believe that in this age a small country by itself is not viable; it has no defense in today's world of developing military technology. Such countries have to join a larger, stronger community if they are to defend their freedom and achieve economic progress. This is a view I hold to this day.

Members of the government descended upon Nikšić on April 14. The party of Croatian ministers and I arrived just before midnight. The following day, we heard that the army's surrender had been decreed, and that in a few hours we would be on our way to Greece by air. We took off at 12:45 and arrived in Greece about 4:00 P.M.

The government had never deliberated the question of a

71

surrender, and no formal decision on it had been made. It was the Premier's personal decision, made in agreement with his closest associates. He was in such a hurry to get everything done that he even forgot to issue orders for the navy to put to sea. Slobodan Jovanović told me that the generals of the high command had openly demanded the removal of the Premier and the accession of someone who could arrange a more favorable armistice with Germany and Italy. Ninčić had been considered as a possible replacement.

In a telegram to Campbell on April 13, Churchill said: "We do not see why the King or Government should leave the country, which is vast, mountainous, and full of armed men. German tanks can no doubt move along the roads and tracks, but to conquer the Serbian armies they must bring up infantry. Then will be the chance to kill them. Surely the young King and the Ministers should play their part in this." He added that if necessary, he would send a submarine to Kotor to evacuate the King and his retinue. Nothing was said about evacuating the government.

The Yugoslav minister in Athens, Alexander Vukčević, told us when we arrived that we had little to look forward to, because there had been a fierce conflict that very day between those Greeks in favor of continuing the war and those in favor of surrender, and that the premier, Alexandros Koryzis, had committed suicide.

Yugoslavia had been completely unprepared for that powerful, rapid, and concentrated attack launched on April 6. There was failure even to effect full mobilization. Skoplje fell on April 8, Niš on April 9, Zagreb on April 10, and Sarajevo on April 15. The Italians crossed the Yugoslav frontier on April 12 at Rijeka and advanced without firing a shot. The Hungarians started their operations between the Danube and the Tisa on April 11 and moved forward without opposition. The Germans took prisoner some 350,000 soldiers and more than 12,000 officers, mainly Serbs. They also captured a huge booty in arms, military equipment, and all kinds of stores. German casualties in this tremendous victory were minute: 151 dead, 392 wounded, and 15 missing.

Yugoslav casualties, on the other hand, were enormous. It is estimated that in Belgrade alone twenty thousand were killed in the savage bombing raids. Battle casualties were on a much smaller scale, because military operations were of short duration. Also, the German attacks split up the planned lines of defense and isolated individual Yugoslav units to such an extent that no real front could be established anywhere. In some places, units put up magnificent resistance, but they were rapidly overwhelmed by a barrage of steel from German tanks and artillery.

The collapse of Greek resistance came eight days after the Yugoslavs' resistance fell, and the withdrawal of the British army began soon after the Greek army's surrender. Embarkation started on the night of April 24, and the bulk of the army remnants sailed for Crete under strong naval and air fighter protection.

The first meeting of the Yugoslav government in exile took place at the Yugoslav legation in Athens on April 17. At times it was very stormy. Debate centered on the statement that Premier Simović was to issue to the press. In the draft, the cause of the rapid collapse of the Yugoslav army was said to be the treachery of the Croatian units. The Croatian ministers and the Yugoslav-oriented Serbian ministers objected, pointing out that the quick collapse was the result of a whole chain of mistakes, shortcomings, and unfortunate occurrences. The military and the Great Serbs were anxious to brush aside any suggestion that the army high command had been in any way responsible. I tried to persuade my Serbian friends in the government that they must at all costs prevent this anti-Croatian campaign from going any further. Simović and his colleagues made a show of yielding; yet in the end they issued the statement according to the original conception of the draft, though toned down slightly.

Although he had announced that he was going to stay in Athens, Simović made arrangements to fly with the King and three other ministers to Egypt. Those who were to be left behind protested violently, until it was agreed thay they should go, too. On April 18, we all flew to Cairo. The King went on to Jerusalem with the Premier and two other ministers, and the rest of the government to Port Said, where they remained for a fortnight before going on to Palestine.

The government now had to declare its stand before the

73

Yugoslav people and Yugoslavia's allies, and explain its future policy. A statement, adopted on May 4, stressed that the Serbo-Croatian agreement of August 26, 1939, remained "one of the cornerstones of state policy," and that the so-called Independent State of Croatia, proclaimed after the German occupation, had been rejected by the Croatian people and their lawful representatives. It expressed faith in the triumph of "our great and painful struggle" and promised resolutely to continue the fight until "our territorial integrity, the independence of our state, the complete freedom of all Serbs, Croats, and Slovenes are re-established." This was the first, last, and only joint statement of a Yugoslav government that had gone into exile with the express intent of carrying on resistance.

It was decided that the main body of the government, together with the young King, should go to Britain, and the remainder to the United States. It was also decided that all evacuated army, naval, and air force personnel should be mustered in Egypt, and the armed forces minister, Ilić, should remain with them. The King flew to London with the Premier and the Foreign Minister at the end of June. The rest of the government left later, those destined for Britain arriving in July, the United States party arriving in mid-September.

During its short stay in Palestine, the government had successfully emerged from its first two crises. They were a foretaste of the great crises that were to arise later in London.

In accordance with his decision of March 27, Hitler immediately proceeded with his plan to carve up Yugoslavia. He had sent agents to Zagreb to induce pro-Axis Croats to proclaim the breakaway of Croatia from Yugoslavia, which was done in the name of Ante Pavelić the moment the first German army units reached Zagreb on April 10.

Mussolini became alarmed lest the German advance to Zagreb put an end to his plans. As soon as he heard that German troops had reached Zagreb and that Slavko Kvaternik, a former colonel in the Austro-Hungarian army, had proclaimed the Independent State of Croatia, he made arrangements for Pavelić and two hundred of his Ustashi ("Insurgents") to be taken to Croatia and given immediate recognition. The previous day, however, the commander of the German forces had offered Maček the presidency of Croatia, with Pavelić as his premier. Maček declined the offer, as he had all earlier ones.

The field units of the Second Italian Army set foot on Croatian soil on April 12, followed by Pavelić's convoy. The German army commander in Karlovac, sixty kilometers west of Zagreb, sent his envoy to bring Pavelić immediately to meet Colonel Kvaternik and Ribbentrop's emissary, Edmund Veesenmayer. Kvaternik asked Pavelić explicitly whether he had made any secret deals with Mussolini. If he *had* entered into such arrangements, Pavelić said nothing about them. Veesenmayer wanted to know whether Pavelić had accepted any commitments to Mussolini that might delay German recognition of the Croatian state. Apparently satisfied with Pavelić's answer, Veesenmayer informed Ribbentrop that there were no obstacles to German recognition. Hitler wanted to recognize Croatia as soon as possible. He felt he then could better persuade Croatian soldiers to desert from the Yugoslav army. In the meantime, Mussolini's emissary, Anfuso, had extracted from Pavelić confirmation of his "earlier agreement with Italy" guaranteeing satisfaction of his territorial demands at Croatia's expense.

Hitler had more than once acknowledged that the Mediterranean and Adriatic were in the Italian sphere of influence, but it had never been precisely established whether this was meant to include the whole of Yugoslavia or merely a territorial belt along the Adriatic coast. The German military advance into Yugoslavia, and Mussolini's general dependence on Hitler, enabled the latter to insure that the greater part of the booty in Yugoslavia would go to himself.

On the eve of Yugoslavia's capitulation, Ribbentrop invited Ciano to negotiations in Vienna on the distribution of conquered Yugoslav territory, and told him that Germany would annex two-thirds of Slovenian territory, leaving Mussolini the remaining third. They agreed that Hungary's right to Bačka and Baranja, and Bulgaria's right to Macedonia, should be recognized. Montenegro would belong to Italy, and the Kosovo-Metohija region to Albania (that is, also to Italy). Ciano wanted to enlarge Albania's share by adding part of southern Macedonia, but Hitler had promised that territory to Bulgaria a few days earlier. Bulgaria was to obtain some Serbian territory also. The Banat was to be held by Germany, to avoid a conflict between Hungary and Rumania. Hitler was out to wreak a remorseless vengeance upon Serbia. And so Serbia was to be pared down on all sides and left as a German occupation zone.

Hitler decided to leave his troops in Croatia to guard German lines of communication in the Balkans. This meant that the provisional demarcation line between the areas occupied by the German and the Italian armies was made permanent. The line ran along the Sava valley, in Slovenia, crossed into Croatia at Bregana, and ran through Samobor, Zagreb, Glina, Prijedor, Banja Luka, Jajce, Travnik, Sarajevo, and Rude, then along the frontiers of Montenegro and expanded Albania and Bulgaria, on to the Greek frontier. West of the German zone Mussolini could do what he wanted.

Pavelić wanted to postpone the awkward talks with Italy for as long as possible, because he was aware of Mussolini's rapacious claims on Croatia. He remembered all his promises to Mussolini, and he knew that his reputation would suffer if he were to satisfy these demands. On May 3, Mussolini sent Pavelić an ultimatum to meet him on May 7 near Trieste. There Pavelić proposed that Croatia enter into a union with Italy under Victor Emmanuel as king of Croatia; he hoped this would soften Mussolini's feelings somewhat. Mussolini accepted the proposal but otherwise remained adamant. Because Hitler was unwilling to intervene, Pavelić accepted all of Mussolini's demands. The signing ceremony was announced for May 18. Victor Emmanuel stepped down in favor of his nephew, Duke Aimone of Spoleto, who thus became King Zvonimir II of Croatia. The tumultuous events that soon erupted in Pavelić's Croatia. however, did not encourage the Duke to come to Zagreb and sit on the throne he had accepted.

Three treaties, all very awkward for Pavelić, were signed in Rome. These treaties, plus the seizure of Croatia's backbone, turned the country into a completely unviable organism, which was precisely what Mussolini had planned. Croatia had to cede to Italy almost the whole of her coastline, together with a wide belt of hinterland. Pavelić was also hard hit by having to cede the northeastern Croatian regions of Medjumurje and Prekomurje to Hungary.

CHAPTER 5

On May 20, 1950, I met Prince Paul for the first time since the war. I was surprised to hear him say that those opposing his regime had been unaware of how strong Yugoslavia's international position had been in the winter of 1940–1941. He had held all the strings controlling the major diplomatic moves and negotiations at the time. He was the only leader who knew all the policy makers in Britain, Germany, Italy, and Yugoslavia's neighboring countries, and he was in the best position to evaluate their plans and play the diplomatic game. Whenever I have reflected on Paul's assertion, I have always come to the conclusion that he had some information about Hitler's policy which convinced him that Yugoslavia could be saved if certain concessions, short of entering the war, were made to Hitler. Paul was on good terms with Göring and Ribbentrop, after all, and he met with them at critical moments.

The more I have studied the German diplomatic documents of 1940–1941, the more I am convinced that I am right in my conclusions. I have discovered there the factors that led Hitler to decide at first against a military attack on Yugoslavia. It was in his interest not to upset his economic relations with this important producer of foodstuffs, raw materials, and ore for Germany. The last thing he wanted was to push Yugoslavia into the arms of Britain and Turkey, which might result in a Yugoslav-British-Turkish-Soviet bloc. A more moderate policy toward Yugoslavia would enable him to take the sting out of any Anglo-Turkish alliance. London was well aware of that.

Safeguarding supplies of Rumanian oil for the German army was the first priority in Hitler's calculations and plans. As long as

77

he was on friendly terms with Stalin, he could rely on oil supplies from Russia. But if that friendship should break up, German military operations would be totally dependent on Rumania. When Stalin extorted Bessarabia from Rumania in June, 1940, and took possession of some islands in the Danube, his troops came within 160 kilometers of the Rumanian oil fields. If Yugoslavia were to side with Britain and place bomber bases at her disposal, the entire Rumanian oil-production industry would be threatened. Hitler was panic-stricken when British bombers arrived on Crete, because they were within range of the Rumanian oil fields. It is easy to imagine how he would have felt if bases had been made available to them in Yugoslavia. The presence of this danger tremendously strengthened Yugoslavia's diplomatic position vis-à-vis Hitler. That position was further strengthened by Hitler's decision to invade Russia, which made the German army completely dependent on oil production in Rumania.

The Führer realized only too well that a prudent approach to relations with Yugoslavia was the only way of insuring Rumanian oil supplies for his Russian campaign. When he decided to attack Greece, his military advisers proposed that the German army enter Greece through Yugoslavia. He rejected that proposal. The bravery of Yugoslav soldiers, along with the mountainous terrain and primitive roads, so suitable for resistance, were among other factors leading to his decision. Also, his encounters with Paul had left him with a certain feeling of good will toward, and confidence in, the Prince. German documents reveal that Hitler was not prepared to go to extremes in order to force Yugoslavia into the Tripartite Pact. That follows clearly from Hitler's declaration to Ciano on March 7, 1941.

Did Prince Paul lose his nerve in the game he was playing with Hitler, and accede to the pact unnecessarily? Or were there some deeper motivations that led him, fully aware of what he was doing, to yield? I think there were deeper motivations behind it all, closely connected with the Prince's personality and his political aims and ambitions.

For years after the coup, he thought continually about what had happened, trying to arrive at an answer to the questions why he had been overthrown and why his policy had failed. Day after day during the first few years after his departure from Yugoslavia, he sat in his villa in Rhodesia, with his legs over one arm of a worn-down chair, in the grip of a deep depression, pondering the causes of his downfall and the tragedy that befell Yugoslavia. Harold Nicolson was given this account by Princess Olga, Paul's wife, when she came to London in the spring of 1943. He, in turn, related it to me a few days later. I found this information very interesting, and I made inquiries among many of Paul's acquaintances concerning the Prince and his days in power.

Prince Paul was a complex person, with definite political views, objectives, and ambitions, which he concealed carefully and skillfully. Bliss Lane remarked that he could have been an "excellent actor." An English friend of mine, who was close to Paul, told me that the Prince never trusted anyone, not even his wife, with his most important secrets. A master of equivocation when he considered it necessary, he was quick to sacrifice others for the sake of his own plans. Because he had a high opinion of his own abilities and a tendency to underrate other people, he surrounded himself with people he was sure would carry out his policies.

Paul had to live a secluded life and was not allowed to meddle in politics during King Alexander's lifetime, though he was exceedingly anxious to play an active political role and felt supremely competent to do so. Djordje Djurić, for many years Yugoslav minister in London, told me of Paul's exhilaration, when, in the autumn of 1925, Milan Stojadinović, then minister of finance, sent him to London to investigate the possibilities of negotiating a loan.

When Alexander proclaimed his dictatorship, Paul had to sever ties with certain personal friends who were opponents of the move. For reasons unknown to me, the King had a law drafted in 1933 that provided for the Prince's banishment. The Prince himself admitted to me that because of the differences between them at that time, he went away to Paris. But in 1934 the whole idea of exile was dropped, and Alexander in his will appointed Paul first regent if he, the King, should die before the heir to the throne had come of age.

I remember well a conversation I had, about a fortnight after the King's assassination, with the leader of the Agrarian party, Joca Jovanović, who had been closely associated with the Prince. He delivered a real panegyric, stressing Paul's superior intelligence, his exceptional political acumen, and his broad education. He said that as regent Paul would blaze a new trail in domestic politics, far removed from the path taken by Alexander.

Prince Paul soon eclipsed the other two regents, and took into his own hands the enormous powers that Alexander had arrogated to himself in the dictatorial constitution of 1931. He did moderate certain crude aspects of Alexander's regime and some of its brutal methods, but the essence of the dictatorship remained. The Prince justified it on the grounds that the supporters of the old regime were still powerful, and that he was not the only regent. On March 16, 1939, he said to Joca Jovanović, "It can't be otherwise. I'm only the custodian of the people's rights. . . . I am not the king but the regent. You don't know my trouble with the regents." Although there was some truth in that, it was for the most part a convenient excuse for not changing the dictatorship.

Had Paul wanted really to change the regime in the direction of parliamentary monarchy and, at the same time, to bring the Croats and Serbs closer together, he could have done it. The dictatorial regime was completely discredited, and the responsibility for the assassination of the King could in part be laid to the regime's supporters. Paul could have followed Alexander's decision, made shortly before his death, to set his dictatorship on a different path and to seek an agreement with Maček. A considerable measure of understanding had been achieved between the Croatian and the Serbian members of the opposition, and these leaders, together with Prince Paul, could have undertaken the responsibility for establishing a democratic regime. If Paul had taken this course, he could have brought to the domestic scene the tranquility and healthy stability so sorely needed for the country's security on the eve of the crisis that Hitler and Mussolini were about to create in Europe.

The inclusion in the government of representatives from the democratic parties would not have hampered Paul's activities in the foreign-policy field. Joca Jovanović, with his extensive diplomatic experience, would have been an ideal choice for the post of foreign minister. He would have known, for example, how to hold the delicate balance between the Franco-British and German-Italian blocs. In this he would have had a staunch ally in

Maček, who was an ardent believer in neutrality. Neither Jovanović nor Maček, nor any of the leaders of the democratic parties, would have stooped to toadying to the Fascist and Nazi regimes; nor would they have hatched any plots with Hitler and Mussolini, as Stojadinović did.

Moreover, Paul could have brought about a union with Bulgaria if he had had the backing of the leaders of the democratic parties.

Paul's idea that monarchs and princes know what is best for their people inclined him, quite naturally, toward an authoritarian regime. He tended to consider the Karadjordjević dynasty the representative of Serbism, and he did not look kindly on the idea that the old Serbian political parties had taken this role upon themselves. He repeatedly made the point that the Karadjordjevićs knew what they wanted, and that they were not prepared to accept whatever conditions the political parties wished to thrust upon them.

His concept of the ideal ruler led him to try to settle the differences between the quarreling national communities arbitrarily and in his own way. Joca Jovanović had a conversation with the Prince in 1939 in the course of which he tried to persuade the Prince not to conduct negotiations with the Croatian Peasant party leader by himself, but to leave this to the political leaders who already had an agreement with him; the regents and the army should be the final arbiters. "Why the army?" exclaimed Paul. "I'm the person who matters; the army has to obey, while I shall decide." The trouble here was that armies in the Balkans were not to be relied upon to obey automatically, as Paul was to learn on March 27, 1941.

It is in the nature of every authoritarian regime to try to divide its adversaries. Prince Paul was partly successful in breaking up relations between Maček and the Serbian opposition leaders; they had made the mistake, in the critical days of April, 1939, of not accepting Maček's conditions for maintaining the proposed combined front. It was this sort of policy that provoked hostility toward the Prince on the part of the combined Serbian opposition. Hostile elements both inside and outside its ranks thus had grounds for launching a large-scale campaign of vilification against him. The campaign gathered momentum, and became particularly fierce after his negotiations with Hitler. Anglo-Greek groups joined the campaign in the hope that a weakening of the Prince's position would turn Yugoslavia against Hitler. It was easy to provoke mistrust for the Prince's foreign policy, because his paths were extremely devious. Nevertheless, his objective remained unchanged: to thwart any Hitler-Mussolini agreement that might be detrimental to Yugoslavia. All the while, he kept his eyes fixed on Mussolini, safeguarding himself by currying favor with Hitler, in the hope of creating a unified Bulgaria and Yugoslavia. Out of this combination he hoped one day to create a Balkan, or, rather, a Balkan-Danubian, confederation of states.

Paul's strategy might have had some chance of success if there had been a *rapprochement* between Germany and Britain. His close ties with the British advocates of an understanding with Hitler strengthened his own inclinations in that direction. Consequently, French proposals for tying the Little Entente more firmly to France and allying it with Russia met with no response from the Prince. He preferred to seek security for Yugoslavia by being careful not to tread on Hitler's toes, while waiting for the British to come to terms with Hitler. But when Britain and France showed their readiness to go to war with Germany over Poland, Paul abandoned caution and was prepared to incur any risk, even war with Germany, in his eagerness to obtain guarantees from Mussolini. Yet his dearest wish was still "a German-English understanding," as he put it to Heeren on April 13, 1940. He expressed the same sentiments in a conversation with Ulrich von Hassell, a former German minister in Belgrade, in March, 1941, when he said that an attack by Hitler on Russia might "constitute a bridge toward an understanding with the West."

It should be mentioned here that the diplomatic documents assert that Hitler had informed Paul of his preparations for an attack on the Soviet Union. In later years, I wrote to Paul asking him if this information was true. The Prince replied, on March 15, 1968, that it was not. I have, however, heard about this from several other sources. My explanation is that the Prince received the report on preparations for the invasion of Russia, not from Hitler, but from our minister in Moscow, and a similar report from our military attaché in Berlin; he passed this information on to the British minister in Belgrade.

Prince Paul was aware that the devious, enigmatic course he was taking in foreign policy was not at all to the liking of the Serbs. During the crisis leading up to the March 27 coup, Mihailo Konstantinović, the minister of justice, told him that he ought not to be conducting both domestic and foreign policies that were unpopular. In an audience with the Prince on March 20, Slobodan Jovanović alluded to the possibility of a *Putsch* that might force Hitler to attack Yugoslavia, the very thing the Prince was trying to avoid. On a number of occasions Paul has blamed various elements in Yugoslavia for accession to the Tripartite Pact. In fact, he made decisions in such a way that the responsibility could always be placed with other people. If he had intended Yugoslavia to resist Germany over her entry into Bulgaria and invasion of Greece, he had plenty of time between the beginning of November, 1940, and the end of February, 1941, to form a combined front with Britain, Greece, and Turkey. Instead, he told the Greeks he might permit the passage of German troops across Yugoslav territory if the Greeks permitted the British to land in Greece to create a Salonika front. In addition, he proposed to Mussolini the demilitarization of the Dalmatian coast in exchange for Salonika, and in March, 1941, he granted Italy credit for 500 million dinars' worth of raw materials and foodstuffs already ordered from Yugoslavia. This credit and the visit that he was due to pay to Mussolini shortly after acceding to the Tripartite Pact were to serve as a consolation prize for Mussolini in the absence of the close Rome-Belgrade pact that he had been dangling before him for some months. It is obvious from the way the secret negotiations were conducted and completed that Paul had no serious intention of signing any such pact with Mussolini.

Cincar-Marković stated at the time that the Yugoslavs, instead of taking up arms and rushing off to fight when the international situation was troubled, were, for the first time in their history, engaged in political negotiations. Obviously he and the Prince considered *Realpolitik* the best safeguard for Yugoslavia's interests. He and Court Minister Milan Antić, who were the Prince's closest collaborators in implementing his foreign-policy decisions, argued that the Western powers would not penalize Yugoslavia for acceding to the Tripartite Pact by favoring her neighbors, who were much more guilty than she was.

Did the Yugoslav negotiators really feel that Hitler would keep Yugoslavia out of the war even if she refused to accede to the Tripartite Pact? Paul claimed he did not know whether Hitler would attack Yugoslavia if she refused to join the pact. It is highly unlikely, however, that Hitler would have promised Salonika to Yugoslavia if she was *not* going to accede. According to Cincar-Marković, if Yugoslavia did refuse, Mussolini, King Boris, and the Hungarian revisionists would be in a much more favored position with Germany, because of their membership in the pact. Yugoslavia, by putting herself on equal footing with them, could prevent such favoritism, while remaining exempt from the provisions of the pact that bound the others. But Hitler's consent to Yugoslav possession of Salonika provided a far stronger motive for accession. Antić was right when he said, "The Serbs would stone us if we failed to make sure of getting Salonika for them."

Cincar-Marković put up an interesting defense of this Salonika policy at a Crown Council meeting, in answer to Maček's objection to taking Salonika away from Greece: "Hitler and Mussolini are offering it to us. It would make them suspicious if we were to refuse. And anyhow, God alone knows what's going to happen after the war."

Paul was aware that many Serbs felt that he had no understanding of their traditions or the things they held sacred. He would be finished if the Italians or Bulgarians entered Salonika with Hitler's backing. This had to be prevented, even at the price of acceding to the Tripartite Pact. If Paul had believed that Hitler was going to win the war, and if he had been planning Yugoslavia's permanent annexation of Salonika, he would not have been opposed to the spread of the war into the Balkans in response to the British landing in Greece. Yet he fought this tooth and nail. He called the British plan to land in Greece a "clumsy move."

As the pressures on Yugoslavia reached a climax, the government began to debate the problem of the King. Was it in the interests of the country to allow King Peter, who was immature, to take over the helm of state when he came of age, in September, 1941? His youth and inexperience would have made this undesirable even in times of perfect peace; but with the world in the grip of the most terrible war in history, it seemed impossible. Thus, the question of extending the regency, along with the problem of relations with Hitler, became the chief worry of the government. The British minister in Belgrade was in favor of such an extension. Discreet steps were taken to inform some of the Serbian opposition leaders that it was in the highest interests of the state to change the article in the constitution providing for the King to assume power on his eighteenth birthday. The idea was to make constitutional arrangements for Paul to remain sole regent for the duration of the war. The opposition leaders would be called upon to share the responsibility for this move in a new government. For National Assembly elections were to be held in accord with the new, liberal, electoral law that, in January, 1940, had replaced the sham electoral law of the dictatorship. Thereby, a few weeks after Yugoslavia's accession to the Tripartite Pact, a new democratic order was gradually to be installed in Yugoslavia.

By handing Stojadinović over to the British, Paul was trying to show them that they should not lose faith in him; he was delivering into their hands the man who, in the interests of Germany, could have done most damage to the Prince's plans in the further course of the war. In September, 1939, he had been prepared to go to war against Hitler and Mussolini. He would have been prepared to do the same again if Anglo-American armies had approached Yugoslavia either on the Balkan side or from Italy, thus assuring him of effective assistance to the Yugoslav army. Turkey would also have been certain to take action when Yugoslavia did. Hungary, Rumania, and Bulgaria were ready to break away from Hitler in the early summer of 1943, and their breakaway could have been co-ordinated with the operations of Yugoslav-Turkish forces, had Yugoslavia not been prematurely hurled into the war against Hitler. An enormous gap would have been opened up in the rear of the German armies that were in gradual retreat in Russia, and Hitler would not have found it easy to close that gap.

It is probable that such a great operation in the Balkans and Italy would have led to Hitler's downfall by the end of 1943 or the summer of 1944. Churchill said in his report to the Combined Chiefs of Staff at the Cairo meeting with Roosevelt on December 4, 1943: "If Turkey entered the war, there would be great political reactions. Bulgaria, Rumania and Hungary might all fall into our hands. We ought to make these German satellites work for us." And if Yugoslavia had still been on her feet at that time, this might have come about earlier and more easily.

Radoje Knežević, the intellectual leader of the March 27 *Putsch,* stated after the war that "if there had been a government with true Serbian representatives, like the Croatian and Slovenian representatives, the pact would not have mattered, if there had been no alternative." In other words, there would have been no *Putsch* on March 27. Slobodan Jovanović told Konstantinović shortly after the *Putsch* that the pact might have been acceptable if the internal regime had been changed. Milan Grol, leader of the Democratic party, who entered the government on March 27, told me later that he would not have accepted responsibility for the *Putsch* if he had known about it.

The rumors circulating in Belgrade to the effect that Paul disliked the Serbs and considered them unreliable caused Serbian dissatisfaction with the political situation to grow into resentment and hatred against him. Anglo-Greek propagandists spread the story that the Prince was going to permit the passage of German troops through Yugoslavia and allow them to occupy Salonika, and people began to get wind of the news that the term of the Prince's regency was to be extended.

During the first three months of 1941, the Prince was preoccupied with his games of chance at the table of international politics. During that time, he granted frequent audiences to the British and American ministers in Belgrade. He was patient to the extreme with them. He put up with their almost daily bombardments, their moral pressures, their inquisitorial interrogations.

Paul's chief domestic advisers bear a great responsibility for not keeping a more vigilant eye on dangerous currents inside the country and for not taking seriously the accurate reports of the conspiracy among the air force officers. They never uncovered the secret British radio stations in Belgrade and Zagreb that were pouring out propaganda against the government, or even the German station in Zagreb. One section of the army was too closely associated with British military personnel in Belgrade. The Yugoslav ambassador in Moscow, Gavrilović, was communicating through British legation channels on exceedingly delicate foreign-policy issues. British, German, Italian, and Greek intelligence agents and propaganda agencies enjoyed far too much freedom. There was no firm hand on the reins on the domestic front at a time when such control was absolutely essential.

The crowning irony of the tragedy that followed the bursting of the dikes on March 27 was that the Prince had intended, a few weeks later, to carry out the internal reforms that could have prevented the ill-fated series of events. Slobodan Jovanović told me that had the *Putsch* leaders been aware of the gravity of Yugoslavia's external position, and had they known that accession to the pact had not involved a promise to Hitler of passage for his troops through Yugoslavia, or any commitment to provide military assistance, they would never have carried out the *Putsch*.

The tragic developments that ensued in Yugoslavia were to show that the *Putsch* ought never to have been undertaken, however justified the leaders were in their objections to certain aspects of Prince Paul's policy. As shall be seen, these leaders did not all have spotless motives for hatching their conspiracy. March 27 was only a prelude to other daring exploits, which were to become a tangled, frenzied skein as the war advanced, creating grave troubles for the Yugoslav government in exile, for the Allies, and even for the enemy. Their baneful consequences still hover over the unhappy people of Yugoslavia.

British military experts are almost unanimous in their condemnation of Churchill's decision to land troops in Greece and to push Yugoslavia into the war. "The sequel was," wrote B. H. Liddell Hart, "that within three weeks Greece and Yugoslavia were overrun, and the British forces driven to a second 'Dunkirk.' . . . It brought appalling misery on the people of Greece and Yugoslavia, and the bitter fruits are still being harvested in the troubles that followed the war." *The Economist* called it "a cardinal strategic error." Lord Harding called it "a major strategic mistake," and Lord Alanbrooke (General Alan Brooke) termed it "a definite strategic blunder." Eden had told Dill that he felt largely responsible for the catastrophe in Greece and Cyrenaica, and said that he was going to resign. However, Dill persuaded him not to do so. George Thompson called the Greek expedition "the most disastrous British blunder of the war."

CHAPTER 6

Even before the March 27 *Putsch* there was disagreement between the leaders of the conspiracy, Dušan Simović and Radoje Knežević. The conflict came to a head over the question of the composition of the government that was to take over after the coup. Ten days earlier, it had been agreed that the Simović government was to be composed only of representatives of the political parties. But then Simović proposed to include certain "distinguished personages," who were, in fact, his personal friends; Knežević resolutely opposed this. Simović had to give way, because Knežević's brother, Živan, was in command of the main body of troops that actually carried out the *Putsch*.

Thus a national coalition government was set up, composed only of representatives of the main political parties. But that government rested on a constitution that gave the king virtually complete power. Since there were no popularly elected representatives, the only figures on the political stage were King Peter, the party representatives in the cabinet, and the military figures who had organized the coup. The fact that the King was the head of state enhanced his position with the British, and later with the Americans.

Britain had made it clear that she wanted a resistance movement organized in Yugoslavia. Arms were issued to members of Yugoslavia's Agrarian party for use against the German and Italian armies. At the same time, the British were looking into plans for a Yugoslav-Bulgarian state. But at the first meeting between Churchill and Simović, priority was given to a Yugoslav-Greek federation, which was to be the nucleus of a Balkan federation.

The British showed every consideration toward the new Yugoslav government. Because of the March 27 *Putsch,* it was held in higher esteem than any other government in exile, and its prestige was enhanced by reports in August of continuing resistance in Yugoslavia. The supreme moment came with a splendid ceremony in St. Paul's Cathedral, on September 12, to celebrate King Peter's coming of age. The British royal family was present, as were many Allied heads of state and members of Allied governments in London.

Shortly after this, however, the status of the Yugoslav government began to decline, and at a time when the people of Yugoslavia were in their direst need. The mass slaughter of the innocent Serbian population by the Croatian Ustashi in Pavelić's satellite state was followed by the Serbian Chetniks' retaliation against innocent Croats, and the beginning of the Communist uprising.

The news of these events made no dent in the extraordinary optimism of the Yugoslav government; we were still certain that all would be well in the end, and that we would go back to our liberated homeland and carry on the game of politics that had been interrupted by Hitler's invasion. This facile optimism was founded on the conviction that Allied troops would free our country and take King Peter and his government back in their wake.

As soon as the first disagreements arose, I began to fear that the government would become completely discredited with the Allies, thus doing immeasurable damage to the people of Yugoslavia. I spoke of this danger at great length with Milan Grol, whose Democratic party was the strongest in Serbia. Night after night in Cairo, he and I thrashed out the government's political problems. Upon our arrival in London, we discovered that the government was on the verge of a new, very grave crisis, which would break as soon as the two vice-premiers, Krnjević and Slobodan Jovanović, arrived. Three weeks earlier, the King had arrived with Simović and Ninčić, both Serbs. They were followed by the finance minister, Juraj Šutej, a Croat. Then came our group, with the third vice-premier, Miho Krek, a Slovene.

At our first meeting, Šutej showed me two telegrams from Ivan Šubašić and Savica Kosanović, who were in Cape Town, en route to the United States. They had heard a radio broadcast summarizing an article in the London *Times* entitled "How Yugoslavia Fell." The article contained a number of gross calumnies against the Croatian people. Šubašić sharply condemned those who had supplied the information to the *Times,* and requested that the King summon him to London immediately. Kosanović also wanted to come to London to help smooth things over. Šutej asked me to discuss the matter with Grol and get his advice on how to avoid a government collapse. I spoke to Grol that same evening, and we agreed that I should find out who was responsible for supplying the information to the *Times.* The paper's diplomatic correspondent, who had been credited with the article, told me that the *Times* military correspondent had talked to Simović and Ninčić, and that the article had come out of that interview. I told Grol that Ninčić should be dismissed for committing such a gross offense against the Croatian people. If in the future, I said, a Croatian minister should misbehave similarly, the Serbs would have every right to demand the same penalty for him. "Unless this principle is adopted," I told him, "it will be impossible for the government to put its house in order. If Ninčić goes unpunished and keeps throwing mud at the Croats, we Croats will be forced to throw mud back at the Serbs. Then we shall both be covered in mud and shame." Grol agreed that Ninčić deserved to be punished.

Krnjević accepted our plan for government changes, and he persuaded Simović to accept it, too. Simović, in turn, asked Krnjević to get Slobodan Jovanović to accept the foreign ministry. Through a leak from some quarter, Ninčić heard about it, and he mounted a successful counteroffensive.

Subsequently, Simović jeopardized his own position by committing certain indiscretions in his conduct toward the King and the Queen Mother. Finally, in the middle of September, King George VI himself had to intervene with King Peter on Simović's behalf to save him from being overthrown. Simović's opponents showed skill in exploiting Peter's coming of age. On September 17, Jovanović told Krnjević: "Simović's government no longer exists . . . the King has taken everything into his own hands, and from now on ministers will report to him directly." And, indeed, after September 25, the King began to preside over the sessions of the Council of Ministers.

On September 30, Simović informed Krnjević that he intended

to reduce the size of the cabinet, bring younger people into it, and make arrangements for Ninčić's removal. While this upheaval was in progress, the situation in occupied Yugoslavia had passed beyond tragedy.

The people of Serbia had been horrified by the swiftness of Yugoslavia's collapse. Serbs living outside Serbia had particular cause for anxiety and fear. The new masters immediately began mass evictions and confiscations of their property. Serbian refugees swarmed into Serbia from Croatia, from the Vojvodina, from Macedonia, and from Kosovo. Many villagers had hidden away a certain amount of war material after the defeat of the Yugoslav army. When he found out about this, the German army commander in Serbia set up a collection center to enable him to extort the last useful scraps from Serbia for the German war machine.

Rumors began to circulate that a certain colonel had surrounded himself with a group of officers, and that in time they would turn against the enemy. It soon became known that this was Draža Mihailović; his group came to be known as the Chetniks. Mihailović, unwilling to accept the surrender of the Yugoslav army, had retreated with a few of his comrades in arms to Ravna Gora, in western Serbia. There they began to lay the foundations for a popular military organization capable of raising a nationwide insurrection when the Allies set foot on Yugoslav soil.

"Why haven't your people killed Pavelić?" Ciano had asked Stakić when the latter visited Rome in February, 1941. And Mussolini had said to Stakić: "It is up to you whether Pavelić becomes an instrument to be used against you or is discarded like a squeezed lemon." At the beginning of March, the Italians told Pavelić that his activities would have to cease. But on March 29, two days after the *Putsch*, Mussolini greeted Pavelić with *"Adesso é il vostro momento"* ("And now your chance has come"). Seventeen days later, Pavelić sneaked into Zagreb late at night. And on the next day, M. Žanić submitted to him, on behalf of the State Council, a draft decree providing a statutory basis for the new regime. Pavelić rejected it, with the curt comment that a ruler could rule without laws. He immediately set about establishing a regime in Croatia based on the Nazi and Fascist systems. He dissolved the Croatian Peasant party and closed down all newspapers but those of the Ustashi. The Ustashi movement, through its militia and secret police, became the mainstay of his personal dictatorship. Its terrorist methods filled the unfortunate population of the Croatian puppet state with fear, particularly the immediate victims of Pavelić's racist legislation, the Serbs and the Jews. Concentration camps were introduced. The opportunities for grabbing Jewish and Serbian property, and the lust for power, drew the worst elements into the Ustashi ranks.

The question of the Serbs was central to the Ustashi program. In Pavelić's Croatia there were just under 2,000,000 Serbs, as compared with 3,500,000 Croats and 800,000 Moslems. The Moslems had come to occupy a key position in Bosnia and Herzegovina; they constituted about one-third of the population, and the Catholics about one-fourth. The remainder were Serbian Orthodox. The Croats, therefore, were unable to insist on their right to Bosnia without recognizing the Moslems as Croats. Hence Pavelić's theory that the Moslems were the "purest Croats."

Even before the fall of Yugoslavia, we knew that Pavelić intended to settle the problem of the Serbs in Croatia with fire and the sword. The Ustashi considered the Serbs in Croatia *injuria temporum* (the sores of earlier ages), and they decided to heal them with evil and barbarous remedies. Mile Budak, Pavelić's right-hand man, gave a clear formulation of the Ustashi aim on June 6, when he said, "We shall kill some of the Serbs, we shall expel others, and the remainder will be forced to embrace the Roman Catholic faith. These last will in due course be absorbed by the Croatian part of the population." Even before that, many Serbs had been murdered. The real pogroms began a few weeks later, after Pavelić met with Hitler at Berchtesgaden and received the Führer's approval of his plans.

Before that meeting there had been negotiations between Hitler and Pavelić about the settlement in Croatia of 250,000 Slovenes whom the Germans were to force from their homes. At the Berchtesgaden meeting, Hitler dwelt at length on his plan. According to the official record, he "took up the subject of the resettlement plans on the basis of which Slovenes were to be transferred to Croatia and in return Serbs were to be sent to

Old Serbia. This type of resettlement was naturally painful at the moment, but was better than lasting harm. . . . If the Croatian State was to be really stable a national intolerant policy had to be pursued for 50 years, because only damage resulted from too much tolerance in these matters."

Maček and I had been extremely worried about the Ustashi plan for exterminating the Serbs. We decided that the Croatian primate, Alojzije Stepinac, archbishop of Zagreb, should be told of Pavelić's plans and asked to exert all his moral authority to get Pavelić to abandon his anti-Christian and inhuman objectives. Seven days before the *Putsch*, I had to go to Zagreb to make arrangements with the Archbishop for the reception of the papal legate who would be attending the Eucharistic Congress of Yugoslav Catholics in May. Maček asked me then to inform the Archbishop of this plan for exterminating the Serbs. I saw the Archbishop on March 22, and I told him that an agreement had been reached for averting a conflict with Germany. However, if Hitler went back on his word, there would be war. Our resistance could not continue for long, and the government would have to move to London and carry on resistance from there. I told him that if that happened, Pavelić and his Ustashi would take over in Croatia; and I described the diabolical plan for exterminating the Serbs. He was extremely disturbed by my revelations, and told me that he was to see Budak that afternoon. He promised that he would speak to him sternly about these matters.

The first detailed reports we received in London on the grave situation in enemy-occupied Yugoslavia came from Macedonia and Slovenia.

In Slovenia, mass extermination of Slovenes was in progress in the area occupied by the Germans and unlawfully annexed to the Third Reich. We heard distressing accounts of violent evictions, removal to concentration camps and forced-labor camps in Germany, ruthless separation of children from their parents, and impressment of young girls for dubious purposes under the guise of some sort of legitimate employment. Young children were being abducted and deprived of their nationality. Many of the unfortunate people fled, either to the Italian-occupied zone, where the population was being treated more humanely, or to Croatia or Serbia.

In Macedonia, the Bulgarians immediately set about obliterating every trace of Serbian influence, to complete the Bulgarization of the country as quickly as possible. All Serbs who had settled in Macedonia between the two great wars were deported to Serbia. The Macedonian Communist party leadership broke away from Belgrade and placed itself under Bulgarian authority.

When Italian troops entered Montenegro, there was a revival of dissension between the "Greens" (those who had voted on green forms in 1918, against the dissolution of the Independent Kingdom of Montenegro) and the "Whites" (those who had voted on white forms, for unification with Serbia). A large proportion of the Greens welcomed the Italians as liberators and accepted status as an Italian protectorate, with Prince Michael, the last survivor of the ancient Petrović dynasty, to be restored to the throne. The Prince refused the offer.

The Communist party of Yugoslavia had been working underground since it was banned in the summer of 1921, and the Comintern had exerted a decisive influence on all its activities. The Yugoslav Communist party's historical archives amply demonstrate to what extent the Comintern manipulated and directed its activities. On the Comintern's orders, for example, the party's program on nationalities was changed twice, in diametrically opposed directions. During the long series of Moscow purges, many of its leaders, including Svetozar Marković, Djuro Cvijić, and Milan Gorkić, were either liquidated or sent to Siberia as Trotskyists, Bukharinists, or saboteurs. In the summer of 1937, the Comintern appointed Josip Broz (Tito) the party's new leader. He was regarded as a well-trained, reliable, genuine Stalinist—in other words, a Kremlin pawn. In accordance with Article 14 of the famous Twenty-one Conditions for admission to the Comintern, the Yugoslav Communist party had to be ready to spring to the Soviet Union's defense against all external threats.

Lenin's teachings—particularly his commandment that every imperialist war should be transformed into a civil war—had become Communist holy writ. "It is simply insane," he wrote in 1914, "to talk about abolishing capitalism without a frightful civil war or a succession of such wars. . . . The duty of Socialists . . . is to transform this war into a war between classes."

Accordingly, the Fourth Congress of the Yugoslav Communist party, meeting in Dresden in 1928, declared that "it must turn any war into a civil war against its own bourgeoisie . . . to defeat the Yugoslav government and insure the victory of the Soviet government." The congress therefore passed a resolution that made it mandatory for party members to organize strikes, sabotage, and riots in the army. The best-known of the Communist-incited army mutinies took place at Karlovac in 1939. After the *Putsch,* Tito sent the following directives to his followers: weaken the resistance of the Yugoslav army; render every assistance to the Ustashi, and to the Macedonian and Montenegrin separatists; and infiltrate the new administration. The Yugoslav Communists carried out no attacks on the German army, and no acts of sabotage, before Hitler's invasion of Russia, because Stalin was being careful not to provoke Hitler.

Soon after Pavelić's arrival in Zagreb, Tito moved to Belgrade, where he began to strengthen his party's military organization. At that time the party had only twelve thousand members, plus a few thousand young apprentices. Long years of underground work, struggles with the police, and an unshakable faith in the Soviet Union had toughened the Yugoslav Communists and raised the discipline in their ranks to the highest level. Not long after Tito placed his men in a state of readiness, the German divisions were withdrawn from Yugoslavia and sent north and east. In Serbia, the Germans left minor units, made up of men of an older age group, to occupy the towns. The countryside, spared the presence of the occupier, was stirring: insurrection was in the very air—but when it would erupt and who would lead it were unknown.

CHAPTER 7

The Serbian population in the Independent State of Croatia was appalled by the rapid collapse of the Yugoslav army, and by the powerful German forces bulldozing their way through Yugoslavia. After returning from Italy, the Ustashi, with their seething hatred, eagerly awaited the moment for action against the Serbs. At the end of April, the first act of vengeance was wreaked on them. A terrorist attack, led by Juco Rukavina, an Ustashi leader, was carried out in Gospić. Rukavina had been severely tortured there in 1932, when he had participated in a revolt that Pavelić had tried to raise in the Lika. Later, when Rukavina realized how many Serbs had fled to the mountains as a result of his reprisal, and how many innocent Croats had to pay for it, he regretted his action.

The first large-scale pogrom against the Serbs took place on April 27, in the village of Gudovec, in the Bjelovar district. One hundred seventy-six Serbs were shot.

After the war, Martin Cikošić, a distinguished member of the Croatian Peasant party of that district, gave me his account of the event. To his misfortune, he was implicated in it from beginning to end. As a result of this shattering experience, which haunted him ceaselessly, he became ill and died. According to his report, a Serb had been put in prison for attempted rioting. His friends responded by organizing an attack on the jail and killing two wardens. The prefect of the Bjelovar district discovered the culprits, and twelve of them were shot. In addition, Dido Kvaternik, chief of Pavelić's security service, came to Gudovec on April 27 and arrested 176 more Serbs living in the vicinity. On Kvaternik's instructions, Cikošić was assigned to have his Peasant

Guard execute them. He objected, on the grounds that these were innocent people, and that those implicated in the murder of the two guards had been shot. Kvaternik threatened to have him shot if he failed to carry out the order, and he added: "We're going to exterminate the Serbs—that has been decided." Following Cikošić's lead, some members of the guard refused to participate in the execution. Kvaternik ordered two army squads sent immediately from Bjelovar, and they carried out the execution. Following this massacre, several hundred Serbs were dragged out of their homes and sent to concentration camps in the Lika, where they lost their lives.

It is difficult, even today, to establish with accuracy all the facts concerning the large-scale massacres. Only the main features of these appalling events and the driving force behind them are fully known. Kvaternik, who organized the massacres, was the living embodiment of that diabolical force. When inspecting the infamous camp at Jasenovac in October, 1941, he sought out Maček, who had been brought there the day before, and told him that the Serbs in Croatia would be exterminated, come what may.

The Ustashi terror assumed major proportions, first in Croatia and Dalmatia, then in Bosnia and Herzegovina. All prominent Serbs were systematically arrested and deported to Serbia or taken away to unknown destinations, where they vanished without a trace. Serbian priests in particular were victims of this barbarous treatment. Early in May, three bishops were thrown into jail and murdered. On May 5, Pavelić issued a decree ordering that Orthodox Serbs be converted to Catholicism, and the Ustashi carried out an energetic campaign to get as many Orthodox as possible to comply, threatening them with deportation, persecution, confiscation of their property, and death. In order to destroy every feeling of solidarity or sympathy between Serbs and Croats, the Ustashi made a special target of prominent Serbs who had worked closely with Croats in politics.

The Serbs appealed to the German military commanders for protection. At the end of June, the German minister in Zagreb brought up the issue of the atrocities against the Serbs with Pavelić's government, and the German army representative, at a meeting with Kvaternik on July 9, pointed out the "acts of terror and the excesses committed by the Ustashi against the Serbian population in many parts of the country." Kvaternik asked him to take this complaint to Pavelić, which he did.

In a report sent to the German foreign ministry of July 10, the German chargé d'affaires in Zagreb wrote: "The Serbian question has become very much more acute as a result of the resettlement of the Serbs now under way. This resettlement which is being carried out harshly and the many atrocities preceding it will heap up tremendous amounts of incendiary material everywhere where Serbs live, and will create centers of unrest . . . which will be difficult to control."

The Ustashi atrocities came as a gift from heaven to the Communists on the eve of their proclamation of the revolution. On the day that Hitler attacked the Soviet Union, the Comintern sent a telegram demanding, "without a moment's delay," the organization of a partisan war in order to assist the Soviet Union. Stalin's call to the Communists of occupied Europe was broadcast by Moscow radio on July 3, 1941. Tito's Partisans began their attacks on July 7, 1941. No other Communist leader or party answered Stalin's call so promptly and so thoroughly. Tito's faith in Stalin was boundless, blind, and fanatical. Only the miraculous strength of that faith can explain how he and his men managed to endure the unprecedented hardships and sacrifices they faced.

On that same day of Germany's attack on Russia, Tito told his followers that the Soviet Union's war was their war, and that the first prerequisite for the success of the uprising was the destruction of the old administrative machinery in Yugoslavia. At a meeting of the Politburo in Belgrade on July 4, it was decided to raise an insurrection in all parts of Yugoslavia. Experienced fighters from the Spanish civil war took over. Young people threw homemade grenades at trucks carrying German troops in Belgrade. Garages were set on fire. German soldiers and military units on the move in the interior were ambushed, and depots were raided for weapons and ammunition. By July 17, a great many people had been hanged or shot.

The uprising in Montenegro, which was launched on July 13, was in every sense a popular uprising. Montenegro was virtually liberated within thirty-six hours, leaving the Italian army in control of only a few towns. Mussolini was furious. He immediately dismissed his high commissioner and replaced him with a military governor, who was authorized to suppress the uprising. Strong military forces were brought in from Albania and Greece, along with units of the Albanian army and militia. Naval bombardment of the coastal areas and heavy bombing from the air were followed by a barrage of artillery fire. Then tanks cleared the way for the punitive expedition, and the infantry moved in with blazing torches to destroy the grain crops. The inhabitants fled to the mountains. "Everything within a stone's throw of the roads became a graveyard and a blazing inferno," recalled one eyewitness. The punitive expedition took a toll of thousands of Montenegrin lives.

With the Communist attacks and acts of sabotage came the lifting of the last vestiges of restraint in the ranks of the Ustashi. This is confirmed in a collection of articles written by leaders of the Communist uprisings throughout Yugoslavia. One of them wrote that "by July 23–24 training had been completed for the Partisan group which, under the leadership of the party organization in Glina, attacked the railway station in Glina and the gendarmery post in Grahovac. After this action, the Ustashi began their massacres in the Serbian villages. The population went into hiding in Šamarica wood, where they encamped, setting up guard posts and observation points from which they could report on the movements of the Ustashi." Another article said that "the massacres of innocent people created a feeling of uncertainty and revealed the true fact of Ustashi rule; this eased the task of the party organizations in forming shock squads and fighting units, and enabled a large number of recruits to be brought into action against the Ustashi and the occupier."

The pogroms against the Serbs reached a peak at the end of July. Unrest was increasing as a result of the Communist call to arms, and many Serbs fled to the mountains. The Ustashi preferred to strike out at peaceful people in villages and towns, who knew nothing of the terrible fate awaiting them. At the end of July, there was a terrible massacre of the Serbian population in the neighborhood of Glina, about eighty kilometers southwest of Zagreb. This slaughter of several hundred Serbs in their church was the most frightful Ustashi massacre of all. According to the published account, a group of forty Ustashi rounded up 1,240 males and took them in trucks to Glina, telling them they were being taken to be baptized. "All these people were herded into their church, where they waited quietly for the baptismal service." The Ustashi then locked all the doors and fell upon the Serbs with bombs, revolvers, and knives. They threw the corpses into common graves in a nearby wood. The church was razed shortly afterward, so that no trace of this appalling atrocity would remain.

When Archbishop Stepinac heard of this, he went straight to Pavelić and said, "God's commandment states—thou shalt not kill!" He then stalked out of the room without uttering another word. Dr. Lončar, a distinguished Zagreb parish priest, asserted that "the Croatian people will pay dearly for this." His words were reported to Pavelić, and he was condemned to death. (His sentence was later commuted to twelve years' imprisonment.) Maček, under house arrest, told his people that they must defend the Serbs with their own hands.

In Bosnia, the pogroms began on August 2. I was told about them by survivors from three towns that suffered most, Prijedor, Bihać, and Sanski Most. Ustashi units arrived in trucks from various points. Collecting the worst of the local riffraff to assist them, they set about killing peaceful men, women, and children. It was particularly horrifying to see the Ustashi employing fourteen- and fifteen-year-old boys to torture and kill innocent people.

In many villages, the Serbian peasants were warned by their fellow villagers, both Croats and Moslems, to hide in the forest. To their great misfortune, they did not heed the warnings. These peaceful people found it incomprehensible that a government could actually organize the murder of its own citizens.

One writer has described the outbreak of large-scale pogroms in the Lika, in Croatia, thus: "The first victims of Ustashi savagery were Communists and other progressive people, regardless of their nationality, though the Serbs predominated. The infamous death camp, Jadovno, was set up in the Velebit Mountains, near Gospić. . . . No accurate details are available, but it is known that the number of deaths here reached the tens of thousands. A massacre of 650 of the inhabitants of Smiljana ensued. During the slaughter, many families were shut up in their homes and burned alive."

An appalling situation developed when the Ustashi began their large-scale pogroms in Herzegovina. S. Prce, a Croatian Peasant party representative, later told me that the Ustashi summoned the Serbs to churches for baptism, then killed the men while their wives and children were inside. Panic-stricken Serbs flocked to the local priests, begging to be received into the Catholic church as quickly as possible. The bishop of Mostar wrote a letter to Archbishop Stepinac, in which he complained bitterly about Ustashi atrocities: "People are being treated like wild beasts. Their throats are cut, they are . . . thrown alive over precipices. Women, children, girls are thrown into pits. . . . On the Mostar-Čapljina line, six railway cars full of women and children unloaded their human freight at Surmanci, from where they were taken into the mountains, and the women and children, still alive, hurled headlong over the cliffs to their deaths. In the parish of Klepci . . . seven hundred Serbian Orthdox were murdered. The prefect of the Mostar district said that seven hundred Serbs had been thrown into a single pit in Ljubinje. In Mostar alone, hundreds were bound, taken outside the town, and killed like cattle."

The fugitives in the mountains were thirsting for revenge. But revenge against whom? Should it be confined to the Ustashi, who had committed these unspeakable atrocities? Or should the entire Croatian and Moslem population be included? Opinions were divided. The followers of the Communist line favored the former alternative. Those imbued with the idea of Serbian nationalism leaned more toward a general retribution. Raids of vengeance on Catholic and Moslem villages further aggravated relations between Croats and Serbs and strengthened the Ustashi position; the Communists therefore set themselves against such tactics. Thus the first outbreak of conflict in Herzegovina was one in which members of Ustashi, Chetnik, and Partisan units all fought against each other. By August such confusion had arisen that the Partisan commissar, R. Hamović, instructed Partisan units to cease all operations for a time.

Many moderate and humane people protested to Pavelić against the abominable Ustashi pogroms. Prce asked him whether he had calculated the inevitable increase in the number of Croatian and Moslem deaths if he failed to stop the Ustashi. The Serbs, he said, were not lambs to be led to the slaughter.

Pavelić replied that there would be no Serbs at all if the Ustashi had killed them all off and burned down their houses. Finally he seemed to give in, and he produced for Prce new regulations, calling for milder treatment of the Serbs. When Prce showed these regulations to the Ustashi chiefs in Herzegovina, they laughed in his face. "Throw them in the waste basket," they said. "We know the real orders. We're settling the Serbian question with bullets, not ping-pong balls." Soon afterward, Prce and other Croats who had survived the Chetnik retaliatory actions were forced out of the area. The whole left bank of the Neretva was swept clean of Catholic Croats, and Moslem houses were burned down in all the villages except Fazlagića Kula.

The growing unrest in Croatia was a godsend to the Italians in their efforts to increase their domination in the annexed provinces of Dalmatia and the Croatian littoral. In order to insure a smooth and quick Italianization program, all prominent Croats in these areas were placed in camps in southern Italy at the end of July. Giuseppe Bastianini, the military governor of the region, worked out a plan with the Serbian refugees in Zadar for the military occupation of as much territory as possible in Pavelić's Independent Croatia (recognized by the Germans as an Italian occupation zone) and for regular aid to the Italian army, to be supplied by the Serbian community. On August 4, the guerrilla detachments' Bosnian headquarters, in Donji Lapac, issued a proclamation that the Italian army would reoccupy three zones: the first, along the coast itself; the second, fifty kilometers inland; and the third, up to the German zone line. Italian officers and men, the proclamation said, were considered friends of the Serbian people and would receive a full guarantee of freedom and peace. There were no Ustashi in the first zone. In the second zone, the Italian army immediately put a stop to the Ustashi terror, expelled a considerable number of Ustashi, and released the Serbs from prison and established safeguards for their life and property. In the third zone, the Ustashi were compelled to accept Italian army supervision. There was an enormous sense of relief, particularly among the Serbs and the Jews. This was the first sign of Serbo-Italian friendship, which was later to develop into close co-operation between the Italian army and the Chetniks.

Not until August 16 was Pavelić informed that the number of

Italian troops was to be increased and that the Italian army was advancing to the Italian-German demarcation line. The Serbo-Italian alliance was a heavy blow to the Ustashi and an encouragement to the Chetniks to carry out reprisals against innocent Croats and Moslems. Thus the bad blood created between the Serbs and Croats was of great advantage to the Italians.

In Bosnia and Herzegovina, the Communists got an enthusiastic response only in the eastern regions, where major atrocities had been committed by the Ustashi. There, army officers from Serbia provided considerable assistance. As in Serbia, where there was peace between Mihailović's followers and the Communists, both sides went into battle together, united against the Ustashi.

In Slovenia, during the early days of the uprising, the Communists took action only against compatriots who refused to accept their ideology. It was in the purely Croatian areas that the Communists had the most difficulty in getting recruits for the insurrection.

In an August 2 letter to Tito, Edvard Kardelj, his right-hand man, who was working underground in Croatia, wrote: "Some comrades (not those in leadership) have a fear of reprisals—destruction of villages, executions, and so on. It is this fear that is the greatest stumbling block to a more determined campaign for recruiting people from the Croatian villages. But it is my firm belief that reprisals will convert the Croatian village to the side of the Serbian village. In war we must not be afraid of whole villages being destroyed. The terror will unquestionably lead to armed action. . . . The terror against the Maček people can only bring the whole of Croatia up in arms."

Between the time of his arrival in Ravna Gora and the Communist call to insurrection, Draža Mihailović succeeded in spreading his organization over a fairly wide field. At that time, the general belief in Serbia was that the Russians would be in Berlin by the end of the year. Many people advised Mihailović to start fighting, so that, when that time came, the Communists would not be the only ones in the firing line. Mihailović finally yielded to this pressure, and he instructed his commanders to undertake minor actions against the Germans. Tito's top men in Belgrade, headed by Alexander Ranković, got in touch with Mihailović's men there. The latter maintained that this was a time for preparation, that major actions should not be started until the Germans had been defeated on the eastern front. They emphasized that it was not worth sacrificing fifty Serbs for "a single German or a section of railway line."

Tito received Ranković's report after his departure for liberated territory at the beginning of September. He decided to continue talks with Mihailović on a personal basis, and the two met on September 19. Mihailović vigorously defended his theory that large-scale attacks on the Germans would result in reprisals that would destroy their own fighting units and cause heavy losses of life and property. Tito rejected the argument. "That's of no importance," he said. "I'm looking further ahead." Interestingly, Tito admitted to Mihailović that he had been surprised by the savagery of his young Partisans, and Mihailović made the same admission regarding his own young guerrillas. No agreement was reached on a joint command; there was merely an ill-defined arrangement for co-operation between Mihailović's and Tito's forces.

The second meeting between Mihailović and Tito took place on October 26. The grave atmosphere created by the German offensive, and the savage reprisals against the entire population, lay heavy on the course of these talks.

The shooting of hostages, and all the other brutal and repressive measures taken by the German masters of Serbia, aided by the SS and the Gestapo, had failed to stamp out the uprising. The government in Belgrade could not get its gendarmes to fire at their own countrymen. Its military actions against the rebels came to nothing, because they avoided frontal engagements, evaporating like mist as they withdrew deeper into the forests. Berlin decided to set up a Serbian government, headed by General Milan Nedić. Nedić formed his government on August 29, with the support of Dimitrije Ljotić, leader of the fanatically anti-Communist Zbor movement. Some two hundred prominent men in Serbia proclaimed their approval of the Nedić government, appealing to the nation for calm.

By the end of August, some of Mihailović's commanders became impatient and joined forces with Tito's Partisans in actions against German troops. Benzler, the German plenipotentiary attached to the military commander for Serbia, informed Berlin that Nedić's government was incapable of putting down the insurrection and that Germany would have to crush it with her own forces. On September 16, Hitler issued the following directive: "I assign to the *Wehrmacht Commander* . . . the task of crushing the insurrectionary movement in the southeastern area. It is important first to secure in the Serbian area the transportation routes and the objects important for the German war economy, and then . . . to restore order . . . by the most rigorous methods."

Field Marshal Wilhelm Keitel, chief of the supreme command of the German armed forces, sent instructions to General Böhme, who had been put in charge of the punitive expedition in Serbia: "In order to nip the agitation in the bud the harshest methods must be employed immediately. . . . A human life is often considered to be of no value in the countries concerned, and a deterrent effect can be attained only through unusual severity. . . . The death penalty for 50 to 100 Communists must be considered an appropriate atonement for the life of a German soldier."

The punitive expedition was sent to Mačva, the rich area of Serbia between the Sava and the Drina, in advance of the main concentration of forces. It left in its path a trail of fire, burning villages, firing squads, gallows, pillaged houses, and the lamentations of innocent people. The indescribable fate of that area, and of its main city, Šabac, was brought up in part at the Nuremberg trials.

But the tragedy that befell the town of Kragujevac on October 20 and 21 was more horrible than anything else during World War II, in Yugoslavia or elsewhere. On October 15, as the Germans began mopping up in western Serbia, a German platoon was captured by Mihailović's forces. The following day, the commander of the 920th German regiment in Kragujevac dispatched his third battalion to rescue the platoon. On its way from Kragujevac it was ambushed. Both Mihailović's and Tito's forces took part in the attack. Ten German soldiers were killed and twenty-six wounded. The battalion returned to Kragujevac, which was reinforced at once with fresh troops under the command of Major König, who had led a great massacre of innocent people at Kraljevo. This was terrifying news for the people of Kragujevac. German security forces had already made a round of arrests in the town; on October 19, some three hundred peasants were shot in three neighboring villages. On the night of October 19–20, all roads out of Kragujevac were blocked, and by 7:00 A.M. the center of the town began to feel the squeeze as the ring around it tightened. All houses were thoroughly searched, and all males between sixteen and sixty were taken to district military headquarters for identification, then to huts overlooking the town. Most of the civil servants were taken away from their offices, and schoolboys over sixteen were taken from the schools, together with their teachers. The roundup continued into the afternoon, when a total of some ten thousand people had been collected. About a hundred were shot that day, mainly after being denounced by local collaborators. On October 21, according to official German figures, 2,300 were shot; according to survivors, however, the actual number was about 7,000, all innocent people. Among the victims was Laza Pantelić, headmaster of the First Boys High School. His name was on the list of those to be spared. When he saw thirty-five of his boys being taken away, he asked one of the Germans, "Where are they being taken?"

"To be shot," replied the German.

"I'm their headmaster. Let them go, and take me instead."

"That's impossible."

"My place is not here—it's with my boys."

Quickly he ran over to the boys and walked along with them to face the firing squad. The boys embraced him; and all hugging each other, they went to their deaths.

On October 29, Benzler sent the following report to his ministry: "In the past week there have been executions . . . of a large number of Serbs, not only in Kraljevo but also in Kragujevac, as reprisals for the killing of members of the Wehrmacht in the proportion of 100 Serbs for one German. In Kraljevo 1,700 male Serbs were executed, in Kragujevac 2,300."

Around this time, reports also reached us in London that the town of Rudnik had been razed, and that in Gornji Milanovac the Germans had brought all the inhabitants to the church and then set about destroying the town systematically with incendiary bombs. Out of 464 houses, only 72 were left, and a great many of the inhabitants lost their lives. In the town of Kraljevo all the railway and aircraft factory workers were shot; in addition, the Germans shot one member of every family in the town.

The co-operation between Tito's and Mihailović's forces was uneasy from the start. Tito's Partisans, anxious to extend their authority and to keep a watchful eye on every activity in the liberated territory, demanded great sacrifices from the population. Mihailović's guerrillas, considering themselves members of a national resistance movement, behaved more circumspectly toward the people. On September 23, Mihailović's forces entered Užička Požega. The Partisans entered the town that same night. Because they were more numerous and better armed than Mihailović's men, they were able to disarm them and send them home. Mihailović's commanders did not accept this with equanimity. They formed new Chetnik units with recruits from neighboring villages, and then made an agreement with the Partisans to return to Požega on October 1 to share the administration of the town. On the appointed day, however, when the first Chetnik units appeared, the Partisans opened fire. After a fierce battle, the Chetniks captured the town on October 2, and held it until November 3, when it fell once again to the Partisans. In the interval, no Partisan passed through without being arrested or murdered. Strained relations between Partisans and Chetniks existed in other places as well, but they continued to collaborate, and for most of this period Mihailović had a delegate at Tito's headquarters in Užice. The final break came exactly one month after the conflict over Požega.

On December 18, 1943, Vladimir Dedijer told me in Cairo that the military mission's radio operator had fled to the Partisans and informed them that he had decoded a message from Simović in London instructing Mihailović to liquidate Tito. Simović's message may not have been the main cause of the armed conflict between Mihailović's and Tito's forces that broke out a few kilometers from Užice on November 2. They had engaged in a number of skirmishes before. Significantly, in the November 2 fight, the main role was played by the same Chetnik units that had fought against the Partisans in Užička Požega a month earlier. Their intention was to capture Užice, where Tito had his headquarters and where there was an armaments factory. Tito dispatched forces to take the Chetniks by surprise, and Mihailović's attack was unsuccessful.

Mihailović requested that the government intervene in Moscow for pressure to stop Partisan attacks on Chetniks. Delegates from the two sides met on November 18 and 20, and reached an agreement for cessation of hostilities, release of prisoners, and continued joint action against the Germans. But events took a different course, and the reconciliation came to nothing. The Germans were advancing on Užice jointly with all the Serbian anti-Communist forces, including those of Mihailović's commanders who had been involved in bloody encounters with Tito's Partisans. Tito just barely managed to escape with his life when these forces converged on November 29.

On December 3, the Germans tried to get Mihailović to join them. Failing in this, they attacked his hiding place on December 7. Mihailović eluded them, but they captured some of his officers and men. Then the old familiar bitter winter was upon them. Mihailović split his forces up into very small detachments, retaining for himself only five men. Traveling by night, they moved to a different village every three or four days.

The news of the Mihailović-Tito conflict in Serbia swiftly spread throughout occupied Yugoslavia. In London, we received a report from Slovenia that the Communists had sentenced Mihailović to death. Mihailović summed up the cause of his dispute with Tito when he said to Christie Lawrence, an Englishman who had fought with him against the Germans: "You have heard of the result of my revolution last autumn . . . ? Of the hundreds of villages burned and the terrible reprisals that the Germans inflicted on our innocent people? . . . When it was over . . . I resolved that I would never again bring such misery on the country, unless it could result in total liberation."

Mihailović was haunted by the horrors suffered by the villages in Mačva and by such towns as Kragujevac and Kraljevo. The memory of all this drew him back to his original plan: to lay the foundations for a national insurrection to be raised when Allied soldiers set foot on Yugoslav soil. Most of the nation agreed with this.

In Tito's camp, the feeling was quite the reverse: there was an icy indifference to the terrible sufferings and sacrifices of the population, accompanied by an equally icy determination to force all other resistance groups to either surrender to the Partisans or become collaborators with the enemy. Communist leaders reacted to the bewilderment caused by their callousness toward suffering by saying that if the Serbs perished in this war, there were enough Chinese to settle Serbian lands. The Partisans proclaimed themselves the only resistance movement and the one to which all power would have to be handed once the enemy was defeated. Therefore, anyone who fought outside their movement was considered a traitor and collaborator and would be sentenced to death. This was a contributing factor in the creation of the worst kind of hell in Yugoslavia: whatever people did was wrong, whether they joined one of the groups in the civil war, or went over to the enemy, or tried to remain on the side lines.

CHAPTER 8

During the summer, many contradictory reports reached London about the tragic developments in Yugoslavia. Dr. Miloš Sekulić, a Belgrade physician, arrived in London, via Istanbul, with a memorandum from the leaders of the Serbian Orthodox church on the massacres of Serbs in Croatia. The memorandum asserted that to date the Ustashi had murdered 180,000 people, among them three bishops and 150 priests. This information was turned over to British newspaper correspondents in Turkey, and the London *Times* published a report on September 29, citing the number of victims as 300,000. Yugoslavs in London were appalled. The strength of their reaction is evident in a remark made by the Serbian vice-premier, Slobodan Jovanović, to the Slovenian vice-premier, Miho Krek: "Yugoslavia no longer exists. The Croats are murdering the Serbs."

My ministry received a telegram from Istanbul about Sekulić's report on October 3; on October 4, I wrote in my diary, "I foresee a great storm in the government." I proposed to Ninčić that a copy of the Istanbul telegram be sent to Krnjević, the Croatian vice-premier, before the next cabinet meeting, scheduled for October 9. He rejected my suggestion because he believed that Krnjević was still conspiring with Simović to oust him from his position as foreign minister. When Ninčić read the telegram, he stated that after the war at least 100,000 Croats would have to be killed in retribution. Thus, when the cabinet session opened, with the King presiding, the air was full of electricity.

Ninčić, the first speaker, immediately accused the Croats of massacring the Serbs. Juraj Šutej pounced fiercely on the allegations that the Catholic church was persecuting the Serbs and that

111

all Croats were following Pavelić. Simović demanded that the facts be established and that appeals be sent to the Pope and to President Roosevelt, asking them to use their moral authority to put an end to the massacres in Croatia. Despite the initial dissension, the session ended peacefully. But other factors soon interfered. The government delegate in Cairo, Jovan Djonović, began urging Simović to "expel the Croats from the government."

Ninčić started working energetically for a Serbian front against the Croats, exploiting the blood of innocent victims for his own sordid political ends. He helped to popularize the belief that Serbia's frontiers had to be extended to the farthest corner of Croatia where Serbian blood had been shed. He proposed a common frontier between Serbia and Slovenia, running through Dalmatia and the Croatian littoral.

The campaign against the Croats spread to the Serbian *émigré* press in the United States. To counteract this campaign, the Croatian *émigré* press began making allegations against the Serbs. In turn, the diplomatic corps, which was 90 per cent Serbian, adopted an anti-Croatian attitude. As the exaggerated, biased reports on the massacre of Serbs continued to emanate from Istanbul, the cloud over relations between Serbs and Croats in exile grew thicker and darker.

The November 10–11 cabinet meeting was the stormiest ever. All the outstanding problems were raised: Sekulić's reports, the dissension between Serbs and Croats in the United States, BBC broadcasts to Yugoslavia, the anti-Croatian propaganda being spread by the diplomatic representatives, the government's territorial demands on Italy, and so on. There were serious altercations between ministers; two men left the debate in tears. Serbian ministers quarreled with one another behind the scenes. Ninčić regarded Simović as a weakling who overindulged the Croats, and he vigorously pursued his hostility both toward Simović and toward the Serbian ministers who regarded themselves as Yugoslavs. Simović was denounced to the King as a republican.

Jovanović informed me on November 11 that a government crisis had developed. The fall of the government was inevitable, he said, unless something unexpected happened to bring about a reconciliation. He begged me to point out to the Croatian ministers the dangers to the Yugoslav people if relations between their representatives in London should break down. It could lead to even more grievous slaughter. He asked me to try to effect a reconciliation between Krnjević and Grol, and said he would try to get Ninčić to make peace with Krnjević. At a meeting at Finance Minister Šutej's home, I pleaded with him and Krnjević to make generous, conciliatory gestures. My appeal was successful, for at the cabinet meeting the following day, Šutej spoke in such a warm, friendly tone that he brought tears to Simović's eyes.

For the moment, the danger of a break between the Serbs and Croats had subsided. It was decided that a joint declaration should be drawn up, embodying the substance of the government's political program. The three vice-premiers—one Serb, one Croat, and one Slovene—completed their draft on November 13. Based on the principles of the Atlantic Charter that deal with the self-determination of nations, and designed to prevent any built-in majority vote among the Serbs, Croats, or Slovenes, it defined in general terms the future pattern of government in Yugoslavia. In addition, the vice-premiers agreed to personnel changes in the government missions in Istanbul and Washington. Ninčić was not satisfied with the declaration because of its reference to the Atlantic Charter. He feared that by strengthening Simović's position, the declaration might help bring about his own downfall.

At a meeting with Krnjević and Šutej on November 26, I told them of rumors that the Serbs were planning Simović's ouster, and that Grol was seeking genuine co-operation with us. Grol was anxious for Krnjević to make a statement in his BBC broadcast severely condemning Ustashi atrocities, to express sympathy for the tribulations the Serbs were suffering, and to take an unequivocal stand in favor of maintaining a united country of Serbs, Croats, and Slovenes in a new federal Yugoslavia. Grol told me that if Krnjević accepted his proposal, the situation would change radically and the demands of the Croatian ministers would be easily satisfied. I told Krnjević and Šutej that Britain's minister of information had expressed similar wishes to Simović, and that Eden was reported to have told the president of Poland that he was worried about Yugoslavia—he did not know what position she could take in postwar Europe, because her representatives in London did not seem to know what they wanted. They were impressed by my arguments, and Šutej said that he was going to have a talk with Grol, since Krnjević was not capable of handling the matter.

Simović's position was shaky, and, having considerable sympathy for him and thinking of the welfare of our unhappy country, I decided to advise him on how to get his cabinet to work together as a team. After I had succeeded in creating a favorable climate for settlement of the many problems, I asked an old and trusted acquaintance of Simović's to try to convince him that the time was ripe for energetic action to bring peace to his government. I was alarmed by Simović's response: "I shall not take action. They can go on quarreling to their heart's content for all I care. As long as they are quarreling, I am safe." As a result, I decided to make a complete break with Simović.

There was enough in the various reports, including Sekulić's, to provide Simović with a motive for taking a firm line in settling the differences in his government. Sekulić had said: "The Serbs have a burning desire to avenge themselves against the Croats." Ivan Avsenek, in occupied Slovenia, reacted to this statement as follows: "Some Serbian ministers wish to settle their accounts with the Croats as soon as they return to the country. . . . The Croatian people are not responsible for the crimes committed by the Ustashi. Do you think that the Croats condoned them? No! . . . If you wish to be objective, you should also condemn the Chetniks. In the area around Bihać alone, twelve hundred children were orphaned through wholesale massacres by the Chetniks of their fathers, mothers, brothers, and sisters. . . . One should try to calm the population by pointing out that it is the design of our conquerors to exterminate us. There is no sense in talking of revenge. . . . On the contrary, it must be emphasized that the criminals will be brought to justice."

Indeed, the government should have been directing all its energies toward solving this problem. And the problem of relations between Mihailović and Tito also ought to have been given priority.

The agreement reached between Grol and Krnjević, at my instigation, enabled Simović's downfall to proceed smoothly. Cabinet meetings were peaceful. Grol was persuaded to cease his attacks on Šutej's handling of government finances. But the Croatian ministers were not yet prepared to topple Simović. They believed they would fare best in an atmosphere characterized by strained relations between Simović and the Serbian ministers. Even the King's speech of December 17 failed to move them, a speech in which he said that although those who had carried out the March 27 coup had been young officers, power had in fact passed into the hands of political party men.

At about this time, Simović recalled Milan Gavrilović from Moscow to take over the foreign ministry from Ninčić. Gavrilović refused. Jovanović and Gavrilović did everything they could to reconcile Simović with Ninčić and Grol, but they failed because Simović was immersed in his convulsive struggle to retain power. In his desperation, he made a series of mistakes that finally brought about his downfall. The first of these was to offer Ninčić a pact against the Croatian group. When the Croatian ministers heard of this, they were ready at once to join with their Serbian colleagues in taking a stand against Simović. The greatest contribution to their success was made by Simović himself—he began attacking the Croatian ministers just as certain Serbian ministers had. He threatened to "use his revolver" before allowing himself to be overthrown. His opponents, who interpreted this as a threat to the King, said that he had been a man of straw in the March 27 coup; that he had completely failed in his conduct of the war; that he had ordered the surrender of the army without the government's knowledge; that he had tried to shift the blame for the rapid collapse of the army to the Croats.

When Simović realized that his broadsides against the Croatian ministers had misfired, he made furtive arrangements for the publication of parts of the report on the massacre of Serbs, hoping thereby to whip up indignation. This was precisely what he himself had been so steadfastly against three months earlier. He told the King that Ninčić and Grol were in contact with the Axis powers via Lisbon, and he lodged the same allegation with the British Foreign Office. This was the ultimate in skullduggery, and it alienated the last of the Serbs who had been defending him. It was decided that Simović should be removed after the Orthodox Christmas holidays. On January 9, the ministers sent a joint letter of resignation to the King, giving as grounds Simović's mishandling of government affairs. Even then, Simović refused to resign, and the King was compelled to remove him from office.

. . .

Simović's fall finally ended the notion that the men of March 27 should be the kingpins of government. The time was ripe for settling awkward political problems, and the prevailing belief seemed to be that they could best be tackled by a government composed of representatives from the major political parties. The logical man to head such a government was Slobodan Jovanović, Yugoslavia's most distinguished expert on constitutional law.

On January 11, a new government was formed, under the premiership of Jovanović. All the ministers in the Simović government retained their posts, with the exception of Armed Forces Minister Bogoljub Ilić, who was replaced by Draža Mihailović. Mihailović was given the position primarily to insure British recognition of the new government. When the British were informed of the impending changes, Eden had expressed concern that Simović's ouster might threaten the resistance forces in Yugoslavia. Taking Mihailović into the government was intended to allay his apprehensions.

There were further changes once the new government took office. Arrangements had been made for General Bora Mirković, deputy commander in chief of the air force and military leader of the *Putsch*, to take over as first adjutant to the King as soon as he had recovered from injuries sustained in an air crash. But he remained in Cairo, and on January 15, Jovanović relieved him of his duties both as first adjutant and as air force commander, and placed Major Živan Knežević, brother of Court Minister Radoje Knežević and commander of the units that had carried out the *Putsch*, in charge of the military cabinet. The following day, Ilić was removed from his position as chief of the general staff in Cairo. This purge of officers of the highest rank inevitably led to even greater upheavals.

Grol and I were invited to meet the new premier on January 20: Grol as the senior Serbian politician in Jovanović's government, and I because of my contribution to the *rapprochement* and my reputation as the most conciliatory member of the Croatian group.

Jovanović told us that the concept of a joint Serbo-Croatian-Slovenian state was in jeopardy, and the new government had to defend it, even if we all sank at sea before the war came to an end. It would be tragic if we were to fall out among ourselves before that time. He proposed a declaration favoring Yugoslavia.

In fact, he said, he would not continue as premier unless he succeeded in obtaining agreement for this basic policy line and an assurance that there would be teamwork. Grol and I both welcomed his decision and promised our full support.

Nevertheless, talks on the joint declaration and efforts to create team spirit in the cabinet progressed slowly and with difficulty. The atmosphere became strained at the very beginning, following a memorandum on Croatia's recent history compiled at Krnjević's request. The memorandum placed far greater emphasis on Croatia's troubles with the Serbs than on the German-Italian occupation. Matters became much more serious at the end of January, when Krnjević announced that he accepted responsibility for the memorandum, a thoughtless move on his part. This incident was resurrected every time a conflict arose between the Croatian and Serbian ministers, and was a stumbling block in the attempts to reach a joint declaration.

Meanwhile, there was growing dissatisfaction among the officers in Cairo. Ilić had withdrawn swiftly and without protest, but Mirković held on to his post and paid no heed to orders from London, even after he was pensioned off on January 27. Most of the officers were on his side. The split in Cairo was disturbing to the British as well, who openly supported Mirković. These events, known as the "Cairo affair," grew increasingly chaotic.

Once we received the first reliable reports on the massacre of the Serbs and the outbreak of armed conflict between the Chetniks and the Partisans, I realized that a united government and genuine Anglo-Soviet co-operation were essential in order to terminate that situation. It was absolutely clear to me that unless Anglo-American troops moved into Yugoslavia, catastrophe would engulf the country. My own task was clear. I had to do everything possible to achieve maximum unity in the government, to keep a close watch on developments in Anglo-Soviet relations, and to make it plain to the British and American officials that they had great strategic interests in Yugoslavia, and great moral obligations to her.

Soviet policy continued to be an enigma. The first steps taken by Simović to obtain Soviet intervention with Tito for an end to hostilities against Mihailović had some effect: the Comintern instructed Tito to stop the attacks that had been launched against Mihailović's forces on November 2. This must be seen in the light of the Soviet Union's desperate military position at the time. Stalin hoped for a secret agreement with Eden acknowledging the Curzon line frontiers with Poland and other acquisitions in Europe. Roosevelt was against any such commitments. During his visit to London in May, 1942, Molotov told Eden, who had refused to recognize Soviet annexation of the Baltic states, "But we would sign at once if you wanted the Rotterdam-Antwerp-Le Havre line." Harold Nicolson told me that Eden had said, "If that had only been a joke, the trouble would not have been half so bad. . . . It shows the Russians have absolutely no understanding of us."

Up to the Moscow conference of October, 1943, the efforts of Churchill and Eden were aimed at insuring that the small states in the Balkans and in central and eastern Europe would join in federations, as safeguards against any future German threat. The British made no secret of the fact that these federations were also meant to be a safeguard against a possible Soviet threat. The first treaty of federal union was signed by Poland and Czechoslovakia in January, 1942. A short time later, a similar treaty was signed by Yugoslavia and Greece. Stalin had asked Eden for a second front by early spring, 1942, either in France or in the Balkans, so he approved Eden's proposals for federations in that area. But when he received neither recognition of the frontiers he wanted in eastern Europe nor a promise of a second front in the near future, he soon showed his displeasure.

Slobodan Jovanović informed me that he had failed in his effort to get the Soviet ambassador, Alexander Bogomolov, to accept his proposal that Yugoslavia and Moscow jointly co-ordinate the activities of Mihailović and Tito. When I saw Bogomolov on January 21, he told me that the guerrillas had sprung from the people; recognition could not be granted to one group and denied to another; and it was not possible to manage their activities from London. "We cannot intervene between Mihailović and the Communists." he said. "That's your internal affair." I also gathered that Moscow was not pleased with Mihailović's appointment as armed forces minister. I realized immediately that our troubles with Russia would grow as the war progressed.

A commission was set up, headed by British experts and composed of Peasant party representatives from all the countries of southeastern Europe, to work out a joint program of economic reconstruction and co-operation in the postwar period. The program laid down certain purely political conditions: there were to be democratic regimes in all the countries, and an end to the extravagant nationalism of the nineteenth century, which had left "a legacy of national strife." The basic assumption was that the three great Allied powers would assent to the program, and that understanding among them would continue after the war.

The optimistic belief on the part of the *émigré* governments of the southeastern European nations that Anglo-American influence would be decisive during and after the war was given a lift by this program. The Yugoslav government's optimism was boosted by powerful propaganda about the fighting exploits of Draža Mihailović and by the satisfaction in British circles that concord between the Serbs and the Croats had been preserved after the fall of Simović. The Serbs believed that Mihailović was the answer to all the dangers that threatened them, and the Croats were satisfied by a guarantee that the Serbs would not oust them from the government until the end of the war, when, in any case, other arrangements would have to be made.

Mihailović's appointment as armed forces minister a few weeks after his clash with Tito led many people in Yugoslavia to the erroneous, if logical, conclusion that Mihailović's war against the Communists was approved by the Yugoslav and British governments. On April 8, 1944, Milovan Djilas (who was leading the first Tito delegation to Moscow via Cairo) told me that many Yugoslav officers believed this and had opted for Mihailović.

British propagandists had welcomed the news of Mihailović's resistance and had been spreading it on the radio and in the press. This, in turn, reinforced Mihailović's belief that the British approved of his war against the Communists. Both the British and the majority of Serbs went too far in their glorification of Mihailović. He had not asked for this, but it did raise his standing in the country and helped him to extend his leadership abroad as well as within Serbia. On January 22, his forces were proclaimed "the Yugoslav Army in the Fatherland," to distinguish them from the self-styled Chetnik groups, some of which were collaborating with the Germans and Italians. Mihailović was promoted to army general the following June. Soon thereafter, supreme headquarters was transferred from Cairo to Yugoslavia, with Mihailović as chief of staff. His reputation grew until the end of the year, in spite of adverse reports filtering out from Communist sources.

What was his actual position during this period? The hard winter and lack of manpower obstructed operations in Serbia. When the winter was over and the Communists had departed, many of his commanders who had gone over to Milan Nedić rejoined Mihailović in the mountains. Those who had abandoned him after the first skirmishes with the Communists also came back, after seeing the bitter resentment of the population against the Communists. Sometimes they clashed with Nedić's forces, but they avoided open conflict with the Germans. Nevertheless, on April 2, the Germans ordered Mihailović and his staff to surrender within five days or their families would be held as hostages. Mihailović appealed to the government in London to stop broadcasting news of his operations and inciting Yugoslavs to rise up in arms. At the end of May, the Foreign Office replied that all measures to this effect had been undertaken. Meanwhile, the Germans were offering a reward of 100,000 gold marks to anyone who captured or killed Mihailović and Tito.

Before Mihailović himself left the area, he appointed a commander for Serbia. In May, 1942, he withdrew into the Sandžak, and in June he set up headquarters in Gornje Lipovo, in Montenegro. He arrived at a time when Montenegro had been almost swept clean of Communists. Mihailović had established contact with the leaders of the 1941 uprising, mainly Yugoslav army officers. Like Mihailović in Serbia, they were faced with the problem of breaking ties with the Communists, whose ill-considered attacks on the Italian army were imposing intolerable sacrifices on the population. When the situation had gotten completely out of hand, the Montenegrin Nationalists had accepted arms from the Italians and joined them in battling Tito's forces. The engagement lasted six weeks, and ended on June 12, when the last of Tito's units were driven out of Montenegro.

The vicious hatred between Communists and non-Communists in Serbia and Montenegro resulted mainly from the Communist military operations, which provoked brutal German and Italian reprisals against innocent people. The Communists expected that the reaction to these reprisals would be so strong that people would be driven over to their side. The reverse was the case: people turned against them in large numbers. Some of the brutalities meted out by the Communists to their enemies are described in detail in a book by M. Mladenović, who was a Partisan in the early stages of the uprising and then went over to Mihailović. Mladenović relates how, for example, in an act of reprisal, the Partisans ambushed and killed a number of Bulgarian soldiers and then took to their heels. The result was a visit by Bulgarian troops, who completely destroyed several villages. It was such incidents that drove the majority of the peasantry into the anti-Communist camp.

Christie Lawrence has recorded the reactions of some outsiders who found themselves among the resistance fighters. A certain Dr. Daniele said it was not the resistance forces, scattered in the forests, who had to pay for their actions, but innocent people. She accused Tito and Mihailović of aiming to set up their own dictatorship, and exclaimed, "Power, power, that's all any of them want." The pressure on Mihailović from his own followers to break with the Communists was very strong. Mihailović himself admitted this to Mladen Žujović, later his representative in Dalmatia, when he said that his men would have deserted him if he had not broken with the Communists.

The reaction of the Montenegrin people was the same. At the beginning of the uprising, a group of captured Italian officers was brought together in Kolašin. The nearby population, fearing Italian reprisals, rose in revolt and on July 29 surrounded Kolašin, demanding that the officers be spared. The Partisans yielded, and the officers were handed over to a unit commanded by Lieutenant Minić, a Nationalist. In the great onslaught against Plevlje at the end of November, Nationalists and Communists fought shoulder to shoulder. The attack was badly planned and badly led. The Communist commissar, a cobbler by trade, assigned the Yugoslav army officers to random positions. The Italians were strongly entrenched in the town and met the attackers with a barrage of artillery and machine-gun fire. The action was a complete fiasco, and some three thousand were killed. After this defeat, a serious blow to Communist prestige, the Communists stepped up their terror campaign in the villages. Their opponents went into hiding in the towns, which had Italian garrisons and were ringed with bunkers and barbed wire.

Yugoslav army officers were astonished to hear the Communists saying that the British would not be allowed to land on the shores of Yugoslavia. Anyone who said anything unfavorable about Russia, or put any credence in German communiqués from the Russian front, was immediately liquidated. Even Dedijer has admitted that "the rapid growth of the revolt in Montenegro was, to a very large extent, a result of the general conviction prevailing there that the war would soon end by a decisive victory of the Red Army over Hitler's hordes. Woe to those who in Montenegro at that time ventured to prophesy that the war would last as much as another six months."

The Communist commanders said in the winter of 1941–1942 that the wheel of the revolution crushed all who stood in its way, and it was futile to look back at its victims. An apt appraisal of the consequences of the tragic conflict between Communists and Nationalists in Montenegro has been given by one who took part in it: "When the civil war broke out, the occupier was left on the side lines. Not a single cottage, not a single human being, was spared the fearful consequences of the devastation. The big and the small, the robust and the sickly—they all carried on their backs the cross of affliction." Djilas and other leading Communists wrote to Tito, complaining that this appalling situation was the result of the Communists' politically incorrect positions on all basic issues. In his book, Mladenović recorded his view of a similar situation in Serbia: "I wanted to fight the occupier, as my patriotic duty; but this fight was soon pushed into the background. Instead of resisting the occupier, we fought our own brothers in the villages and mountains, while the occupying forces sat in peace and mocked us." The unanimous view of all who have talked to me about these sad events and their own part in them can be summed up thus: "We can never forgive the Communists for forcing us to accept enemy arms to defend ourselves against them."

Julian Amery has written that the reprisals against noncombatants was the occupiers' principal weapon against the resistance, a weapon aimed at driving a wedge between the resistance fighters and those on whom they depended. As a result, Tito had to withdraw from Serbia, while Mihailović was compelled to "return to a passive policy and on these terms was received back by the peasants, even was driven to accommodation with the

German enemy in order to resist the more immediate threat from the Communist forces of Tito."

In January, 1942, a massacre of Serbs under Hungarian rule added some twenty thousand victims to the casualties, according to Yugoslav sources. Thousands of bodies were thrown into the icy water of the Danube and the Tisa. A full inquiry into these terrible happenings was instituted by Nicholas von Kallay when he became premier of Hungary. He wrote: "The story was the most dreadful that has ever taken place in the course of Hungarian warfare: a tale of horrors perpetrated by lunatics, criminals, and cowards. More than two thousand [sic] innocent people, including women and children, were murdered and thrown into the Danube. The motives behind the criminal action are still a complete mystery to me to this day." On the basis of the inquiry, five officers, all of them Hungarians of German extraction, were sentenced to death. With the help of SS units they escaped to Germany, only to return as German officers when the German army occupied Hungary in March, 1944.

All subsequent developments in occupied Yugoslavia, and in relations between Yugoslavia and her allies, clearly showed that it had been a monumental blunder to place so much responsibility on Mihailović's shoulders. He was in no position to exercise control and had no chance of receiving major assistance from his own government or from his allies. He was appointed at a time when conflict had broken out with Tito. His contacts with the resistance forces in his immediate vicinity were poor; with those farther afield they were nonexistent. For nearly four months he had had no radio contact with London, because he was constantly changing hide-outs. What policy and what machinery could he employ to establish a network stretching from Slovenia to Macedonia?

Eastern Bosnia was most accessible for him, and it was there that the war had broken out between his forces and the Communists. In eastern Bosnia Major Dangić's bands had been receiving German help against the Communists. Thousands of innocent Moslems had lost their lives, and their villages had been burned down. Serbs have told me that Mihailović, as a representative of law amidst chaos, should have executed those guilty of violence against innocent Moslems.

In the same way that Glina, Jasenovac, and Jadovno became synonymous with Ustashi bestiality, so Foča became synonymous with Chetnik brutality. At the beginning of December, the Italian army evacuated the town as a gesture of good will toward the Chetniks; a small Croatian garrison of Domobrans (the regular Croatian army) and Ustashi also left. The Chetniks entered without firing a shot and immediately began hunting down the Moslems and the handful of Catholics in the town. Some were murdered in their homes; others were taken to the bridge and slaughtered like cattle or thrown into the waters of the Drina. The number of victims was estimated at one thousand. The towns of Goražde and Čajnice suffered a similar fate. Tito's forces captured Foča on January 23, and Tito made it his headquarters for the next three months. The town again fell into Ustashi hands, and on August 19 once again into Chetnik hands, when several hundred more Moslems were slaughtered on the Drina bridge.

The guerrilla commanders who had come to an agreement with the Italians, and later in Bosnia with the Germans, for joint action against the Communists, claimed allegiance to Mihailović. Mihailović's explanation was that the alliance had been formed in order to insure that his forces would be supplied with arms. Some of my British friends said that the British had to accept this stratagem because they themselves were unable to provide him with arms on a major scale. Reports from Yugoslavia reaching the Croats in London spoke of collaboration between Chetnik leaders in Dalmatia and Herzegovina and the Italians. We were asked whether Mihailović and the British and Yugoslav governments approved of this, and were urged, whenever the Chetniks mounted a large-scale expedition against Croatian and Moslem villages, to take a strong stand against it. On July 16, 1942, Radio Free Yugoslavia, which was controlled by the Comintern, attacked Mihailović for his collaboration with the enemy. These events made it imperative for the government to make a serious study of the situation without delay, and to declare its position unequivocally.

According to Avsenek's report, the eyes of all serious-minded people in Yugoslavia were on the *émigré* government in London. It could not have been otherwise, for the people under occupation were enduring an apocalyptic season that encompassed even the most remote villages. They lived in constant terror. They often lost their bearings, for they received contradictory news about what was going on. Only the political leaders in London, they felt, were able to keep themselves well informed; they alone could make a thorough examination of all their problems and make the appropriate decisions. They alone were in a position to anticipate the disasters that were bound to befall the people of Yugoslavia.

The BBC transmitted four broadcasts to Yugoslavia daily. At the risk of their lives, thoughtful men sent desperate appeals to the government in London to establish unity and begin speaking in a single voice. At the height of the inflammatory campaign against the Croats, in October, 1941, Žarko and Boško Todorović, close associates of Mihailović, sent a message to the government in his name, asking that a unified Yugoslav policy be conducted, "because Serbian and Croatian separatism is playing into the hands of our greatest enemies, and is therefore very harmful to us." On February 26, 1942, Voja Djordjević, a former minister, sent a message stating that the government was "not doing its job properly." Shortly after that, he was arrested by the Germans and killed in a concentration camp.

In a circular dated April, 1942, the premier's office acquainted the members of the cabinet with a report from two Serbs on conditions in Yugoslavia. They declared that while decent and honorable Croats condemned the ghastly Ustashi killings, they were powerless to stop them. However, there were areas, Kupres and Belo Polje, for example, where the Croatian peasants had not allowed the Ustashi to touch a single one of their Serbian neighbors.

Encouraging news also came from Croatian sources. A. Juretić, a priest who had been sent by Archbishop Stepinac to Switzerland to keep in contact with us, told us that two Serbian villages in the Metković district had been protected by armed Croatian peasants. A Croatian church dignitary in Rome informed the Croatian ministers on June 10, 1942, that "over 85 per cent of the Croats are not in sympathy with the Ustashi movement, condemn the persecution and murder of Serbs, consider Dr. Maček their leader, and want the return of a Yugoslavia in which everyone would have equality and freedom." It is to the great credit of the

Moslem community that their leaders unequivocally disassociated themselves from the Ustashi massacres, which they condemned in a series of resolutions in the autumn of 1941. On September 2, the same Croatian clergyman urged that the government issue "a declaration from London regarding the federal basis of the Yugoslav state after the war, with guarantees of full national and religious freedom." In a later report, he warned of the horrors that would ensue if the government did not adopt policies designed to stop "the internecine war of mutual extermination between Croats and Serbs."

Some of the Serbian and Croatian ministers were falling under the spell of a chauvinism that made them blind to the horrors in Yugoslavia, and deaf to the agonizing cries of the people. Parents were frequently forced to watch their own children being butchered before being killed themselves. Not everyone was able to flee to the forests. It has been rightly said that the real heroes stayed at home. Many families were divided. I have heard of cases where a Chetnik was killed by his Communist sister, who was then killed by their father; where a Communist was killed by his father because he had killed his Chetnik brother and then fired shots at his own mother; where brother had killed brother because one was a Communist and the other an Ustasha. One Montenegrin woman lost all three of her brothers: one was killed by the Communists, one by the Ustashi, and one by the Chetniks. The Žilić family in Herzegovina lost fifty-four of its fifty-six members.

No one will ever know how much looting, pillage, and murder was done by men with criminal tendencies who had joined various resistance groups, and how many innocent people were herded into camps as a result of the mean, vengeful, and grasping proclivities of the occupation forces and their henchmen. There is no outrage or torture to which the victims of camp or prison were not subjected, while their families starved or froze, waiting for the worst. Thousands were constantly in frantic flight from the battlefields or the paths of punitive expeditions. The occupiers sent thousands more away to forced-labor camps in Germany or other parts of occupied Europe. At the Nuremberg trials, the court heard that Yugoslav prisoners in Norway had been stripped naked in midwinter, buried up to their waists, and then sprayed with water. When the water froze, the men died, statues of flesh in blocks of ice. Some of the tortures were even more fiendish, beyond human imagining.

The flower of the nation, the 350,000 prisoners of war, lived in camps in Germany and Italy, barely managing to survive, receiving terrible news from their families. About forty thousand Croats were interned in Italy. There was no end to the indescribable sufferings of the population in occupied Yugoslavia. The old adage came true: when the leaders err, it is the common people who pay.

CHAPTER 9

While the government was procrastinating over a solution to Yugoslavia's problems, events within the country as well as on the international scene were moving ahead relentlessly. The crucial problems that should have been tackled—the armed conflict between Mihailović and Tito, relations between Mihailović's forces and the Italian army of occupation, and the opening of the anti-Mihailović campaign—demanded maximum confidence and unity in the government. Confidence and unity never came, nor did any real discussion of the vital problems.

Colonel Vladimir Vauhnik, the Yugoslav military attaché in Berlin, described to me how he worked out a plan in 1942 to send King Peter to Yugoslavia so that Serbs and Croats might rally under his leadership. "The Germans were bogged down in Russia . . . and . . . the Italian soldiers could easily have been persuaded to turn a blind eye to what was going on," he wrote. The plan was to send a number of Croatian army brigades into Bosnia to join with the King and raise an insurrection. "I sent the proposal," Vauhnik said, "to the head of the intelligence service in London, and I trust it met with unqualified acceptance. . . . Where then was the hitch?" My own view is that disunity in the Yugoslav government in London was one of the reasons the plan was never seriously considered. The other was fear for the King's safety.

In December of 1941, the Slovenian economist Vrhunec sent a report to Simović, informing him that the Croatian army was preparing a *Putsch* against Pavelić, that General August Marić, chief of the Croatian general staff, had been arrested, and that Colonel Vauhnik had escaped to Ljubljana, where he was still in contact with the pro-*Putsch* officers. The Italian army was anxious to help. The Croatian officers, he said, wanted a liaison with Mihailović, who would be given the task of capturing Sarajevo. Vauhnik told me that Mihailović had refused to accept any close liaison with Croatian army officers. For their part, however, they sent him arms and supplies.

In 1941, Mihailović took a Yugoslav line, whereas nine months later he viewed the Serbs as the liberators of Yugoslavia. Why this reversal? In the first place, in April, 1942, he had received instructions from certain *émigré* Serbs to discredit the Croats in his reports; and, second, his two chief political advisers, Dragiša Vasić and S. Moljević, were Great Serb extremists. A message from Mihailović reached London at the end of June, 1942, at the time of King Peter's visit to Roosevelt, stating that one million Serbs had met their deaths at the hands of Croats.

Reports from Vrhunec and from the military correspondent of the London *Times*, which reached me on December 31, 1941, suggested that Generals Badoglio and Soddu of Italy were pro-British. Consequently, I was on the lookout for possible secret Anglo-Italian contacts. My interest was aroused when I heard that Vrhunec had been arrested and sentenced to twenty years imprisonment, only to be rescued by General Ambrosio, commander in chief of the Italian army of occupation in Yugoslavia. Ambrosio's successor, General Mario Roatta, showed even more zeal for establishing contact with the British through some of Mihailović's commanders. "If the Central Powers win," he told them, "Italy will be able to help establish a strong Serbian state in the center of the Balkans as a counterbalance to German omnipotence. If the Western Powers win, the Serbs will testify at the peace conference to the humane conduct of the Italians during the occupation." Roatta's machinations were aimed at letting the British know that, at the right moment, the Italian army would be ready to go over to the Allies and start fighting hand in hand with the Chetniks against the Germans.

Eden had these machinations in mind when he asked Eduard Beneš, the president of Czechoslovakia, why the Yugoslavs did not give some thought to the danger from Italy. Eden found the disunity in the Yugoslav government a serious obstacle in his efforts to achieve greater co-operation among the various resistance movements in Yugoslavia. On May 19, in a note that strongly stressed the desirability of keeping Yugoslavia together as a state, Eden made a formal plea for unity. He made it absolutely clear that Britain would not support any separatist plans.

The Great Serb members in the cabinet were not at all pleased with Eden's note. Jovanović failed to inform the rest of the cabinet of it, and no effort was made to formulate a political credo. One faction in the government was toying with the idea of getting America and the Soviet Union to help. As a result of Eden's opposition, however, Ninčić failed to secure a treaty of alliance with the Russians when Molotov visited London. The Anglo-Soviet Treaty of Alliance was signed on May 26, 1942. We were overjoyed with the clause which declared that the signatories were "not seeking territorial aggrandizement for themselves" and bound them to "noninterference in the internal affairs of other states." Ninčić induced Eden to propose that the Soviet Union and Great Britain agree not to conclude treaties with exile governments without prior mutual consultations and agreement. The British maintained that this agreement would be applicable everywhere, not just to Greece and Yugoslavia, as the Russians asserted. Moscow was desperately anxious to conclude an agreement on reciprocal spheres of interest in Europe, and was prepared to surrender Greece and Yugoslavia to the British sphere of interest in return for a recognition of Soviet hegemony in eastern and southeastern Europe.

The British were not pleased with the rumor that King Peter might move the seat of his government to the United States. The King visited the United States and Canada from June 22 to July 29. One of the main purposes of his visit was to glorify Draža Milhailović and request American aid for him. Complaints about the British handling of the Cairo affair and about their refusal to allow the Yugoslav government direct communication with Mihailović met with President Roosevelt's understanding. He remarked that all the armed forces of the small Allied nations in the Middle East (Polish, Greek, Free French, and Yugoslav) should be organized under American command. Ninčić informed the cabinet that he and the King had accepted this. Churchill, who was in Washington at the time and had a talk with the King and Ninčić, commented on the Cairo affair with considerable acerbity, pointed out that all the high-ranking officers responsible for the March 27 coup had been dismissed, and warned that "the Yugoslavs are beginning to exhaust all their best friends."

On July 19, the Soviet news agency, Tass, reported that there had been a Yugoslav resolution condemning Mihailović for allowing some of his units to collaborate with the Italians. The following week, the Yugoslav government issued a note demanding withdrawal of these allegations. The Soviet reply came as a sharp blow to Yugoslavia—not only did the Russians not retract their earlier statement; they cited specific examples of such collaboration.

Shortly after this, the Soviet government began to adopt a milder attitude. On September 16, it offered training facilities in the Soviet Union for Yugoslav airmen so that they could then bring in Soviet help to Mihailović—with the stipulation that Mihailović guarantee that he was fighting the occupiers. Jovanović turned down the offer and refused to engage in any talks on further co-operation unless the Russians ended their radio and press campaign against Mihailović and agreed to have the Partisans placed under his command.

My frequent talks with the Russian ambassador, Bogomolov, convinced me that his government was anxious for talks with us without the British as intermediaries, because Moscow believed this was the way to increase their influence in Yugoslavia after the war. Bogomolov once said to me: "It doesn't matter if you are anti-Communist—but you mustn't be against the Soviet Union."

While the Yugoslav cabinet was busy debating, three distinct political trends emerged among the Allies. The British government was working for a federation in eastern Europe and the Balkan Danube basin. Russia was insisting more and more emphatically that she must have "friendly governments" in neighboring countries, but gave no indication as to which specific countries she had in mind. Roosevelt stood by the Atlantic Charter and the agreement to set up a United Nations organization after the war. On two occasions he had opposed Stalin's attempts to conclude a secret agreement with Britain on Russia's postwar frontiers in Europe. Thus he was the idol of the eastern European Allies in London, their bulwark against Soviet domination. The Great Serb faction made a special effort to foster in him hopes for the postwar period. This was in large measure responsible for their intransigence toward the Croats in the face of British pressures.

Constantin Fotić, the Yugoslav minister in Washington, had a great deal of faith in Roosevelt, and Serbs were adamantly opposed to Fotić's transfer, a move that would have helped bring some measure of good will into the government and reduce the tension between Croats and Serbs in America. Fotić relates in his memoirs that he sent Roosevelt a memorandum on the massacre of the Serbs, and that Roosevelt asked him on December 20, 1941, "how, after such horrible crimes, we could expect to live in the same state with the Croats." In October, 1942, Roosevelt told him of Churchill's proposal for a joint declaration on "the reconstruction of Yugoslavia" and again wondered whether "the Serbs would be willing to live in the same state with the Croats." And on an earlier occasion he had said that "it would be for the Serbs to decide what sort of community they intended to retain with the Croats after the war, and that the future for the Croats looked 'cloudy.' " On several occasions Roosevelt spoke of Serbia, not Yugoslavia, in his public utterances. This put Fotić on the good side of the Great Serbs. Besides, Sumner Welles instructed A. J. Biddle, the ambassador to Yugoslavia, to "make it clear in every appropriate way that Fotitch has an exceptional position in Washington where he has gained the respect of all of us. From the standpoint of the best interests of Yugoslavia . . . his replacement at this time would be highly prejudicial."

Roosevelt harbored feelings of great sympathy for King Peter, because of the heavy burden that had fallen on him at such an early age. He was aware that his own pressures on Yugoslavia to enter the war were largely responsible for the indescribable disasters that had occurred, and for the plight of the young King. We all expected that the President's strong sympathy for King Peter and his feeling of responsibility would be major factors in getting things settled to the advantage of the King and the Yugoslav people. The Yugoslavs' faith in Roosevelt was unshakable. Undoubtedly, their certainty that Roosevelt would resolve the situation to their satisfaction led the members of the Yugoslav cabinet to take a rather lackadaisical attitude toward settling their problems themselves. The harsh and uncompromising anti-Communist statements made by Americans in the lower levels of government led their Yugoslav counterparts to believe that Yugoslavia would never be abandoned to the Communists. The chief of the State Department's Yugoslav section, Cavendish W. Cannon, always had a ready answer for those who blamed Mihailović for collaborating with the Italians: "Isn't it all to the good that they are collaborating with an enemy that is the lesser evil against an enemy that is the far greater evil?" Statements like this were passed on to Mihailović, and he accepted them as the firm policy of the people who really mattered in the United States.

In mid-August, the American government proposed that Yugoslav diplomatic representation in the United States be elevated from legation to embassy. Similar changes of status had already taken place in Britain and in the Soviet Union. The decision the Yugoslav government now had to make was whether to appoint Fotić ambassador in Washington. A few moderate Serbs, and some Croats, advised Krnjević not to give his consent. Other moderates, however, felt that Fotić should not be made such a crucial issue, since the urgent question was really whether Jovanović's government could agree on the basic political problems still outstanding. Krnjević accepted this view, and Fotić was appointed.

The cabinet was now engaged in a fierce debate that lasted for three months. Ninčić was attacked for aiding and abetting diplomatic personnel in anti-Yugoslav activities, for failing to report on his talks with Molotov and Roosevelt, and for advocating a Serbo-Italian understanding, the same policy he had favored during the 1923–1926 period. Another charge was that he was protecting Fotić, who was behind the anti-government and anti-Yugoslavia campaign carried out by *Srbobran*, the Serbian newspaper of Pittsburgh.

Miloš Trifunović, a Ninčić supporter, made a number of accusations against the Croats, raking up all the Serbo-Croatian quarrels since before World War I. He declared himself against the 1939 agreement that gave Croatia autonomy. With the consent of the moderates and the members of Grol's party, I managed to persuade Krnjević to show a tolerant and conciliatory spirit.

Jovanović, however, refused to side with the moderates until all the Serbian cabinet ministers agreed on a policy. As this was impossible, we agreed to ask A. J. Biddle to help.

On October 19, Biddle advised Ninčić that the King should first come out with a royal proclamation of national unity, followed by a joint declaration with the Premier. Ninčić agreed. Biddle's efforts were aided by George W. Rendel, the British ambassador, who informed Jovanović on November 7 that Britain was "wholeheartedly in favor of Yugoslavia." I asked Biddle to make a similar approach to the Premier, because Jovanović had told Krnjević a few days earlier that "he had to take Serbian feelings into account and could not declare himself in favor of Yugoslavia." On December 1, the King announced over the BBC that "the Yugoslav state will be restored in its entirety, because it is as imperative to the vital and enduring interests of all of us as it is for the peaceful future of Europe." The efforts of the American and British ambassadors were only partially successful, however, for the government never made its declaration. The King expressed his dissatisfaction to Biddle, saying that he only wished he could "get rid of a number of old fossils" in his government.

In a telegram dated December 30, Secretary of State Cordell Hull congratulated Biddle on his zeal in promoting unity in the Yugoslav government. His message concluded: "Because of America's deep interest in the future of Yugoslavia, it is hoped that the few leaders available will rise to the responsibilities of these times." His words threw the tragedy of the Yugoslav situation into sharp focus; the implication was that if the leaders did not meet their responsibilities, the Yugoslav people would pay very dearly for their failure to do so. I had an ominous feeling at the end of 1942 that "the few leaders available" would bring catastrophe to millions in Yugoslavia.

The government was incapable of concentrating on the real issues. No sooner had the Cairo affair been settled than a breakdown occurred in relations with the ban (governor) of Croatia; Fotić was kept on in Washington, and the government still had not laid down its policy line. The Soviet press stepped up its attacks on Mihailović. Reports reached us that Mihailović's forces in eastern Bosnia, Herzegovina, western Bosnia, and Dalmatia were massacring Catholics and Moslems under the pretext of waging "war against the Communists." A rumor was circulating that King Peter had fallen in love with Princess Alexandra of Greece, and wanted to marry her, but the leading Serbs were against the match. Finally, I was informed by my British friends that dissatisfaction with Mihailović was growing because of his war against the Communists and accommodation with the Italians.

On September 23, 1942, I saw Douglas Howard, head of the Foreign Office's Southern Department, who said that Yugoslavia was giving him more trouble than all the other countries put together. He predicted that we would have a lot of trouble with Mihailović. "Before the war ends he will be absolute master," Douglas told me. "He's self-confident and thinks for himself." At first I didn't understand what he was getting at; but I soon realized he meant that Mihailović was uncompromising in fighting the Partisans. He said that the Mihailović-Partisan conflict could have serious consequences for Anglo-Soviet relations. The British were helping Mihailović, and he was fighting the Partisans, who were receiving aid from the Russians. This was civil war, not resistance against the Germans and Italians. In practical terms, there was now an Anglo-Soviet war in Yugoslavia, and this had to stop. Mihailović was not so much anti-Croat, Howard said, as anti-Communist. I realized immediately the serious import of this conversation, and I reported it back to our ministers.

On November 23, I saw Major Peter Boughey, who was liaison officer between the Yugoslav government and the Special Operations Executive (SOE). I learned from him that there had been great political upheavals over Mihailović, in which Gavrilović's Agrarians and some friends of Major Knežević were involved. In their anxiety not to have the London people drawn into these quarrels, the British had refused them direct radio contact with Mihailović. Meanwhile, the British government had not sent any political directives either. Boughey said, however, that "Mihailović must carry out Allied policy if he's to expect help from the Allies. He's a dictator, and that's why he won't recognize the Partisans. If he doesn't mend his ways, we shall find someone else and make him leader, as we did Mihailović. . . . We ascribe importance to all resistance, however resentful your military cabinet may feel about this."

Because the British considered Mihailović's organization the only one capable of becoming the nucleus of a regular army, they asked him to carry out various tasks. General Harold Alexander sent Mihailović a personal telegram before the 1942 offensive against Rommel, requesting him to carry out large-scale attacks on enemy lines of communication in order to impede the transport of German war materials to Salonika, from where they were being sent by sea to Libya. In response, Mihailović ordered a civil-disobedience campaign in Serbia. This brought brutal reprisals from the Germans and Bulgarians. Several thousand troops surrounded the villages of Kriva Reka and Mačkovac; seventy houses were set on fire, and more than a hundred people were herded into a church, which was then set on fire. In the end, nearly seven hundred people lost their lives. In addition, thousands were arrested: some were taken hostage and shot; others perished in camps. Communists today claim that they were carrying out certain military actions in that area at the time. It is probable that this was an instance of the kind of Communist tactics mentioned by Churchill in his memoirs: "The partisans deliberately violated any agreements made with the enemy by the Cetniks. . . . The Germans then shot Cetnik hostages and in revenge Cetniks gave the Germans information about the partisans. . . . It was a tragedy within a tragedy."

These events made it imperative for the government to settle its differences. But Ninčić did everything he could to prevent the cabinet debate from concentrating on essential decisions. He sabotaged government declarations, because he knew that implementation of the principles embodied in such declarations would injure him and Fotić. In mid-November, declaring that there was an "anti-Serb majority" in the government, he and Trifunović maneuvered Grol's Democrats into a corner, so that a "Serbian front" could be created against the Croatian ministers and the two Serbian ministers from outside Serbia. The latter were to be dismissed from the cabinet if they refused to join the front. Krnjević insisted that Ninčić submit to the cabinet a report on his talks with Allied leaders, which he refused to do. So the debate became a series of personal clashes. This would have dragged on for months had Ninčić not arrived at a position that proved untenable.

Ninčić's relations with Eden were not good. Eden considered Ninčić responsible for his not being allowed to come to Belgrade after the March 27 coup. (In this he was wrong; it had been a government decision.) Relations between the two were further impaired when Ninčić, without prior consultation with Eden, offered Molotov an alliance and tried to arrange for the King to visit Stalin. Then, in November, 1942, Ninčić did himself great harm by writing a personal letter to Eden in connection with Mihailović's report on the massacres in Kriva Reka and Mačkovac. The text of the report was made known to us by the premier's office in a top-secret memorandum dated November 5.

The memorandum stated that mopping-up operations had been carried out and horrible atrocities perpetrated in the two villages by "Croats in German uniforms" as well as by Germans and Bulgarians. I immediately asked my English friends to check this. Ten days later, they informed me that no Croatian soldiers had taken part in operations in Serbia. Krnjević promised to raise the matter of Mihailović's report at the next cabinet meeting. When the people in German-occupied Yugoslavia heard about the report in a BBC broadcast, they sent us strong protests: "It is gratuitous and unwise to feed the flames from London, to undo the work of all of us here who are convinced that our sworn enemies are trying to make us exterminate each other."

Meanwhile, each time there was an attempt to find a basis for agreement and to make some concessions to the Croatian ministers, insidious attacks on the Croats, instigated by Ninčić's associates, would appear in the British and American press. Mihailović's report was part of that campaign. Ninčić and the Great Serb faction again attempted to get the Croatian ministers and the two Serbian ministers from Croatia removed from the government. Biddle acknowledged that two influential Yugoslavs had asked him whether the Americans would recognize the *émigré* government as a "Yugoslav government" if it had no Croatian Peasant party members. On December 8, I again met with Major Boughey. This time he spoke even more sternly about British objections to Mihailović, who was acting without receiving any political directives from the Yugoslav government. The British did not have the authority to give Mihailović such directives, since he was minister of the Yugoslav armed forces. Their liaison officer with the Chetniks, Captain D. T. Hudson, was unable to exert any influence on him, and Mihailović was now working with the Italians for the establishment of a Great

Serbia. Boughey also came down severely on Jovanović's military cabinet. His organization, he said, now had no choice but to work with the Croats directly.

This conversation merely confirmed my conclusion that the situation in Yugoslavia was far more serious and intricate than I had once thought. The members of the cabinet were like children playing in the garden while their house was going up in flames. I had firmly made up my mind to tell Krnjević that he must unflinchingly set before the cabinet all the problems it was so carefully evading, that he must declare his intention to resign, and inform the Allies of his reasons for taking this extreme step, unless agreement could be reached on all the following major questions: a joint political program; a single propaganda line to occupied Yugoslavia; a reconciliation between Mihailović and Tito; the consolidation of a united front of anti-Axis forces; an end to mutual recriminations between Serbs and Croats; the liquidation of the hotbeds of intrigue in the Middle East and the dismissal of people engaged in such intrigue; and a determined effort to co-ordinate our policy with that of the Allies.

On December 12, I saw Churchill's parliamentary secretary, George Harvie-Watt, who told me that on December 9 King Peter and his mother, Queen Marie, had seen Churchill. He told them that in order to fulfill its responsibilities, the government would have to make certain changes. The Allies were obviously ready to help the government out of the morass and away from the catastrophes threatening Yugoslavia. I was unaware at that time that the King had given Churchill a strange memorandum against his own government and that he had informed Eden on December 11 that he wanted to get rid of Ninčić.

After my lunch with Harvie-Watt, I saw Krnjević, who had just received a report on joint Chetnik and Italian attacks on Croats in Dalmatia and the Croatian littoral. I again urged him to make a categorical demand for a government inquiry into Mihailović's report of November 5, and into Ninčić's letter to Eden. Krnjević had promised earlier to do this, but since I knew his propensity for shifting responsibilities onto the shoulders of others, I insisted it was his duty to act at once because he was deputizing for Maček. "Why," I asked, "are these discussions dragging on endlessly? Why doesn't someone stand up and say bluntly what the debate is all about?" But, for all that, he demurred. He simply wanted to go on with his protests and pinpricks, creating incidents that would enrage the Serbs. I told him that unless he changed his strategy and put a stop to the political infighting, he would bear a heavy responsibility before his own nation, and before history, for the tragedies that would continue to befall the Croatian people. This was our last political talk until mid-February, 1945.

I waited three days for Krnjević to make a decisive move in the cabinet. He failed to act. I then saw Jovanović myself and lodged my complaint about the outrageous smear made by Ninčić against the Croatian people. I also told him I was no longer willing to stay on as assistant foreign minister under Ninčić and that Eden would not enter into any important discussions with Ninčić because high officials in Britain believed that Ninčić was aiding and abetting Mihailović in his pro-Italian policies. I had no wish, I told the Premier, to make any trouble for him, because I had great respect for him; nevertheless, I would have to make public the reasons for my resignation. The highest interests of the nation and the state were at stake, and that was why I could no longer keep silent. He asked if I could be patient for a few days, because the Ninčić issue was going to be resolved along with other matters. I knew that a great battle was in progress over the reshaping of the cabinet. I went away satisfied with his promise.

Attempts to solve the government crisis took an unsatisfactory turn for the Croats and the moderate Serbs, because Krnjević refused to engage in any genuine debate regarding the future of Yugoslavia. He made a show of indignation before Jovanović on December 21, when he and Miho Krek, the other vice-premier, saw him. Jovanović told them that the cabinet would have to be reshaped because the King and Queen Mother had been advised by Churchill of the need to settle the differences in the cabinet and Eden had asked for Ninčić's removal. Jovanović told Krnjević and Krek that the three of them, together with Mihailović, were to remain in the new cabinet, and that he would appoint three Serbs from the Serbian party. Krnjević protested against the dismissal of Srdjan Budisavljević and J. Banjanin. Grol supported Krnjević in his protest against the removal of these men. The Great Serb elements began to plan the removal of Juraj

Šutej. They suggested that this was being demanded in official quarters in Britain because he had "voted for the Tripartite Pact." Šutej was terrified of being thrown out of the cabinet, and urged Krnjević not to raise any questions. Krnjević, unfortunately, followed his advice and so lost the chance of playing a historic role by bringing about an effective settlement. In order to remain in the government, he even accepted Jovanović's condition that he support Mihailović fully.

By the end of 1942, it had become quite clear that both Mihailović and Tito were out to impose their respective dictatorships on Yugoslavia after the war. Mihailović wanted a narrow Great Serb regime headed by the King; Tito wanted a Communist system dependent on the Soviet Union. In the summer of 1942, it was said that there was a government in Kolašin, centered around Mihailović, called the Central National Committee (CNC). In early December, 1942, the CNC Youth Congress adopted a draft constitution for postwar Yugoslavia. Yugoslavia was to be a Chetnik state, in which "the Chetnik organization . . . in agreement with the Crown, will . . . carry sole responsibility for governmental authority in the country." There were other outrageous provisions, such as the abolition of "politics" and the "legal profession." On November 12, 1942, Tito informed the Comintern that "preparations are going ahead for the establishment of a body that will have the character of a government." The Comintern had replied that "this Committee should not be in opposition to the exile government, nor raise the question of the monarchy or give prominence to a call for a republic." Then, in Bihać, on November 27, an assembly of fifty-four delegates elected the Anti-Fascist Council for the National Liberation of Yugoslavia (AVNOJ). Immediately after that, in order to show that the Communists wanted a federal system rather than the centralistic one being urged by Mihailović, a resolution was adopted establishing identical bodies in all the historical provinces of Yugoslavia.

My later talks with British acquaintances increasingly confirmed my conviction that the British government wanted to see radical changes in Yugoslavia and within the Yugoslav cabinet. Hugh Dalton, the British minister in charge of SOE, told me that the British government was in favor of Yugoslavia, and that Churchill would come out very strongly against those destroying it. Boughey felt that we ought to have a strong premier, and said that the British would "have to use the stick" if our government did not settle the crisis soon. Ambassador Rendel believed we should have a smaller, more efficient cabinet, which would come out with a clear declaration on the future order in Yugoslavia. Boughey was outspoken to the point of brutality when on December 29 he said to Knežević, chief of the military cabinet: "General Mihailović is openly collaborating with the Italians, and his detachments are being transported . . . to western Bosnia in Italian trucks to fight the Partisans side by side with Italian troops." On December 31, he told me everything he had said to Knežević, including this: "We don't consider Draža Mihailović a god . . . and neither should you. . . . He should be told from London: 'We want a free Yugoslavia. The people will decide on the system . . . if that is not what you want, you should resign.' We are asking the Foreign Office to demand a declaration to this effect from the Yugoslav government."

Grol tirelessly urged the government to begin working on the settlement of the most pressing problems. Većeslav Vilder, Budisavljević, Banjanin, Krek, and I gave our wholehearted support to these efforts. Grol thought the initiative ought to come from Krnjević, who first had to be clear in his own mind whether he favored the combined Serbo-Croatian-Slovenian state, and whether he was prepared publicly to condemn Ustashi policy, making clear that it was incompatible with the democratic and humane principles of the Croatian Peasant movement. Grol promised that once Krnjević had committed himself unequivocally on this, he and his friends would be prepared to help Krnjević in any way they could—either by remaining in the government or by resigning. But Krnjević was unwilling to make such a commitment. E. M. Rose, in his minute of January 5, 1943, called this "an extraordinary feature" of the government crisis that began on December 28, 1942, and ended on January 2, 1943, negatively from every point of view. Rose added: "Mihailović is after all only one of several leaders and the sensible thing for the Government to have done would have been to declare their policy of supporting all resistance, Mihailović's as well as the others.

Instead with inglorious haste they rushed to pin their colours to Mihailović's alone, thereby sacrificing at one stroke their independence and their power. . . ." Krnjević should have raised the question of organization of Croat resistance, and its link with Mihailović's and Tito's in a united front.

The new cabinet did not include Ninčić. After the war, Jovanović told me that Eden had recommended his dismissal to the King. Eden accused Ninčić of attempting to take the King on a visit to Moscow without prior consultation with the British. Five Yugoslav-minded ministers connected with our information center in New York were also excluded from the new cabinet, a victory for Fotić and his Great Serb policy.

While Grol's refusal to take any initiative on the delicate Mihailović question was understandable, the reluctance of the Croatian ministers to raise the question in a forthright and statesmanlike fashion was not. In spite of Krnjević's breach of relations with me, I informed him that Boughey was in favor of his bringing up at cabinet meetings everything he had told me and Knežević. Moreover, Boughey had said that "many people in Britain and the United States are demanding that Mihailović be treated as a Quisling and relations with him broken off." I was not surprised when the BBC refused to broadcast a New Year's message for 1943 from the Premier to Mihailović.

The attitude of the Croatian ministers was entirely at variance with the messages from politicians in Croatia, who were demanding that their voice in the government be raised against Mihailović's collaboration with the Italians. These demands put the Croatian ministers in a very awkward position. It was difficult for them to raise the matter of Chetnik atrocities at this time, because a year earlier they had failed to express their abhorrence of the Ustashi massacres of innocent Serbs. It was not difficult for me to do so, however, because I, as a man, as a Christian, and as a Croat, had condemned these atrocities; and so, on January 4, 1943, I was in a position to take up the cudgels also against the brutalities of the Chetniks and Communists. Had I not been a close observer of events in the Yugoslav government in London, I could never have understood how the political elite could have gone so far astray or why they had failed to live up to Cordell Hull's hope that they would "rise to the responsibilities" of the harsh days of war. In April, 1943, Wickham Steed quoted the late president of Czechoslovakia, Thomas Masaryk, as having said of the Yugoslavs during World War I: "These Yugoslavs only make guesses about the future; they never sit down to work out the practical problems."

CHAPTER 10

The situation in occupied Yugoslavia was indescribably tragic and complex. It called for men of exceptional moral fiber, intellectual caliber, and breadth of vision—men with experience in international affairs, capable of grasping the intricacy of the situation and maneuvering within it. If even one of the leading political figures in exile had possessed these qualities, the fate of Yugoslavia at the end of the war would have been different. On more than one occasion, Churchill said to King Peter: "Your people are suffering tremendously, and you need a strong man here." In the absence of a strong man or a group of exceptionally talented people, a team of lesser men who possessed sufficient integrity and determination could have saved Yugoslavia. But Yugoslavia was denied even that. The massacre of the Serbs by the Ustashi made the *émigré* Serbs frantic and resulted in the emergence of a narrow chauvinism that left no room for any human feelings and led both Serbs and Croats into strange paths and unpredictable schemes.

The King was young and inexperienced. His first premier had failed because he was politically incompetent and power-hungry. His subsequent advisers were Slobodan Jovanović, Milan Grol, Momčilo Ninčić, Milan Gavrilović, and Miloš Trifunović, Serbs; Juraj Krnjević and Juraj Šutej, Croats; and Miho Krek, a Slovene. The first clashes in the government arose from the unwarranted accusation that the Croats had favored the Tripartite Pact and betrayed Yugoslavia. The two sides would eventually have been reconciled had it not been for the Ustashi massacres and the irrational reaction of the *émigré* Serbs. When Krnjević saw that the Serbs wanted to exploit the situation to indict the entire Croatian nation, his indignation was enormous. He could not believe that there had actually been massacres on such a scale. He sincerely thought the reports were fabrications designed to discredit the Croatian people in the eyes of the Allies, so that after the war the Serbs could work their will on the Croats with Allied approval. This was why, he explained later, he found it so difficult to speak out against the atrocities and why, when he finally did raise his voice, his condemnation was not wholehearted. He failed to denounce the forced conversions to Catholicism, and he made only sporadic references to the restoration of a united Serbo-Croatian state. As a result, the majority of *émigré* Serbs were convinced that Krnjević's aspirations were merely a disguised version of Pavelić's, and this created a gulf of suspicion that proved unbridgeable for the duration of the war. All subsequent disputes in the cabinet, and the final collapse of the government, had their origins in this mistrust. When the Premier asked me, at the beginning of 1942, to take charge of the government's information directorate, I declined, because the government had no unanimous policy. In London alone, there were seven separate centers supplying separate and mutually contradictory information to the Allies and the people in occupied Yugoslavia.

This confusion and strife was well described by C. L. Sulzberger in his survey of Yugoslavia, published in the New York *Times* early in 1943. On January 17, I advised Sulzberger to start his inquiry with the Serbs. He told me that he had already talked to them. Some had only the vilest things to say; they reported seeing "Croatian girls wearing Serbian tongues on strings around their necks" and even "wagonloads of Serbian eyeballs." I had heard these stories from the same people seven months before, as well as from Stojan Pribićević, *Time* and *Life* correspondent in London. At first it was said that the Italians had been spreading the stories, but Sulzberger was told they came from Mihailović, and that was what gave them weight. We were able to reject the former version as enemy fabrication; whereas the latter we found nauseating. When Sulzberger's survey was published, some of my conversations with him were included as the Croatian point of view. I described the appalling situation in Yugoslavia and the dangers of discord in the government, in the hope of awakening sympathy in official United States circles.

At the same time that Sulzberger's survey appeared, Tito issued a new appeal over Radio Free Yugoslavia for an Anglo-American-Soviet delegation to go to occupied Yugoslavia. Sulzberger, Pribićević, and I agreed this was the only way to bring some sort of order into the tragic chaos.

After he had formed his second government, Jovanović summoned me several times. He had a number of sensible ideas, but he was incapable of seeing them through. At our first meeting, on January 6, 1943, he said: "I have asked to see you because . . . you are the most reasonable of all the Croats here. . . . The massacres at home have been carried out by enemy mercenaries, not by the people. . . . Communism now has a hold on the mixed Serbo-Croatian areas. . . . We ought to try to get Mihailović and Maček . . . to start co-operating with each other." He asked me to discuss with my influential British friends ways of repairing the government's reputation. On January 25, I sent him the following memorandum: ". . . The faith of the Foreign Office and of public opinion here in the possibility of Yugoslavia's restoration has been shaken. In the view of the people I talked to, the first prerequisite is unity in the royal government. The second, a clarification of our relations with the Soviet Union. . . . The third, co-ordination of Serbian and Croatian propaganda. Mutual recriminations must be stopped at all costs. . . . It is known to British officials that *Srbobran* is being subsidized by the Yugoslav ambassador in Washington, and [is being] used . . . to stir up anti-Croatian feeling."

I saw the Premier again on February 3. Inevitably, our conversation turned to the dissension in the cabinet, and I was quick to point out that petty, hit-and-miss methods were no longer any good. "No," he agreed, "we talk of new arrangements, but our ideas keep turning in the same groove." We then spoke of relations with Russia. Jovanović asked me to offer the following plan to Bogomolov: first, a truce between the Chetniks and the Partisans; second, a joint plan; and finally, only after the first two had been accomplished, a unified command. When I saw Bogomolov on February 6, he replied at once that he could not submit this plan to his government as long as "your government maintains the attitude that it is dealing with 'bandits.'" I reported this back to the Premier, who said he would search his files to see if the word "bandits" had ever been used. On March

8, Bogomolov said to me, "We do not trust Mihailović at all. This does not mean that we shall break off diplomatic relations . . . but Yugoslavia cannot expect any help from us as long as this situation continues."

I did not see the Premier again until March 13. We of course discussed the recurrent theme of the discord in his cabinet. Once again he asked me to do everything possible to get the ministers to settle their differences. I told him I still believed this could be done, but only if they would realize that the real problems were not the ones they were squabbling over. I regretted having to speak in such a forthright manner to a venerable old man, but I was driven by a sharp awareness that the future of my country lay in the hands of five men: it was they who would decide whether the war would bring deliverance or a new catastrophe. It was my countrymen's fate to drink the bitter cup of suffering to the last drop, and my fate to watch the events unfold, as in a Greek tragedy. I came to know, all too well, the truth of Churchill's assertion that it is an extraordinarily difficult and thankless task for someone in a subordinate position "to initiate a dominant plan or policy."

The cabinet's Great Serb wing nurtured a dream that Mihailović and the Americans would finally bring the situation under control and give them what they wanted. They refused even to entertain the idea of opening up talks with the Partisans. The Croatian ministers firmly believed that the British and Americans would establish a federation in the Danube basin and southeastern Europe, allowing the Croats to decide at their leisure whether to join it or to break away from the Balkans by joining a league of Danube basin Catholic states under British protection. Lest they jeopardize their extravagant postwar aspirations, neither the Croatian nor the Serbian chauvinists were prepared to declare themselves in favor of Yugoslavia and a Serbo-Croatian reconciliation.

The greatest service the Yugoslav government could have rendered to its people would have been to listen to those who were crying out for unity and clear directives. The worst offenses were committed by the Yugoslavs in exile: they sent death-bringing messages to the country, and, in their error, led others, good people, astray. If the Yugoslav government had welcomed military co-operation between the Serbs and Croats, it would have done a great deal for the Allied cause. Moreover, this would have involved the Croats in the war effort. I maintained that in order for a united Serbo-Croatian resistance movement to be raised, the Croatian ministers had to declare that they would not remain in the government unless they were given the opportunity to organize resistance in Croatia against the Ustashi and their German and Italian masters. If the Great Serb wing refused to let the dispute be settled in the best interests of the Allied war effort, then the Allies would be justified in acting as arbiters. The Mihailović-Tito conflict also had to be settled, as well as the question of the Soviets' negative attitude toward Mihailović. Confronting these problems would compel the Allies to come to grips with the whole deplorable tangle of the Yugoslav crisis. I devoted all my time to the problem, enlisting the support of the British and American ambassadors and my influential British and American friends. A good climate was created everywhere, but the Croatian ministers refused all my appeals to raise the major questions in cabinet.

Krnjević was so anxious for Allied intervention that he often engineered clashes in the cabinet in the hope that they would intervene and impose their own solution. He was hoping, obviously, for a solution favorable to the Croats, leading perhaps to a dissolution of the Serbo-Croatian partnership, if not during the war then certainly after it. Meanwhile, he considered it his duty to keep the Serbo-Croatian dispute going. Whenever he felt he was in danger of being ousted, he declared himself in favor of the King and Yugoslavia. His Croatian colleague, Šutej, did the same whenever he was in similar danger. In private, Šutej did not hesitate to express himself in the most offensive terms: "I am pro-Yugoslavia at the moment because the Serbs are anti-Yugoslavia. . . . I will not work for the restoration of Yugoslavia. I am here to sabotage it." Had there not been a corresponding Great Serb wing in the cabinet, also working against Yugoslavia, the Serbs would easily have been able to expel the Croatian ministers. Instead, the Great Serb wing accepted the situation as a necessary evil and adapted itself to it. In practice, the government was run by Jovanović and the military cabinet; the Croatian ministers were not kept informed about anything. Since the Croatian ministers would hold on at all costs, it was easy to keep them in this humiliating position.

I was anxious for Allied intervention so that the differences might be settled and the government set on the right path for action against the enemy. This would help Yugoslavia approach the war's end with as few upheavals as possible. Krnjević wanted intervention so that the Allies might partition us; he therefore carried on with his obstructionist policies. He refused to see that with a war on their hands, the Allies could not resolve such problems. At his first meeting, in August, 1941, Eden had told him that the British government had no intention of interfering in the internal affairs of other Allied governments. On June 24, 1942, I told Cordell Hull that the fear of Communism kept many people in occupied Europe from resisting Hitler and that resistance could be strengthened if the Allies would commit themselves beyond the Atlantic Charter and provide guarantees for democratic systems in those countries. I pointed out that Hitler and Mussolini were exploiting the fear of Communism, particularly in occupied Yugoslavia, where they had sown seeds of discord between Serb and Croat and between Mihailović and Tito. He replied that the Allies had to concentrate all their energies on winning the war, and that any diversion to deal with purely political problems would surely lead to inter-Allied conflicts. And in March, 1943, when I told Harold Nicolson that a large proportion of our government's difficulties arose from its belief that the British would settle all our difficulties, he exclaimed: "Good God! Can't they see we are simply surrounded with difficulties of our own?"

Grol and I suffered most as a result of the failure to achieve unity in the cabinet. He actually wept at a meeting with Krnjević and Šutej in February, 1942. A year later, he told Vilder and me, "My head is splitting. I spent a whole hour with the Premier. I told him I could not be in the same cabinet with Croats if it is true that they 'had a wagonload of Serbian eyeballs.'" After Vilder assured him that this was a crude fabrication, Grol urged Jovanović to issue a correction to this news item, and accused him of being irresponsible. "Slobodan must have views of his own. He can't just shut his eyes and say, 'I'll put my signature to whatever your three parties decide.'"

Jovanović and Krnjević had one trait in common: they made no effort to anticipate events. Krnjević once said to me, "Why worry about disasters that might happen? I never do." And

149

Jovanović once told me he never allowed problems to bother him, and he never looked even as far as three days ahead. Jovanović was an extremely intelligent man who was well aware of the disunity in his cabinet, but he had neither the desire nor the determination to put an end to that disunity. He said to me one day, jestingly, "What do you expect? Back home there's a guerrilla war going on—so there's one in my cabinet."

Like everyone who lives solely for an idea, Krnjević was exceedingly obstinate and intolerant. He brooked no criticism and found it extraordinarily difficult to make positive decisions. He once admitted that it took him as long as six months to make a decision on a political problem. His vacillation about condemning the Ustashi atrocities was to have fateful consequences. All of us Croats, except Šutej, did everything we could to get him to see the dangers of his silence. He had to speak out in a loud voice against the Ustashi atrocities, regardless of whether Serbs were going to condemn Chetnik atrocities, because vital Croatian interests were at stake. When he finally spoke, he grudged every word. There was a tremendous difference between this half-hearted protest and the fulminating condemnation in the leaflets distributed on All Souls' Day, 1942, by the Croatian Peasant party in Zagreb. The leaflets, which also condemned the vindictive Chetnik expeditions into peaceful Croatian villages, led by the common enemy of both Croats and Serbs, contained this message for the Serbs: "The enemy does not lead you against the Ustashi, the father of all evil. He drives you into peaceful Croatian villages . . . to make you soil your hands with the blood of your kin. And this gives the Ustashi another pretext for more massacres. . . . We want our shared misfortunes to bring us together. The burnt-down family homes, the smoking shells of our villages, our dead . . . must . . . bring us together as partners determined to live under the same roof. . . . This is what the enemy fears most." Had Krnjević's activities been inspired with the spirit of this message, the government crisis might have been resolved.

It was clear to me that we would eventually have to open talks with Tito, and that these talks should be conducted by the main political parties of Yugoslavia, not by some government of civil servants. The party leaders were most entitled to defend democratic principles against dictatorial ambitions from the right or left, and were best equipped to ward them off. Wickham Steed said to me, in late March, 1943, "What good will a government of civil servants do Yugoslavia? She needs a government that can speak with authority." Had the government been united, it could have spoken with authority to Mihailović. It was my belief that contact with Tito would bring the ministers to their senses and compel them to face reality. Once they saw what the Communists were after, and what their methods of warfare were, they would draw closer together.

In my view, it was essential that contact with the Partisans be established while the Communists were still weak and Russia was not within striking distance of Yugoslavia. I considered this vital for our Allies. In January, 1943, I advised the Premier to invite three delegates each from both sides to London, so that we could have both points of view and bring about a reconciliation by creating a new resistance organization. In Cairo, in April, 1944, Djilas told me that Tito had been willing to send delegates to London and, subject to certain political conditions, would even have recognized King Peter. He repeated this to me at Princeton in October, 1968, and gave me explicit permission to quote him in this book.

As a Croat, I felt that such a course of events would accord best with the interests of the Croatian nation. It would make it possible for a majority of Croats to join the new combined resistance and make a significant contribution to the Allied war effort. The resistance forces would also provide a safeguard for Croatian national rights. Croatian officers would join because this would give them a satisfactory way out of their terrible dilemma: whether to remain with Pavelić, thus incurring the stigma of treason, or to eradicate that stigma by fighting the Ustashi regime, the Germans, and the Italians. Some of them had been assisting Mihailović in various ways, even though he had rejected any combined plan of operations. This could not happen if there were a joint resistance, because the government in London would be unable to reject offers from Croats to fight in a common resistance. In May, 1943, General I. Prpić, chief of staff of the Croatian army, sent a message, through Father D. Mandić in Rome, saying that he could easily dispatch a large force to Dalmatia to cover an Allied landing there. The Yugoslav chargé d'affaires in Madrid refused to pass the message on to London, because, he said, "it is not my job to save the Croatian army." This was at a time when the Western Allies were trying to gain a bridgehead on the Dalmatian coast to hasten Italy's surrender, and is but one example of the damage done the Allied war effort by the Yugoslav government's failure to put its house in order.

Another thing that was clear to me, and I mentioned it to Krnjević, was that one of the extremist groups, either Mihailović's or Tito's, was going to come out on top in Yugoslavia unless the London government, with the support of the Allies, promoted some moderate course of action. Krnjević did not agree, and he sent messages to people in Croatia telling them that when the war ended, the Croatian army must safeguard Croatia's frontiers on the Drina—this at a time when Tito's forces were already operating in the vicinity of Zagreb. He also sent word that the Croatian army should not enter into any agreement with either Mihailović or Tito. Obviously, he opposed my plan for Mihailović and Tito to send delegates to London. For completely idiotic reasons, he maintained that the worse relations were in the government, and between Mihailović and Tito, the better it was for the Croatian national cause; and he was totally obsessed with the idea that the Allies would, for that very reason, intervene on Croatia's behalf. He even told Rendel that he was "concerned about Croatia's rights, not about the total situation." The Ambassador was astonished that a vice-premier of Yugoslavia could fail to see that rights go hand in hand with obligations.

Much of the population in Yugoslavia was frightened of the possibility of a Communist regime; and the Croats were afraid of a possible Great Serb military dictatorship under Mihailović. Many democratically minded Serbs, among them Živko Topalović, the Yugoslav Socialist leader, were also afraid of this. When Topalović joined Mihailović in the mountains of Serbia, early in 1944, Mihailović himself talked about an agreement with Tito: "Genuine serious, peaceable negotiations are only possible with Allied mediation abroad." Unfortunately, in the period between the proposal of this plan and Mihailović's decision to accept it, the Yugoslav government fell and Churchill decided to make a complete break with Mihailović.

The lessons of history have taught me that the facts of life turn men from the path of fatal error to the path of reason. My interpretation of Tito's appeal to the Allies was that the harsh realities he had experienced since the beginning of the uprising had prepared him for compromise with other political forces in Yugoslavia. At that time, no one knew about his disillusionment with Stalin over the aid he had been awaiting since the summer of 1941. He went on clamoring for that aid all through 1942, and his clamoring grew louder at the beginning of 1943. Djilas said to me in Cairo: "Don't imagine that we have learned nothing from this struggle. If we had not had the support of our people, we would have gone under long ago." And in Princeton he told me: "The bitter experiences of our struggle compelled us to change from being internationalist to becoming increasingly nationalist." I presumed that there must have been tremendous changes in Tito's attitude, and so I favored making contact with him, in the hope that we might set up a united resistance that could claim the protection of the Hague Convention.

I felt that both Tito and his opponents had right on their side. I thought it was the Yugoslav government's duty to seek a compromise on this basis. The same idea has been expressed admirably by Walter Lippmann: "The great and difficult controversies are precisely those in which there is something . . . to be said on both sides. . . . And controversies of that magnitude are never resolved and concluded unless men arise who will look for solutions not in the errors and evils of one side or the other but in whatever truth and virtue can be discerned on both sides." I hoped that a sufficient number of such men would be found in the ranks of the Yugoslav government. I was grievously mistaken; and my country had to pay a terrible price.

Tito was right in favoring resistance to the enemy, but he was not right in inciting enemy reprisals against innocent people as a way of spreading the Communist revolution. Mihailović was right in wanting to avoid excessive casualties, but he should not have permitted the accommodation with the Italians to pass into open collaboration, into a war against his own countrymen. The Croatian and Slovenian elements were right in demanding command of their own units within the framework of a combined resistance front. The Western Allies were right in drawing Stalin's attention to the damage to the joint war effort resulting from an unbridled Communist revolution in Yugoslavia. Churchill expressed this forcibly, with regard to the Greek Communists, in a message to Roosevelt on June 23, 1944: "It would be quite easy for me, on the general principle of slithering to the left, which is so popular in foreign policy, to let things rip when the King of Greece would probably be forced to abdicate and EAM [the National Liberation Front] would work a reign of terror in Greece, forcing the villagers and many other classes to form security battalions under German auspices to prevent utter anarchy. The only way I can prevent this is by persuading the Russians to quit boosting EAM and ramming it forward with all their force."

This assessment was far more applicable to Yugoslavia in 1942 than to Greece. The Yugoslav government in London should have presented these same arguments to Churchill early in 1943, long before the question of establishing a combined resistance had to be tackled. On January 11, Jovanović lodged a complaint with Eden regarding the BBC's bias in favor of the Partisans. Eden responded by warning him that the Chetniks had to stop fighting the Partisans, and that the Allied forces would be co-operating with the Partisans. He advised Jovanović to establish close ties with the Soviet Union. Jovanović did not reveal to his government the substance of his talks with Eden. However, in a speech he gave four days after their meeting, he acknowledged publicly for the first time the existence of Tito's resistance forces. Once he had done that, it was quite logical for him to try to establish contact with Tito.

Eden's advice to Jovanović showed that he expected Jovanović to conduct a policy in line with the British view of the situation. On January 5, I learned from John Ennals, who was on the staff of the Political Intelligence Department, that the aim of British policy was to detach Mihailović from the Italians and bring him to a closer understanding with the Croats. He showed me a Turin newspaper article of December 2 on Chetnik-Italian collaboration, and he expressed the hope that the current campaign against Mihailović would induce him to co-operate with the Croats at least, if not with the Partisans as well.

On February 25, Ennals showed me the text of a message sent to Krnjević by August Košutić, Maček's deputy. It read: "At the beginning of February, delegates representing General Mihailović visited Zagreb for negotiations with the Croatian Peasant party. They demanded that all activity in Croatia be subordinated to Mihailović's command. The Croatian Peasant party replied that . . . they would not turn over control to Mihailović until the Chetniks in Dalmatia . . . ceased collaborating with the Italians. The Croatian Peasant party further demanded that Mihailović begin active warfare against the Axis in Serbia."

I knew immediately that this information would help me continue my struggle to get the government to establish a united resistance. I waited a few days for Krnjević to place the message on the cabinet agenda. When this failed to happen, I went to the Premier and proposed that since there seemed to be a problem about asking Tito and Mihailović to send delegates to London, we might send three government delegates—a Serb, a Croat, and a Slovene—to Yugoslavia to convince Mihailović of the need to change his attitude toward the Croats and the Partisans. I was well acquainted with his two chief political advisers, Vasić and Moljević, and I was prepared to go myself. If the mission was to succeed, the government had to agree on a program, make it public, and have it approved by the Allies. Jovanović liked my idea. He said he would give it serious consideration and discuss it with me later. Our next meeting did not take place until mid-March, when I had learned of the German plan to destroy Mihailović's and Tito's forces.

I received several reports on Mihailović's relations with the Italians. Professor R. W. Seton-Watson told me that the sculptor Ivan Meštrović had reportedly witnessed attempts on the part of the Italians and some of Mihailović's men in Split and Dubrovnik to block the restoration of Yugoslavia. R. Bruce Lockhart told me he had seen an "ultra-secret document about co-operation between a Great Serbia and Italy at the expense of Croatia."

Since Krnjević was not on speaking terms with me, I delivered my report on Mihailović's relations with the Italians to Šutej on January 25, 1943. Once again I advocated energetic action by the government in the critical days ahead. Šutej told me that he and Krnjević had read my January 25 memorandum to the Premier and had found it satisfactory. When I tried to engage him in a discussion, he lost his temper and threatened me. I just left. The following day, he called me in for further talks, but I could tell that he was not going to budge an inch unless he felt himself in danger of being ousted from the cabinet.

Soviet complaints about Mihailović's collaboration with the

Italians, and the desire of the British military in the Middle East for guerrilla warfare in the Balkans, induced Eden to demand that Mihailović cease fighting Partisans and begin battling the occupier. During their January 11 meeting, Eden had also told Jovanović that it might be necessary for Mihailović's forces to withdraw into Serbia in order to put an end to the clashes with Tito in other areas. His proposal was well timed: eight days later, the Germans launched their biggest offensive against Tito, with the support of the Italians and all the local anti-Communist forces. Would they be joined by Mihailović as well?

CHAPTER 11

The Anglo-American offensives at both ends of North Africa reawakened Hitler's interest in Italy and the Balkans. He concluded, quite logically, that as soon as the African campaign was over, Allied troops would land either in Italy or in the Balkans. Consequently, he put pressure on Mussolini to launch full-scale offensives against both Tito and Mihailović. On December 18, Ribbentrop told Ciano that they must "exploit the warm relations which [exist] between some of our commands and the četnik elements to lay a trap for Mihailović and to hang him as soon as he [falls] into our hands." It was agreed that a military plan should be drafted for the operation against Tito and Mihailović. The operation was given the code name Weiss. The Germans were forced to permit the Chetniks to operate jointly with the Italians against the Partisans, but only on condition that the Chetniks had no contact with the German army or the Croatian regular army. They also agreed that action against the Chetniks would be delayed until the Partisans had been liquidated.

Obviously, Hitler's main objective was to put an end to the co-operation between the Italians and Mihailović, and to destroy the latter completely. In a letter dated February 16, and delivered by Ribbentrop, Hitler outlined to Mussolini the dangers Mihailović's movement held for the Axis. In a conference with Ribbentrop, General Roatta, who had established a wide network for co-operation with the Chetniks, defended it as useful, arguing that only after the Chetniks had been used to destroy the Partisans should they be disarmed. Bastianini came to Roatta's support, maintaining that there was no chance of a reconciliation between Tito and Mihailović, and since only minor operations could be conducted in such mountainous country, the number of divisions was not crucial.

Because the Italians planned to withdraw as many of their forces as possible, they rejected the German plan for pacification operations in occupied Yugoslavia. General Ambrosio argued that it was impossible to fight both the Chetniks and the Partisans at once. In order to carry out Hitler's pacification plans, he said, they would have to have a large standing army at their disposal. Ribbentrop and General Walter Warlimont spoke of the necessity of smashing at least the main centers of resistance in order to prevent the outbreak af a general revolt if and when the British landed. Warlimont reported that since the launching of Operation Weiss, five thousand Partisans had been killed out of a fighting force of fifteen to twenty thousand, and that the remainder had withdrawn into the Neretva valley, where they could be destroyed. Ambrosio asserted that the joint German-Italian operations would not succeed, that disorder would break out again within a fortnight, and that the Italians could not spare any troops for such operations because all of their reserve divisions were needed to defend Italy herself should the British land there.

Mussolini replied to Hitler's letter on March 8. Anxious to assuage Hitler's displeasure, he wrote that the Italian generals in Montenegro had been told to stop giving arms to the Chetniks, and that the Chetniks would be completely disarmed as soon as it was felt that the Partisans were no longer a threat. At the Hitler-Mussolini meetings of April 7 and 10, the desirability of disarming Mihailović's forces was again stressed. Mussolini wanted withdrawal of Italian troops from Russia and the Balkans, a separate peace with Russia, and a declaration of freedom for the European nations. He obtained none of these.

Hitler believed that there were hidden motives behind the Italian relations with Mihailović, and he returned to this subject in some harsh letters six weeks later. Through Mihailović, Roatta made a desperate attempt to reach an agreement with Britain and the United States that would provide for the dissolution of Yugoslavia in exchange for an Italian reversal against Germany. Out of the rubble of Yugoslavia, a Great Serbia was to arise, and Italy was to keep everything she had obtained at the expense of the Croats and Slovenes in 1941. Ciano complained to the Germans, as well as to Pavelić's minister in Rome, that he had no influence on Roatta's policies. It is unlikely that Mussolini knew about Roatta's schemes, since they were directed against him. In early April, 1943, Mussolini expounded his policy toward occupied Yugoslavia to Nicholas von Kallay, the Hungarian premier. He said that "the Italians were supporting Tito because . . . he was the weaker of the two. . . . Supporting Tito was the way to disrupt the unity of the Yugoslav resistance. There was no danger of Yugoslavia going Communist. . . . The question of Communism was to be resolved on the battlefields of Russia."

There are strong indications that the Italian army helped Tito indirectly. Dedijer has described in his diary the critical position of the Partisans in their retreat from Serbia: "The Germans stormed on to the heights above Uvac and raked us with machine-gun fire. . . . On the other side, two hours' march away, the Italians were in Nova Varoš. If the Axis Powers had been working together, they would have caught us in this hole." He later cites the information about Operation Weiss given by General Löhr, commander in chief of German troops in the Balkans, at his interrogation after the war. According to Löhr, the Partisans' line of retreat was not cut off at the beginning because the Italian divisions from Karlovac did not reach their positions in time. The Italian army in Herzegovina retreated before the Partisans crossing from Montenegro in June, 1942, and did not allow Croatian reinforcements to prevent this. On August 6, the German minister in Zagreb complained to Ribbentrop that the Italians were not hunting down the defeated Partisans fleeing into their zone; and on August 11 he requested Berlin to make arrangements for Italian troops to defend the bauxite area in western Bosnia, "because German troops are not allowed to enter an Italian operational area." In early March, 1943, in an area in the Neretva valley held by the Italians and Chetniks, Tito managed to extricate himself from a very dangerous situation when the Germans were unable to complete the encirclement of his forces. Could all of these events have been pure coincidence? Captain D. T. Hudson had told the SOE in June, 1942: "The Italians are apparently sitting in the towns in those portions of the country occupied by them and are giving arms both to the Partisans and to the Chetniks and leaving them to fight it out."

Roatta succeeded in drawing Mihailović into his schemes. As early as July, 1943, Roatta had been optimistic about getting favorable terms from the Allies in return for deserting the Germans. General Robotti, then commander of the Second Army, revealed that there were two plans: the Roatta plan, and the Italian high command plan. He told Pavelić's representatives that the Allies had missed a golden opportunity by not turning Italy against Germany, because Italy, in agreement with the Balkan peoples, could have opened the Balkans to the Allies. Pavelić passed this information on to Ribbentrop on August 10. Roatta even thought he could bring Croatia in with Italy, and both he and the Italian minister in Zagreb advised Pavelić to democratize his regime. Obviously Roatta wanted to use Mihailović to help Italy get the Western Allies into the Balkans. On August 2, Harold Macmillan informed Harry C. Butcher, General Eisenhower's adjutant, that five Italian divisional commanders in Yugoslavia had told British secret agents that they wanted to surrender to the Allies. After the war, King Peter told me that in 1942 the British had sent a man to Split to make contact with General Badoglio through Ilija Birčanin, Mihailović's representative there. Mladen Žujović, Birčanin's successor in Split, later told a friend of mine in Paris how sorry he was that Mihailović had been unable to do anything about Roatta's plan for a separate peace. A letter written by Žujović after the fall of Mussolini was quoted at Mihailović's trial: "If the Italians capitulate they will probably help us. The British spoiled everything by putting emphasis on unconditional surrender. They should have agreed with the Italians." F. W. Deakin told me, in April, 1972, that he had found, in the Italian archives, a telegram from the governor of Dalmatia to Rome, in the spring of 1943, saying that he had had a long conversation with Žujović on the projected agreement between Italy and the Serbs, according to which Mihailović's people would help Italy by working for an Italo-British armistice and the Italians would help Serbs establish their rule in Dalmatia and elsewhere.

As soon as I heard of Roatta's relations with Mihailović, my one fear was that this master of intrigue would lead Mihailović astray. Cut off from the world, Mihailović was in no position to understand the complex international game. The Premier shared my concern. I heard that Mihailović's couriers had delivered

Roatta's plans to our chargé d'affaires in Madrid, who in turn delivered them to Jovanović in early February, 1943. "What are we to do?" the Premier complained to Stojan Pribićević. "Draža has made some arrangement with Roatta." On March 24, I had a long talk with Jovanović; I told him of the important information showing that Mihailović had gone astray, and emphasized that he had to be rescued. He replied, "Yes, there's confusion over two plans—a separate peace, and anti-Communism. . . . Quite clearly, the Croats are right to be suspicious, if Mihailović is collaborating with the Italians." On April 12, he told me that there had been a sudden deterioration in relations between Mihailović and the British, and that he had sent Mihailović the following message: "Don't discard long-term British auspices for momentary advantage from Italians. Repulse Partisans if they attack you." When he said Ambassador Rendel had told him the message was "highly satisfactory," I replied, "Let's not fool ourselves. Our position is very precarious. The British must have a military plan and want Draža to sever his connections with the Italians."

Four days earlier, Rendel had said to me: "Your government is not a government. . . . I have warned Jovanović, Krnjević, and Šubašić that the international situation is serious for the small nations . . . there is skepticism about the restoration of Yugoslavia, and the present discord in your government could do a great deal of harm." He had gone on to say that Mihailović would be in great trouble if the government fell. The British would be forced to abandon him and help others, because resistance in Yugoslavia was essential. "Mihailović's forces are weak," he pointed out. "He would be in an impossible position if we cut off aid to him. . . . I understand he doesn't know what the government's policy is, and some of his people are collaborating with the Italians." Finally, he said, "I see Communism in Yugoslavia, unless you settle your differences."

On March 29, Churchill wrote a historic letter to Jovanović, protesting a speech made by Mihailović at the christening of a child of the man at whose home he was staying. The drinks flowed freely, Mihailović's tongue was loosened, and he made a toast. According to another guest, Colonel S. W. Bailey, a delegate of the British military command in Cairo, Mihailović said that "the Serbs were now completely friendless; that the British, to suit their own strategic purposes, were pressing them to engage in operations without any intention of helping them . . . that the British were trying to purchase Serbian blood at the cost of a trivial supply of munitions . . . that his enemies were the Ustashi, the Partisans, the Croats, and the Moslems; that when he had dealt with these, he would turn to the Germans and Italians."

Churchill concluded his letter thus: "His Majesty's Government cannot ignore this outburst nor accept without explanation and without protest a policy so totally at variance with their own. They could never justify . . . their continued support of a movement, the leader of which does not scruple publicly to declare that . . . his enemies are not the Germans and Italians, invaders of his country, but his fellow Yugoslavs . . . who at this very moment are fighting and giving their lives to free his country from the foreigner's yoke. . . . Unless General Mihailović is prepared to change his policy both toward the Italian enemy and toward his Yugoslav compatriots who are resisting the enemies, it may well prove necessary for His Majesty's Government to revise their present policy of favouring General Mihailović to the exclusion of other resistance movements in Yugoslavia."

Mihailović replied that if he had relied solely on the aid from the British, he would have been able to equip only two hundred men. He was accepting assistance from the Italians because he could not get it from anyone else. He regarded the Partisans as sworn enemies with whom there could be no reconciliation. I told the friend who had given me this information that Jovanović had said to R. W. Seton-Watson that Mihailović was not one to take orders, but to be obeyed. I explained that that was precisely why it was so urgent to settle the internal differences in the cabinet, so that grave problems like this could be tackled. He promised my little group his help. Three days later he asked to see me. He handed me a sheet of paper, which read: "The Japanese ambassador, on the basis of a talk with Bastianini, informed his government that at a recent conference in Rome, Ribbentrop demanded that Italy disarm Mihailović's forces. The Italians parried the demand by saying that they were still useful, as long as the war against the Communists was going on; but when that came to an end, then the possibility of disarming the Chetniks could be considered."

Spurred on by this report, I stepped up my efforts to get the cabinet members to reach some agreement. I arranged for Vernon Bartlett, a friend of Eden's, to warn the Yugoslavs to come to their senses, which he did, in the *News Chronicle* on March 26, 1943. He demanded that the Yugoslav government send "strict and united orders" to the various resistance groups in Yugoslavia. This caused a great commotion in the cabinet. That same day I was summoned by the Premier, who knew that I was on good terms with Bartlett and thought I had prompted him to write the article. He only asked whether I had seen Bartlett recently. He also told me that he wanted to get in touch with Šubašić, who was in London, and he talked about the Croatian Congress that had been held in Chicago earlier that month. The congress had paid tribute to Tito's movement as the only focus of resistance, and had condemned the London government for its anti-Croatian policy. It had especially condemned the Ustashi regime.

I told the Premier that these were trifling matters compared with the problems of Mihailović's relations with the British and the Soviets. I said that now was the time to take up my suggestion and invite Tito's and Mihailović's delegates to London, because both sides were in deadly peril. He feared that Mihailović would not consent to Tito's being placed on the same footing as himself. I reminded him that he had acknowledged the existence of Tito's guerrillas and therefore could not accept such an attitude on Mihailović's part. Furthermore, I recommended that Mihailović disown Jevdjević and Djujić, the two Chetnik commanders most under attack for collaboration with the Italians and massacres of Croats and Moslems; this gesture would improve Mihailović's position both with Moscow and with the Croats.

In proposing the invitation to delegates from occupied Yugoslavia, I was also concerned with the confusion in people's minds regarding relations among the Allies. The Nazis had been spreading rumors of the impending disintegration of the Anglo-American-Soviet alliance. Many people, particularly those in Mihailović's orbit, firmly believed this. The Communists in

Yugoslavia still believed in Soviet omnipotence. I felt that these mistaken notions could be corrected if we got together and talked things over. The delegates would be able to tell us a good deal we didn't know about the tragic events at home, and we would explain to them the Churchill-Roosevelt "unconditional surrender" policy, which had been adopted at Casablanca in January, 1943, as a guarantee to Stalin that the West would not make a separate peace with Hitler. "Unconditional surrender" meant that Italy could not demand conditions from the Allies in return for a cessation of hostilities, but would have to surrender unconditionally and let the Allies determine her fate. This is what I wished to make clear to our people who mistakenly believed that the Italians could arrange with the Allies for the creation of a Great Serbia, with Italy holding Croatia and Slovenia as a reward for her break with Germany.

Churchill's strategic plans were in complete accord with his political plans. "It would be a measureless disaster," he wrote to Eden in October, 1942, "if Russian barbarism overlaid the culture and independence of the ancient States of Europe. . . . I look forward to a United States of Europe. . . . I hope to see a Council consisting of perhaps ten units, including the former Great Powers, with several confederations—Scandinavian, Danubian, Balkan, etc." His war plan against Germany and Japan, which had been drawn up at his first conference with Roosevelt, in late 1941, envisaged a return from the Pacific to the European continent in 1943, via the Mediterranean, Turkey, and western Europe itself. The Russians would look after the eastern sector, the Americans the southern sector, and the British the western sector.

However, early in the spring of 1942, Churchill showed signs of a willingness to concede certain frontiers in eastern Europe to Stalin as a means of preventing him from concluding a separate peace with Hitler. Roosevelt thought that Stalin would reduce his pressure on Churchill if the Americans and British brought the dialogue with Stalin around to the opening of a second front. In April, 1942, Roosevelt sent a military mission to London to persuade Churchill that a landing in France should take place in early July, 1943. After meeting with Roosevelt in May, however, Molotov, through a shrewdly worded communiqué, created the impression that Roosevelt had promised a second front in 1942. Churchill had to correct this, and several weeks later he went to Washington, where he made a plausible case for not invading France until 1943. He recommended that a landing in North Africa be planned for that autumn, followed by landings in Italy and an invasion of the Balkans through Turkey. He claimed that this would be the quickest way of helping Russia. Churchill showed Stalin the Anglo-American plan when he saw him in August.

On November 9, at a conference with Eden, Ambassador John G. Winant, and General Walter Bedel Smith, Churchill spoke enthusiastically about the plan for a Balkan invasion with the help of forty-five Turkish divisions. On January 17, 1943, he met Roosevelt in Casablanca. They agreed that Anglo-American forces should occupy Sicily after the North African campaign in order to expedite an Italian surrender, and that "Turkey lies within a theater of British responsibility." Accordingly, Churchill went to Adana to meet President Ismet Inönü, of Turkey. His mind was now entirely occupied with the dual maneuver of getting the Italian army to come over to the Allied side and getting Turkey to enter the war. This maneuver would require the participation of Bulgaria and the guerrilla forces of Yugoslavia and Greece. In order to allay Turkish and Bulgarian apprehensions regarding Communist activity in Yugoslavia and Greece, it would be necessary to reconcile the nationalist and Communist forces in the two countries and put them under the command of the British army in Cairo. Eden, in Cairo in November 1943, had tried to calm Turkish fears that Stalin would plant a Tito in their country by saying: "We shall correct the situation in Yugoslavia."

But Britain was also demanding postponement of the northern France landing, because the North African campaign had lasted several months longer than expected. Roosevelt and Churchill conferred in Washington from May 12 to May 25. Churchill maintained that the entire German flank in southern Europe would be devastated if the Italian divisions in Greece and Yugoslavia could be induced to surrender or to join the Allies. This prize would be well worth the cost of a few weeks' delay in the invasion of France. Roosevelt told Churchill on May 12 that he was against landing anywhere in Italy other than Sicily and Sardinia. Churchill was intent on obtaining an American commitment to a deeper involvement in Italy, and he refused to accept such limited Mediterranean operations; he advocated an invasion of Italy with possible extension to Yugoslavia and Greece. But the American chiefs of staff were worried that opening a Balkan front might lead to a grand campaign that would jeopardize the invasion of France. It was decided to postpone the invasion until 1944. Eisenhower later wrote that after the conference with Churchill, General Alan Brooke had advocated abandoning altogether the invasion of northern France, and that he and General George C. Marshall had rejected the suggestion.

It is clear that the people who mattered on the British side were anxious that the military operations in the Balkans be as powerful as those in northern France. Churchill denied this at the time, but, in a speech on May 3, 1944, he said that if he had had his own way, he "would have been in favour of rolling up Europe from the South-East and joining hands with the Russians." On October 14, King George VI declared himself in favor of this plan, which would save many southern European nations from falling under the Communist yoke, and expressed his firm hope that Churchill would not give way to the American strategic plan. On the eve of the "Big Three" meeting in Teheran, the British spokesmen at the Cairo conference advocated "vigorous and all-out prosecution of the Mediterranean campaign," Eisenhower later wrote. Such concentration, they felt, "might lead to an unexpected break that would make the Channel operation either unnecessary or nothing more than a mopping-up affair."

A reconciliation between Mihailović and Tito would have been very useful to Churchill at this time. It was evident that Stalin was exploiting Tito's movement in order to obtain concessions in other parts of southeastern Europe and thereby disrupt Churchill's plans for federations there. In addition, the date for the invasion of Sicily was not far off. The Germans and Italians had to be led to believe that landings would occur in the Balkans as well. A sudden reversal on Mihailović's part would be a warning to the Italians to accept unconditional surrender rather than wait for more favorable terms. The time was approaching when the Italians in Yugoslavia might well side with the Allies; they would have to be told which resistance movement to join. Britain also had to decide whether to send arms and supplies to Mihailović or Tito, and she had no wish to become involved in the civil war between them. Churchill felt that the conflict between Tito and Mihailović might keep Turkey from entering the war, because Turkey feared Communism.

At Adana, Inönü agreed to the terms of a memorandum given him by Churchill. Among other things, the memorandum advocated stepping up arms to Turkey because of the German menace and stated that the fall of Italy would bring Allied troops up to the western Balkans and into contact with the resistance movements in Yugoslavia. Another memorandum, given to the American ambassador in Turkey by the British ambassador, stated that "even should Germany not attack Turkey, Turkish interests may dictate that she intervene in the Balkans to prevent anarchy. . . . Thus the possibility of Turkey becoming a belligerent must be considered." Stalin's consent to Turkey's entry into the war was given on November 28, 1942, in a message to Churchill: "It would be desirable to do everything possible to have Turkey enter the war on our side. . . . This would be of great importance in order to accelerate the defeat of Hitler."

At that time, Turkey was making energetic moves to get Bulgaria, Hungary, and Rumania away from Germany. Hungary and Rumania were trying to persuade Italy to join them in breaking away from Germany. In a speech broadcast over the BBC on March 21, 1943, Churchill advocated a European council composed of a number of federations. The speech was intended to support Turkey's activities in this direction as well as Eden's efforts in Washington, where he had arrived for talks on March 12. At the request of the BBC, I broadcast two messages to Yugoslavia on the significance of Churchill's speech. In February, Eden had instructed the British ambassador in Moscow to find out from Molotov what the Soviet attitude was toward a confederation in eastern Europe. On March 10, Ivan Maisky, the Soviet ambassador in London, told him that the Soviet government "might not oppose a confederation which excluded Roumania . . . but their attitude to a Polish-Czech confederation would depend on the complexion of the future Polish Government." Harold Nicolson told me after the war that, following the Adana meeting, Stalin rejected the plan for a Turko-British landing at the Rumanian Black Sea port of Constanza. This can only have been in response to the British rejection of his proposals for partitioning the Balkans and eastern Europe into Russian and British spheres of influence.

On March 15, Eden discussed a number of problems, including Yugoslavia, with Roosevelt and Harry Hopkins. Eden, in his memoirs, recalled that "Mr. Roosevelt favoured separating Serbia from Croatia and Slovenia. I told him that in principle I disliked the idea of multiplying smaller states, I hoped the tendency would now be reversed and that we should aim at grouping. I could not see any better solution for the future of either the Croats or the Slovenes than forming some union with the Serbs." This is Hopkins's version of that conversation: "The President expressed his oft repeated opinion that the Croats and Serbs had nothing in common and that it is ridiculous to try to force two such antagonistic peoples to live together under one government. He, the President, thought that Serbia, itself, should be established by itself and the Croats put under a trusteeship." Roosevelt mentioned to Churchill on May 19, 1944, the possibility of three separate Yugoslav states "with separate governments in a Balkan confederation" which "might solve many problems."

In early April, Roosevelt and Eden proposed to Jovanović that there be a thorough examination of the possibility of restoring the Kingdom of Yugoslavia as a confederation held together by the crown, with a joint, two-chamber national parliament, and including an independent Croatia and Slovenia.

Jovanović did not inform the cabinet of the proposal. Even so, a handful of us were working hard for the same cause. I first appealed for help to those trusted friends of Yugoslavia, Steed and Seton-Watson, and on March 12, I went to see Biddle. I told him that Šubašić and Fotić would be in London soon, and their visit would present a good opportunity to resolve the government's problems. On March 15, I told Richard Law, Eden's right-hand man at the Foreign Office, that the differences could be settled with Eden's help. He had only to convince Jovanović and the two vice-premiers that unity in their ranks was essential to the Allied war effort, and offer a program for settling major problems. Law replied that Eden's intervention had not yielded results previously. I told him that Jovanović had not informed the cabinet of Eden's earlier suggestions, and that was why I was now proposing that he meet with all three top members of the government.

I saw Biddle again the following week and told him of the initiative I had taken with Seton-Watson, Steed, and Law. Once again, I appealed for his government's assistance in our efforts to bring unity to the Yugoslav government. He said he had been in contact with Washington on our behalf after our last meeting, and had already received approval to render that assistance. "I shall rush to your aid," he said, laughing, "as soon as you press the button."

Eduard Beneš and his two closest associates, Jan Masaryk and Hubert Ripka, took a keen interest in our efforts. They felt that if Yugoslavia could be saved from Communism, so could Czechoslovakia. Beneš discussed the Yugoslav situation with Churchill, who expressed skepticism as to whether the Serbs and Croats would be able to live together after the war. On March 22, I told Biddle of the German plan for dealing with Tito and Mihailović. I also told him that everything had gotten bogged down because the Premier was siding with the Great Serb faction against the majority in the cabinet: he could do nothing useful without the majority, and the majority could do nothing useful without his support. Vilder and I suggested to Grol and Vlaić that they come to an understanding with Trifunović, because we believed that Jovanović was planning to give prominence to Mihailović's Central National Committee, which was opposed to the old political parties in Serbia. On March 21, Grol told me he was preparing a memorandum to Jovanović demanding a final commitment to either a Serbian or a Yugoslav policy. "Our relations with Jovanović," he said, "are coming to an end in a couple of days; this will be confirmed in writing. I left the country as a Yugoslav minister, and I want to return as one. Anyone who thinks a Great Serbia is feasible, let him go ahead with it. . . . But I don't believe in it. I believe we all have a lot to lose if we break with each other. . . . I think we ought to conduct a campaign to get a reconciliation among the fighting forces at home. . . . We know what the Soviet Union wants, but we've got to use different tactics."

Grol submitted his memorandum at the end of March. He ended it with: "What are our allies to do in their diplomatic and political activity? And what are their armies to do if they suddenly find themselves in Yugoslav territory? And our own countrymen, what are they to do, left without representation unless the government proves capable of keeping a firm grip on the national interest . . . ?" Jovanović wanted to resign after reading Grol's memorandum, but his close friends persuaded him not to.

Steed made a speech at a ceremonial gathering of the British Yugoslav Association on March 31, with several members of the Yugoslav cabinet present. He stressed the dangers of discord among the Yugoslav *émigrés*, and warned that it had to come to an end. Grol made a broadcast to Yugoslavia over the BBC on March 27, and I did the same on March 31. Grol praised Partisan resistance, while I hit out at the people who were carried away with ideas of a Great Serbia or a Great Croatia, warning them that such ideas had no chance of succeeding and would instead do great damage to Croats and Serbs alike. I stressed that the Serbian and Croatian conceptions of the state could be reconciled in a federal Yugoslavia built on a democratic base with a just social system. A few days later, we were both attacked by Mihailović's CNC.

On instructions from his government, Rendel had been trying to work out a *rapprochement* between the Serbian and Croatian ministers even before Eden's visit to Washington. He painstakingly examined their views on the thorniest question of all, that of defining the frontiers between Croatia and Serbia. It was a matter of fixing the boundary between them "under a Yugoslav federal monarchy," as he put it in a letter to Krnjević on March 9. He told me in April that he had not yet received a reply from Krnjević on this matter, and he asked me what boundaries would be acceptable to Maček. His feeling was that only Maček could solve this complex problem, and he asked whether I thought Maček would come to London if we could arrange his escape. I replied that he most certainly would, if he were told what was involved. Rendel accused Krnjević of "straining after straws and avoiding the main issue." I promised that I would get Krnjević to reply to Rendel, and I kept my word. His reply, demanding Croatian boundaries that no Serb could possibly accept, provided no basis for serious negotiations.

My talks with Rendel made it clear to me that the British were very anxious to salvage the Yugoslav democratic system under a monarchy and to protect Mihailović by getting him to adopt a reasonable policy toward the Croats and Partisans. According to friends of Rendel's, the monarchy represented continuity and legitimacy in the stormy times ahead, and the majority of the British believed in both of these things. "Every government in exile has to have a resistance movement in its own country," they explained. When I set out all the Croatian objections to Mihailović, they said it was our job to see that Mihailović rectified his policies.

Jovanović told me that Rendel always toned down the instructions he sent to Mihailović regarding collaboration with the Italians, because he felt the British were to blame for not sending him the arms he needed. On April 2, Churchill wrote to General Hastings Ismay: "It must be considered a most important objective to get a footing on the Dalmatian coast, so that we can foment the insurgents of Albania and Yugoslavia by weapons, supplies, and possibly Commandos. I believe that, in spite of his present naturally foxy attitude, Mihailovic will throw his whole weight against the Italians the moment we are able to give him any effective help." Churchill also showed compassion for Mihailović. According to Llewellyn Woodward, Churchill felt that "since we could do nothing for [Mihailović], he might well ask how he was to keep alive until the United Nations could bring some help to him. He was certainly treating us wrongly; [Churchill] thought that he was also 'double-crossing' the Italians. His position was terrible, and it was not much use preaching to the 'toad under the harrow.' "

CHAPTER 12

The Partisans experienced their darkest hour during Operation Weiss. They were under constant attack from all sides. Their most serious problem was caring for the thousands of wounded they took with them as they retreated. Some forty thousand refugees also joined them, fearing bloody enemy reprisals. Most of them were unable to get very far: some died of hunger and cold; some were caught and shot; some were sent away to camps. Some wandered for days on end through deep snow in desolate mountain regions. At the end of February, 1943, Tito's forces reached the Neretva River. They were completely surrounded. Dedijer wrote in his diary: "The sky is still above us, but it is filled from dawn to dusk with aircraft."

Mihailović concentrated his main forces at the Neretva to prevent the Partisans from penetrating into southern Herzegovina, the Sandžak, and Montenegro. The Partisans were attacked from the west by the Mihailović detachments that had been sent to Dalmatia in the early autumn to help the Italians clear the area of Partisans. These units committed many atrocities against Croats and Moslems. Mihailović had assigned them the task of linking up with the Chetniks in the Lika and the Bosnian marches so that eventually they could form a reception line for the Allies, who were expected to land on the Dalmatian coast. Tito was fortunate that the Germans had not accepted cooperation with the Chetniks; as a result, the Chetniks from the Lika and northern Dalmatia were unable to inflict any heavy blows on his forces as they retreated south. The Italians showed little interest in these operations, which further handicapped the Chetniks. And the Chetnik units in the north failed to break through to the Rama valley because they were unable to co-ordinate their operations with the Germans, against whom the Partisans had used their best units. On the other side of the Neretva, to the east, Mihailović's forces were deployed on the slopes of Mount Prenj. Tito chose this direction, and on March 6 his troops, with their wounded, began to withdraw across the river. Nine days later, having overcome all obstacles, they broke through to the high paths of Mount Prenj leading to the Kalinovik plateau, where Mihailović had his temporary headquarters.

Mihailović had to throw in his reserve force, Major Djurišić's units from the Sandžak, in an attempt to stop the Partisans from entering the Sandžak and Montenegro. (Earlier, Djurišić's units had carried out two large-scale massacres of Moslems, doing enormous damage to the reputation of Mihailović's movement.) Djurišić's units joined Mihailović's at Kalinovik, where they engaged in bloody battles with the Partisans. The Partisans took Kalinovik on March 25, and Mihailović withdrew to Gornje Lipovo, his position considerably weakened by heavy battle casualties as well as by mutual recriminations among his commanders as to who was to blame for the defeat. The Chetniks, in the wake of a great defeat, were plagued by doubts: many were unhappy about fighting against their own kin, and many were puzzled by the BBC broadcasts in favor of the Partisans.

Finding himself in a difficult situation, Tito had sent a series of telegrams to Stalin, pleading for help. "Is it really impossible," he asked, "after twenty months of heroic, almost superhuman fighting, to find some way of helping us?" Moscow replied that every attempt was being made to send help. In his next telegram, Tito asked, "Can we expect at least some assistance from the Allies? Please answer, as it is not clear how long we can stand [the] strain. . . . We are suffering huge losses, and our wounded are badly in the way of fighting."

Djilas has described the desperate plight of Tito's army in his book *Conversations with Stalin:* "The bulk of the revolutionary army, and thousands of our wounded found themselves in mortal danger, and we needed every break we could get." In this desperate situation, only the Germans could offer any hope, and Tito decided to pursue this course. Djilas maintains that the main purpose of negotiating "lay in getting the Germans to recognize the rights of the Partisans as combatants so that the killing of each other's wounded and prisoners might be halted. . . . Moscow had to be informed about all this, but we knew full well . . . that it was better not to tell Moscow everything. Moscow was simply informed that we were negotiating with the Germans for the exchange of the wounded. However, in Moscow they did not try to project themselves into our situation, but doubted us—despite the rivers of blood we had already shed—and replied very sharply. I remember . . . how Tito reacted to all this: 'Our first duty is to look after our own army and our own people.' . . . This was the first time that anyone on the Central Committee openly formulated our disparateness to Moscow." Tito's reply to the Comintern was even sharper: "If you cannot send us assistance, then at least do not hamper us."

The first detailed account of Tito's attempts to come to an agreement with the Germans appeared in *Die Kroaten,* a book by R. Kiszling, an Austrian general, published in Austria and Germany in 1956. Kiszling relates that Edmund von Glaise-Horstenau, the German army representative in Zagreb during the war, told him that he had been approached by Vladimir Velebit, one of Tito's generals, with a strange offer. Tito proposed that the German army and Tito's Partisans form a joint front to repulse the landing of Anglo-American troops in Dalmatia.

Determined to get to the bottom of this story, I went to Vienna in the summer of 1957 and got in touch with General Kiszling. He told me that Glaise-Horstenau himself had given him the account a few days after he had seen Velebit. I asked Kiszling what had happened to Glaise-Horstenau's memoirs. He told me a long story of how they had been preserved from Tito's secret police, and had finally been placed under lock and key in the Austrian State Archives. They will not be available for public scrutiny until 1996.

An Austrian source told me that one of Glaise-Horstenau's former adjutants, Major von Pott, had been living in Voralberg in 1946. Tito's agents brought him a letter from his brother-in-law in Zagreb. A few days later, they drugged him with chloroform and transported him to Yugoslavia. There has been no trace of him or his brother-in-law since then. Thus the only witness to the conversation between Glaise-Horstenau and Velebit was eliminated.

Early in 1965, I went to Bonn, where I obtained permission from the German foreign ministry to examine cables sent by the German minister in Zagreb, Siegfried Kasche, to Ribbentrop. I had the feeling that these messages might contain some reference to the Velebit-Horstenau talks. I was very pleased to discover, in volumes 4 and 5 of the Croatian section, Kasche's report on the talks, which took place between August, 1942, and the beginning of September, 1943. He reported that, at the beginning of August, 1942, the Partisans had captured eight Germans, members of the Todt Organization (an organization, named after the German engineer General Fritz Todt, responsible for building bridges, roads, railways, and so on, in the area around the German front), working in the bauxite mines near Livno. One of them was released, and he took with him a message for Glaise-Horstenau to the effect that Tito was prepared to release all eight Germans in return for eleven of his own men. Because most of these men were in Italian hands, Glaise-Horstenau got in touch with Roatta. Kasche reported this to Ribbentrop on August 14, and asked for his help in getting the Italian government to release these men. Further contacts with the Partisans followed, culminating in Tito's offer to make an agreement with the German army.

On March 17, 1943, Kasche informed Ribbentrop that the negotiations for the release of a German major in exchange for some Communists had widened in scope. Here I quote verbatim from Kasche's telegram to Ribbentrop: "The possibility has arisen that Tito may cease hostilities against Germany, Italy, and Croatia, and withdraw to the Sandžak to settle accounts with Mihailović's Chetniks. In such an event, there is the possibility that Tito would unequivocally turn his back on London and Moscow, who have left him in the lurch. What the Partisans want is to fight the Chetniks in the Sandžak, a return of the Chetniks to their own villages, and peace in the Croatian and Serbian villages; a return of fugitives, after being disarmed, to their own villages; while we for our part should stop shooting and hanging their leaders. My view is that this opportunity should be seized, because the defection from our enemies of this world-famous fighting group would be of enormous significance. . . . I refer you to my earlier messages and to my oral report given personally to State Secretary von Weizsäcker. I await instructions." He added that the Italian minister in Zagreb, and M. Lorković, Pavelić's foreign minister, would approve an agreement with Tito on the above basis.

Nine days later, Kasche sent Ribbentrop another telegram, informing him that two of Tito's plenipotentiaries—Petrović, a Croat, and Marković, a Montenegrin—had arrived in Zagreb for negotiations with the German, Italian, and Croatian military authorities. Once again they offered a cease-fire in exchange for peaceful passage to the Sandžak. Kasche commented that these latest talks "revealed an increasingly strong desire for a cessation of hostilities" on the part of the Partisans: "I see the chance returning for us to achieve a crowning success which could have a significance far beyond the frontiers of this part of the world." In his reply, Ribbentrop forbade Kasche to have any contact with Tito's delegates, and asked him to justify his optimism regarding Tito's offer. Kasche replied with a detailed account of the course of the negotiations, concluding with this evaluation: "The worth of Tito's promises has been proved by events. Solid guarantees will be forthcoming in the shape of the surrender of leading associates as hostages." Kasche's optimism had also been evident in his March 17 telegram: "There is no danger of our being tricked, because we have been kept informed about everything that goes on in Tito's camp."

A few days after his arrival in Zagreb, Petrović identified himself as Vladimir Velebit, the son of a former colonel in the Austro-Hungarian army. Glaise-Horstenau immediately reported Velebit's offer to the German high command. Hitler's reaction was swift and direct: "One doesn't negotiate with rebels; one shoots them." Ribbentrop accordingly sent a telegram to Kasche: "We cannot allow any attempt at the dexterous tactical game of playing off Chetniks and Partisans against each other; both have to be destroyed."

Dedijer revealed in a note added to the third edition of his diary, in 1972, that Djilas accompanied Velebit to Zagreb, and that Koča Popović had signed an armistice agreement at the same time in Sarajevo, though the German delegate, at Hitler's order, finally refused to sign it.

In view of the fact that, since early 1943, Hitler had been energetically demanding that Mussolini stop helping the Chetniks and consent to their being liquidated, his decision regarding the negotiations with the Partisans was perfectly logical. He believed that the British and Americans would eventually land in Dalmatia, and that all the Chetniks would automatically go over to their side. How, then, could he possibly accept Tito's offer, when he had compelled Mussolini to accept, however reluctantly, the liquidation of the Chetniks?

At a conference at Hitler's headquarters on August 30, 1943, Kasche made one final attempt to persuade the Führer to make an agreement with Tito. Others present at the conference were Ribbentrop, Keitel, Jodl, and Warlimont. The whole situation in Croatia was threshed out, and once again Kasche brought up his proposal for the pacification of Croatia on the basis of Tito's offers. In his report on the consultations, he noted that although Hitler had made an observation against the proposal, "he did not come out resolutely against it."

Tito was aware that the near future held in store even greater difficulties and the possibility that the backbone of his army would be destroyed. Paul Leverkuehn has given an account of how the Klagenfurt office of German military intelligence attempted on its own initiative to make contact with Tito early in 1943. This, however, came to nothing, because the German high command could not accept Tito's demands. Leverkuehn has also described an attempt to establish contact with Mihailović, which failed because the German high command refused to accept his terms. The German commander who made the agreement was removed from his post; Mihailović went into hiding in Serbia, while his chiefs of staff, Djurišić and Pugović, were taken into custody by the German secret police and removed from the country. After their arrest, the German army began disarming Mihailović's units with the utmost brutality. Leverkuehn believes that Tito would not have been able to survive the next German offensive, Operation Schwarz, if the Germans had accepted Mihailović's conditions. After Mihailović's defeat at Kalinovik, his units were disarmed and his men taken prisoner and sent to camps. A part of Mihailović's forces was saved from this fate by the Italians. Hitler sent a protest note to Mussolini on May 19, attacking the governor of Montenegro, General Pirzio Biroli, and the commanders of the Second Army, and calling the rescue of Mihailović's Chetniks "sabotage." In his May 22 reply to Hitler, Mussolini said that Operation Weiss had failed because the bulk of the Partisan forces had escaped from the German-Italian trap by fleeing into Montenegro; consequently, the conditions requiring the Chetniks to be disarmed were not in effect.

Tito's original plan was to strike south from Montenegro and join the Albanian Partisans. The Germans realized this, and they launched Operation Schwarz in a modified form, with the aim of hemming in Tito's forces from that side as well. In addition, they reinforced the units of Operation Weiss with troops specially trained for mountain warfare. They also brought in one Bulgarian division.

Operation Schwarz was launched on May 29; the ring around Tito tightened, squeezing him on to the Piva plateau, between two high mountains, Durmitor and Maglić. Because of the bombing, Tito had to move his forces into the more inaccessible terrain around Mount Maglić. The Partisans were now faced with the most severe ordeal of the entire war. This was the fifth offensive, in every respect the most grueling of the seven launched by the Germans. The prospects of breaking out of this ring were very slender. Inside were twenty thousand fighting men, Tito's finest units, and the surviving cadres of his party. The Germans employed mobile forces alongside heavily armed units, and they had air support. The Alpine division units seized all the peaks and sealed every exit out of the ravine, with one possible exception. They trained fire from artillery and from the air on every inch of the mountain track along which Tito's Partisans were trying to escape. The German commander issued a victory order on June 10: "A strong enemy force, with Tito, is squeezed into the narrow Sutjeska-Piva region and is solidly surrounded. . . . Order: no able-bodied man to leave the ring alive." Many sources of drinking water were poisoned. Tito himself was wounded in the retreat by fragments of a bomb that fell nearby. The weary Germans were unable to hold on to the exit at Zelengora, and on June 12, the long column of Partisans broke through and crossed the Kalinovik-Foča road into the dense forests beyond.

In Cairo, in December, 1943, Dedijer told me about the grueling days and nights of the retreat through Zelengora, when some twelve thousand Partisans were killed, a loss that weighed heavily on Tito's mind. Once Tito arrived safely in eastern

Bosnia, he decided to deploy his remaining forces in several places, to prevent this experience from ever being repeated. Mihailović also had to find new headquarters. They would have performed a service to their country if they had decided then and there to stop their mutual slaughter. Mihailović had begun to lose British patronage; and Tito, in spite of frantic appeals, had received no help, except in the form of propaganda, from the Soviet Union. One liaison officer from the British had joined Tito, Captain F. W. Deakin, a young Oxford don and a friend of Churchill's. He parachuted in near Tito's headquarters at the foot of Mount Durmitor on May 28, and at once found himself accompanying Tito in the retreat, during which he was also wounded. From that time on, the British were in communication with both Mihailović and Tito, while the Yugoslav government maintained relations only with Mihailović. This anomaly could not last long. The grim hardships suffered by both Mihailović and Tito, and their disappointment with the powers in whom they had placed such great hopes, could have provided a basis for putting an end to their hostilities. Exhaustion had led Tito to try to make some arrangement with the Germany army. Why then should he not be ready to approach his own countrymen to find a solution? Would the members of the government in exile seize this last opportunity to exert themselves in this cause?

On May 10, Grol told me that Jovanović had not been in favor of a government declaration in February and had urged Trifunović and Gavrilović to oppose it as well. But now that the Allies demanded it, he had to get them to come out in its favor. Grol did not want his memorandum to be discussed in the cabinet, because this would open up debate that might ultimately lead to the government's downfall. He asked Jovanović to decide the particular policy needed, and to inform the cabinet of it when the session opened. Grol gave me a translation of his memorandum to show to Wickham Steed, who promised to pass it on to Orme Sargent.

The government had a new problem to face: King Peter's desire to marry Princess Alexandra, daughter of the late King Alexander of Greece. The Serbs were against the King's marrying during the war; Krnjević said that this was the King's private affair; and Šutej actually urged him to get married. The crisis started on May 12, when the Serbian ministers refused to approve the announcement of the betrothal.

I learned that on May 7 Eden had sent Jovanović a letter outlining a plan for settling the problem of forming a united resistance in Yugoslavia. The letter contained some of the ideas I had been advocating for the past year, and I realized its tremendous importance at once; but I knew that it had not even been mentioned in the cabinet, which had been wasting precious time on the minor issue of the King's betrothal. I could also see that some ministers were trying to ingratiate themselves with the King and exploit the sympathy gained in order to get a government of a certain composition. And all the while, the main problem, that of reconciling Mihailović and Tito, was left untouched. I decided to bring this disgraceful charade to an end by exposing it. On May 27, I saw the United Press correspondent J. Parry, who was on good terms with King Peter and with Princess Alexandra's mother. I told him about the government's refusal to tackle the main problems on the grounds that they had to deal with the King's marriage first. The following day, reports to this effect appeared in American newspapers and were broadcast by radio networks. This caused a great commotion in the cabinet, and for the moment the King's marriage was pushed into the background.

Schemes for a new government were already being hatched. Ninčić was hoping to return to power as a result of his stand on the royal marriage. Šutej was in the King's favor because he had advised him to get married. Simović was warned of the impending crisis, and he wrote to the King advising him to form a government without the senior politicians. One day I discovered that one of Simović's friends, Colonel Beaumont, had recently threatened to "drive the majors out of the Premier's military cabinet." On May 31, I learned that the majors had actually received orders from Jovanović to go to Scotland on June 2 for a parachute course. Now we all felt that some secret power was at work behind the throne.

Immediately after Churchill's letter to Jovanović of March 29, censors got busy in both London and the Middle East. The frequent praise of Mihailović in the war cabinet's broadcasts to Yugoslavia was deleted; the Karadjordjević radio station in Jerusalem was closed on April 1 because of its Great Serb propaganda. At the end of February, the British government informed Moscow that it wished to establish contact with the Partisans, not to influence them ideologically, but for the sake of the war effort. The Soviet government replied that it was not helping the Partisans and would not help the British make that contact. Early in April, Molotov told the British ambassador that, in the Soviet view, the Yugoslav government was fomenting the Chetnik-Partisan conflict. The Soviet government therefore could not try to influence the Partisans to press for a reconciliation, since that would amount to interference in what was strictly a matter for the Yugoslav people. London decided that they were now free to go ahead on their own. The Yugoslav government was not informed of this; the British felt there was no point in "presenting a bitter pill if . . . they are not going to have to swallow it."

Since Eden had stoutly defended the policy of maintaining Yugoslavia, he had to get some sort of settlement of the Yugoslav government's troubles and reconcile the Yugoslav fighting forces. Urgent military requirements also prompted his initiative. It was hoped that it would only be a matter of months before the Italians surrendered: the North African operations were successfully concluded on May 7, and an Anglo-American landing in Italy was to follow within a few weeks. It was therefore not in the Anglo-American interest for Italy to withdraw her divisions from Yugoslavia for the defense of the Italian mainland. In addition, the British military in Cairo were impatiently demanding action from Mihailović's forces against the Italian army. Hudson reported in August, 1942, that "Mihailovic had done virtually nothing against Axis for nine months." The Foreign Office decided to prod him by bringing up the Partisan resistance. In a telegram of November 15, Hudson explained Mihailović's opposition to sabotage against the Italians in terms of Italy's speedy collapse. If Mihailović were to undertake action against Italian troops, the Germans would occupy Montenegro, and he would not get Italian arms. He also feared the "cessation of Italian food supplies for the Četniks." A series of telegrams, 240 of them, sent by Hudson in January and February, 1943, was, according to Deakin, "in great part instrumental in the reexamination of British policy towards the situation within Yugoslavia." Bailey and Hudson proposed in March that: "The time has come to treat

Mihailović firmly. He must be made to realise that we can make or break him. In return for former, we demand frank and sincere cooperation." Bailey had enumerated conditions which Mihailović "would have to accept in the negotiations between British and Yugoslav Governments for an agreement on the aid to him." Howard wrote in April, 1943, that "SOE which up till now had been blindly in favour of Mihailović became very eager to prod him to action and make him accept on the dotted line our conditions for continued support." This sudden and unexpected change took place because the Chiefs of Staff were urging the increase of guerrilla warfare in the Balkans.

London was not satisfied with Mihailović's answer to Churchill's letter. On May 7, Eden asked Jovanović to send a note to Mihailović containing the following points: (1) Mihailović's primary objective was to be resistance. If there were any elements of resistance with whom he could not co-operate, he was to try to avoid conflict with them. (2) There was to be close and constant collaboration between Mihailović and the British Middle East commander-in-chief, to be co-ordinated through Colonel Bailey. (3) All collaboration, even on a local level, between the Italians and Chetniks was to cease. Exceptions could be made only with the approval of the British commander-in-chief (through Colonel Bailey) and the agreement of the British and Yugoslav governments. (4) Special efforts had to be made to co-operate with guerrilla forces in Croatia and Slovenia; in any case, no operations were to be undertaken against any Croats or Slovenes other than those actively co-operating with the Axis. Assistance was to be given to any British officers assigned to contact Croatian and Slovenian groups for the purpose of unifying all Yugoslav resistance. (5) Every effort was to be made by all concerned to reach a peaceful settlement with the Partisans. No operations against them were to be carried out by Mihailović, except in self-defense.

Eden wanted Jovanović to make a strong recommendation to Mihailović to accept these proposals, and he wanted the King to associate himself with the proposals as well.

The note reached Mihailović on May 28, and he replied on June 1, declaring himself ready for the "closest co-operation with British Middle East command." Along with the note, Colonel Bailey handed him an order from Middle East command to withdraw with his forces to Kopaonik, in Serbia, that is, to the other side of the Ibar River, which Tito's forces were not permitted to cross. Hence the name "Ibar telegram" was given by the British to this message. Bailey was instructed to demand an "immediate and unequivocal acceptance" in writing from Mihailović. Mihailović, disgusted by the order, sent it to the government for official cognizance, with the comment that it was "incompatible with the Constitution of the Kingdom of Yugoslavia and with Yugoslav army regulations." He concluded: "I received with . . . consternation the demand that I take my faithful officers and men into exile in Kopaonik. . . . My fighting men and I did not accept the capitulation imposed upon us by our enemies, and we shall be even less likely to accept capitulation to our Allies."

While Eden was opening up prospects for tackling a vital question affecting the future of all the national communities of Yugoslavia, Jovanović's government was moving into its final crisis. After he left office, Jovanović told me that Eden had assured him that if Mihailović had accepted the agreement, he would have announced to the House of Commons that Mihailović's forces were to be integrated into the British army. Churchill was very anxious for this to happen, as can be seen from his September 9 memorandum to President Roosevelt, in which he offered munitions and supplies to "all forces that will obey our orders," and said every effort should be made to give them "good direction." The Greek guerrillas, both Nationalist and Communist, had accepted the authority of British general headquarters in Cairo since the beginning of July.

CHAPTER 13

Jovanović's government condemned itself to death when it failed to accept Eden's proposals with open arms. I told the Croatian members of the government, and some of the Serbs, about Eden's letter, and emphasized that it was their duty to demand that the Premier place that letter before them for a thorough debate. The debate, however, degenerated into a discussion of minor problems.

Finally, at the beginning of June, Jovanović drew up a draft governmental declaration and submitted it to the cabinet. It was accepted in principle, but a crisis ensued on June 9, when Krnjević declared that he had no faith in the Premier, because he did not believe that he would carry out the new policy that the declaration demanded. Jovanović informed the Foreign Office of the situation that same evening. I heard about it from Douglas Howard, whom I saw the following day. I could tell from what he said that Jovanović had put the blame on Krnjević. I said Krnjević was right to demand a guarantee that the new policy would actually be implemented. He told me that the Foreign Office would have to take action now, because Eden, Alexander Cadogan (under secretary of state for foreign affairs), and Orme Sargent all demanded both a declaration and a reconciliation of Chetniks and Partisans. I returned to my earlier suggestion that Eden should see the Premier and the two vice-premiers. He told me that it would be awkward for Eden, who thought such a meeting would be obvious interference in our internal affairs. "Why shouldn't Churchill himself do it?" I asked. Howard told me that Churchill was exceedingly interested in Yugoslav affairs, and that he had asked for a situation report, which Howard had given him. It was not, he added, a very optimistic one.

"I had hoped," I said, "that the German offensive would bring the Partisans and Chetniks closer together."

"So did we," Howard said. "We are trying to insure that our short-term policy does not conflict with our long-term policy. Our main task at the moment is to beat the Axis, and we shall help anyone in Yugoslavia who is fighting the Axis." He said there was a great need for the moderate people in Yugoslavia to get real guidance from London. Once again I made an appeal for firm action from the British. "If this government cannot settle its differences by itself," he replied, "then something drastic will have to be done. We have to know whom we shall be working with in Yugoslavia." I told him that the British had better take action before Jovanović's resignation.

Eden, through Rendel, asked Krnjević to withdraw his contentious demand to Jovanović. Krnjević refused. He did not want a cabinet debate on either Churchill's letter or Eden's. He told both Rendel and the King: "The declaration will be adopted two hours after Jovanović has ceased to be Premier." The King, who believed Jovanović to be against his marriage, asked certain ministers to support Krnjević's attack. The group of ministers favoring the marriage were ready to exploit the crisis for their own ends. The ministers from Serbia wanted Jovanović to stay on at all costs. My friends and I were anxious that there should continue to be a government of politicians, but one that would adopt a clear-cut policy and get down, once and for all, to settling the vital political problems.

Eden saw the King on June 17. Holding a note from Krnjević containing ammunition to be used against Jovanović, the King described the difficulties in the cabinet: Jovanović was too old, he said, and was keeping all the most important ministries in his own hands. According to Krnjević, Eden told the King that if all the accusations were true, then he was prepared to accept Jovanović's fall. That afternoon, the King saw Jovanović. Sharp words were exchanged, and the Premier offered his resignation.

Grol was outraged at the way the King had forced Jovanović out. He himself favored Jovanović's remaining in power, provided he was prepared to accept and implement the new policy. Grol certainly had no wish to succeed him, for he would have a great many awkward problems to settle, and he knew he could expect no help from the main political figures.

On June 18, the King began seeing the party leaders. To spare Jovanović further offense, Grol begged not to be asked to form a government. He proposed instead that Jovanović remain at the head of the new government, with the stipulation that he accept the new conditions. The King rejected this, on the grounds that it would be interpreted by his people as capitulation. My chief concern was that a government of party politicians be retained. After an English friend told me that Churchill was "fed up with Mihailović and your government," we decided to appeal to our Czech friends for help. Masaryk promised to arrange with Lord Cherwell, Churchill's personal assistant, to withhold any documents relating to Yugoslavia from Churchill for at least three days. Masaryk and his colleague Ripka were due to accompany Beneš to a dinner for Eden on June 24. They persuaded Beneš to tell Eden that he must on no account settle the Yugoslav crisis by handing over the government to irresponsible elements. We asked Beneš to try to convince Grol to accept the premiership. On June 23, I warned Biddle of the irresponsible elements that were lobbying around him. Since Biddle was a great admirer of the King, I suggested that the King choose between two candidates nominated by the cabinet. This appealed to him. The following afternoon, the King summoned the ministers and asked them to nominate two candidates, one of whom he would select as premier. They nominated Grol and Trifunović. Two days later, the King entrusted Trifunović with the task of forming a government. Trifunović broadened his cabinet by taking in two members from each of the Serbian parties, as well as a third vice-premier—Slobodan Jovanović. Grol was made foreign minister.

On June 28, Saint Vitus's Day, the Serbian national holiday, the King broadcast a speech to his people over the BBC. He greeted all resistance fighters, regardless of their affiliation, and did not even mention Mihailović's name. The speech had been written in English and translated into Serbo-Croatian for the King, but no one knew who had written it. He had rejected an earlier speech, written for him by Court Minister Knežević, who resigned shortly afterward.

Outwardly, the Trifunović government appeared strong, but its fundamental weakness was soon to be revealed. No consensus had been achieved on how to settle the problems raised by the Churchill and Eden letters. It soon became obvious that Churchill was conducting his own policy toward Yugoslavia, without regard for the Yugoslav cabinet. With the publication of the American diplomatic documents, I learned that the Foreign Office had informed Ambassador Winant on June 30 that "after careful and thorough consideration on the part of the Prime Minister and the War Cabinet a modification in British policy . . . has been decided upon"; that Mihailović's reply had been "considered generally satisfactory"; that reports from liaison officers with the Partisans had been favorable, and that "the British have consequently now decided to give them material aid on a fairly substantial scale"; and that they would continue to assist Mihailović on condition that he used the arms they supplied only against the Axis. The British, the document concluded, would inform both the Soviet Union and the Yugoslav government of this decision.

Further developments bore out my fear about the fragility of the Trifunović government. On July 2, J. Parry asked me to see him on an urgent matter. He told me that the King was not satisfied with the new cabinet, because it lacked young blood. The Croatian ministers were no longer being as helpful as they had been regarding the Yugoslav unity declaration, which absolutely had to be made. America and Great Britain were standing by the King. "We have promised freedom to the occupied nations," he said, "and we shall give them freedom."

Then he said he wished to speak to me confidentially, on a personal matter. "I have been talking to the King about you," he began, "and I warmly recommended you as a sincere, loyal, and sensible man. The King also has a high opinion of you. Would you be prepared to accept office in a cabinet of younger men? And are there any younger Serbs like yourself?"

I replied, "If the political leaders have disqualified themselves by keeping up old quarrels, I would certainly give the matter due consideration. But first of all we must give them one last chance."

He asked if I would see the King. I replied that I would be delighted to, but it would be improper to do so behind the backs of my political superiors; I could do so, however, if they were informed by the King of our meeting. Later in the day, I told

Šutej that he and Krnjević would have to be careful, because forces were at work to destroy the Trifunović government.

At the cabinet meeting that day, some amendments were made to the draft declaration, including the confirmation of the establishment of the Banovina of Croatia, and the condemnation of all those collaborating with the Axis. The Serbs were unwilling to accept either of these amendments. The latter they interpreted as a condemnation of Mihailović. The moderate Serbs and Miho Krek did everything they could to get agreement, but their efforts were in vain. Thus yet another government crisis occurred. At that point, the King asked Trifunović to announce his bethrothal to Princess Alexandra. Grol was firmly set against this. Once again we had a lunatic situation on our hands, with Serbo-Croatian relations in turmoil and one faction of the Serbs disgruntled with the King. Šutej told me that he and Krnjević had put forward the amendments because on more than one occasion Trifunović had declared that he did not recognize the 1939 agreement establishing the Banovina of Croatia. They were anxious to get him to do so by including it in the declaration. I told Šutej that the cabinet should have worked on establishing a united resistance, so that the major part of the Croatian army could be rescued, instead of condemning them all as Axis collaborators. "That's what the Croatian Domobran troops are," I told him. "Can't you see you're condemning them? You ought to be trying to save them and Mihailović's forces on the basis of Eden's proposals to the cabinet." Grol was eager to have the crisis center on the King's impending marriage rather than on Serbo-Croatian relations. He expected that the Serbian ministers would support him in his opposition to the marriage, but he was wrong. Without the cabinet's knowledge, Trifunović sent a document to Eden approving the King's betrothal. Rendel returned the document to Grol on July 15, with the comment that the Foreign Office had "never in its history received a document of this nature."

On July 15, Eden sent an ultimatum to Krnjević insisting that he accept the declaration and warning him that if he failed to do so, he would have to take the consequences, which would be grave for his people. Krnjević requested a meeting with Eden, but Eden refused. He tried to see Orme Sargent, but he also refused. Finally, Krnjević asked Wickham Steed for help. Steed, in turn, wrote to Sargent, asking for his advice. "We often feel extremely sympathetic to Krnjević and the Croats," Sargent replied, "but on this occasion we feel that his present attitude is not to be encouraged, and I am sure you will not do so. We have given very careful consideration to the matter, and far from feeling that something should be said to the Serbian members of the Yugoslav Cabinet, we have found ourselves compelled to put it to Dr. Krnjević that his present obstinate attitude is seriously damaging the Yugoslav and with it the Croat cause."

The cabinet had again become bogged down in squabbles over side issues; it still had not tackled the main problem—the British demands on Mihailović and the establishment of a united resistance. In July, in accordance with the war cabinet's decision about helping Chetniks and Partisans, Churchill urged both leaders to make a solemn pledge not to attack each other. Aid was to be contingent on this. The Yugoslav government should have immediately set about establishing a joint resistance plan on the basis of Eden's proposals, which Mihailović had accepted. First, however, it had to settle a dispute over orders from British general headquarters in Cairo requiring that the BBC broadcast the names of people co-operating with the Italians and brand them as collaborators. On July 14, Grol was called to the Foreign Office, where Sargent informed him that the following warning was to be broadcast the next day: "Every Yugoslav who has been in touch with the Italians, for whatever reason, must discontinue such contact forthwith. Anyone who continues to assist the Italians is a traitor to his country. All who now belong to organizations having any sort of contact with the Italians must leave these organizations immediately and, if possible, join one of the patriotic units. . . . It is in the interests of the Allied cause, as it is also in the interests of the Yugoslav people, to bury these dissensions so that Yugoslavia may be liberated as soon as possible." Some days later, I was worried by a casual remark made to me by George Harvie-Watt: "Those around Mihailović who have been banking on the Italians are going to regret it." But how could the Yugoslav government set about smoothing over the Mihailović-British quarrel when it was not in possession of all the relevant facts? A single conference on this was held at the Foreign Office, with Rendel and the four senior ministers from Serbia present. Thus the last chance to get the whole cabinet involved slipped by. From that moment, the Yugoslav ship of state steamed toward the rapids. Only the arrival of Allied troops in Yugoslavia could save it from being sucked down.

Biddle asked to see me on July 8 at the U.S. embassy. When I arrived, the embassy counselor, R. Schoenfeld, introduced me to the military attaché, Colonel Solbert, and the three of us had a talk about the government crisis. Solbert said, "Your political parties have lost all influence among your people. Other forces have arisen. The mandate for the liberation of your country is in the hands of the United Nations. . . . If the King does what we and the British want, everything will be all right."

When Biddle arrived, I followed him to his office. "Your military attaché has just told me some very serious things," I said.

"They have to be taken very seriously," he replied. "The King acted constitutionally in the last crisis. He left it to the politicians to elect the premier. If they fail to agree this time, the King will have the right to set up a small 'emergency war cabinet.' Public opinion everywhere, sick of your squabbles and crises, will welcome this."

"I have heard from many quarters," I said, "that the King has been assured of your complete support for some mysterious political maneuver. I interpret this as meaning backing for Yugoslavia."

"Quite right," he replied. "We regard the King merely as a symbol of Yugoslavia."

I warned him that, even so, they would have to take care that the King did not choose a man with an overloaded past. I was thinking of General Petar Živković, deputy minister of the armed forces.

He replied, "You will be the senior member of the cabinet that will succeed the politicians if they fail to settle their differences. You are our candidate for that cabinet. I hope you will not refuse, because, as a former close associate of Dr. Maček, you are a very important person." He continued to shower compliments on me.

I then went back to Schoenfeld's office and gave him some information about the cabinet members. He said, "And now some information about yourself, please. You are our candidate for the emergency war cabinet."

I saw Šutej that same evening, and reported to him on my talks at the embassy. He listened without blinking an eye. "My conclusion," I said, "is that the candle of party government is burning at both ends. You'll have to be very careful now, you and Krnjević, about what you do. I would advise you to raise all the problems now in a dignified manner, and see how the Serbs react. If you can't find a basis for a decent understanding, then you will resign, giving the Allies a full explanation. Stop the game of Serb-baiting and pinpricking. Get down to the real problems the Allies want to see settled; then you have nothing to fear." I asked him to pass this on to Krnjević.

I had a talk with Harvie-Watt on July 23. He spoke of the King as being a person who really mattered politically. "The King's name," he said, "if he keeps on the right lines until the end of the war, is the best rallying symbol for the Serbs, while Dr. Maček will fulfill the same role for the Croats."

Krnjević was again being used by the King to overthrow the cabinet, and I warned Šutej of the dangers here. Churchill was disgusted at the game being played by the ministers over the King's marriage. On July 11, he wrote to Eden: "A bundle of Ministers that has been flung out of Yugoslavia are rolling over each other to obtain the shadow offices of an *émigré* Government. Some are in favour of the marriage, some are not. . . . My advice to the King, if you wish me to see him, will be to go to the nearest Registry Office and take a chance. So what?"

On July 26, it was officially announced that, at the request of the British government, the King and his government were moving to Cairo. This was what British Middle East command wanted, and Churchill agreed to it. The majority of the Yugoslav cabinet were against it. The Croatian ministers did not wish to leave London until their demands had been satisfied. Once again, we turned to our British friends for help.

On July 30, Parry told me that the King wanted to see me. I explained that it was impossible for me to meet with him. The next day, the King sent one of his advisers to see me. I sent him back with the following message: "The King must have a government of politicians, because only politicians can give status to his government. . . . If this fails, the King should try to form a broad coalition government. . . . As a last resort, he will have to form a government of the most distinguished civil servants in exile; and I would be prepared to take office in such a government if called upon."

I was well aware that I had been considered for a cabinet position since the summer of 1942, and particularly since the spring of 1943, after Eden had told the King to put me into the cabinet if it became impossible to work with Krnjević. Eden had made the same suggestion to Jovanović and to Beneš. My answer was always the same: "I shall be prepared to accept office in a cabinet that will conduct a clear policy founded on democratic principles and a federal system of government, dedicated to reconciliation among the peoples of Yugoslavia and their fighting men; but Krnjević would not accept that policy." It was on the basis of these principles that I had been pressing my demands for punishment of those fomenting dissension between Croats and Serbs and for the removal of Fotić from his Washington post. I was aware of the harm that had been done years ago, when various politicians came to King Peter's father on the sly with intrigues against their leaders. I did not want to be like them. I was open in my opposition to Krnjević's political line, which I considered harmful to the interests of the Croats and all the peoples of Yugoslavia; but I protected him from stabs in the back by the Serbs and the Allies.

Eden was anxious for party government to be preserved. On July 21, he told Grol, "Don't have another cabinet crisis, because you've no idea how they bring you into disrepute." Howard told me on August 6 that Eden had said our government must not go to Cairo if the move meant a split between the Serbs and Croats. The crisis moved toward its climax; I suggested to Šutej and Vlaić, the minister of justice, that they broaden the cabinet debate to include the larger issues, and then resign if Krnjević and the Serbian reactionaries were unwilling to take them up. I was against their resignation, but if they decided on this course, it would have to be a starting point for the clarification of all outstanding issues. On July 28, Vlaić and I, along with Vilder, made another attack on the problem. Vlaić said it was easier for his party to bring the crisis into the open if the main issue was the King's marriage rather than Fotić's removal; he added that Trifunović was adamant about keeping Fotić. I replied that the government would fall ignominiously unless it took a resolute line, regardless of pressures from the right or left. Vlaić wanted to know whether we could get the Allies to use their influence on the King, Krnjević, and the Serbian group. I replied, "The Allies are the key factor in our tragedy. You can depend on them. Your policy is in line with theirs. I can very easily arrange for your memorandum to reach Churchill, Eden, and Biddle; but it must be clear and constructive. You'll have to suggest a solution, and you'll have to ask for help, admitting frankly that without it the present crisis cannot possibly be settled." Vilder supported me completely. I advised Grol to set the matter of the King's marriage aside, and to raise the important issues: the maintenance of Yugoslavia as a state; reconciliation of the resistance groups as proposed in Eden's letter; and strong measures against those sowing hatred between Serbs and Croats.

CHAPTER 14

Eden informed the Premier and his colleagues on August 3 of the war cabinet's decision to move the Yugoslav government to Cairo, emphasizing that it was in their own interests to agree to the move. There was an alternative plan, which he was not in a position to reveal, that was less acceptable. The following day, the cabinet met to discuss the decision. Krnjević did not attend. Šutej made a fervent appeal to the Serbs to accept the Croatian demands before taking any further steps; this was rejected. He then read a prepared statement to the effect that he and Krnjević were convinced that their Serbian colleagues were unwilling to co-operate with them because they did not want them to be anything more than "observers" in the cabinet.

On August 5, Rendel told me that he was resigning. "I am leaving my post, because the Premier and Mr. Eden have made some arrangement with your king without informing me. Your situation is more confused than ever. . . . I can't see any alternative to splitting up. My successor is a good man; perhaps he will be able to steer you out of this impossible situation." I tried to calm his fears by telling him of my proposals. "That will be fine, provided the cabinet can get the declaration out before leaving for Cairo. I'll do my very best to help you." He then raised the subject of Krnjević. "He has sunk very low in our estimation," he said. "With his insistence on including the 1939 Serbo-Croatian 'agreement' in the declaration, he has come up against a brick wall. . . . Why did he have to challenge the Serbs by demanding a reaffirmation of the agreement? . . . He can't find fault with the new premier, so he attacks the declaration. . . . We had great sympathy for him and the Croats. . . . We know the

Serbs, their self-assertiveness, and their Balkan mentality; but Dr. Krnjević has been greatly at fault too. He should have reacted at once to the Ustashi atrocities. . . . And why didn't he accept the declaration, since it approved the federal basis, with only the crown left as a common factor?"

When I asked him if the situation could still be put right, he replied, "Only by agreement." I asked about the Mihailović-Partisan situation. He replied, "My proposals for this were not adopted, and that's why I am leaving. The War Office has adopted another policy." As we parted, he said, "What a pity that Dr. Maček did not come out. There would have been no difficulties. It would have been much wiser than staying in the country." I recounted my conversation with Rendel to Šutej, and we agreed that I should inform the Democrats and Howard of it.

I saw Howard the next day. He went over more or less the same ground as Rendel, saying that the Yugoslav situation was more complex than ever, and asserting that 90 per cent of the blame was Krnjević's. Later that day, I called on the Court Minister, who had asked to see me. He asked me a number of political questions, assuring me that he was asking on the King's behalf. I answered by repeating the statement I had sent to the King the previous week, and I advised that the King summon Šutej to answer the same questions. That evening, I had an informal talk with Vilder. He said that Grol and Vlaić thought Trifunović was impossible, and that Jovanović, Čubrilović, and Gavrilović were in favor of maintaining the agreement with the Croats, while Trifunović was strongly against it.

Šutej saw the King late that night. After their meeting, Šutej mournfully told me that arrangements had been made for a civil-service government.

The following day, I told Grol of my talk with Howard. He complained bitterly about Krnjević's cabinet speech accusing the Serbs of duplicity. A while later, Šutej told me that Trifunović, Krnjević, and Grol had been summoned to a joint audience with the King that afternoon, and that it was essential that Grol and Krnjević not quarrel in front of the King. He asked me to tell Grol that the situation could be saved if he would submit to the ministers' conference a decree appointing Jukić to Washington. "As for Fotić," he said, "they can send him wherever they like, give him whatever they want. If Grol does this, I will deal with Krnjević concerning the declaration. If the Democrats don't accept this, anything can happen."

Accompanied by Vilder, I went to see Grol. Vlaić was with him. I delivered Šutej's message, adding, "We can make it if you hurry. I am sorry that my name has to appear in the message; but that can easily be dealt with once the other thing is settled." (I meant the removal of Fotić.)

"I'm in favor of concessions," Grol replied, "but Trifunović won't give any ground."

"Talk to him," I insisted. "The main thing is to avoid a clash in front of the King, giving him an excuse for heaven knows what. The situation is dangerous, believe me. I realize the decree can't be drafted and submitted to the King for signature immediately, but his promise would help."

"We can tell the King," said Grol, "that we shall continue our talks today and tomorrow, and come to him with an agreement on Monday."

I asked the Court Minister to advise the King that if the party government broke up, there would be a danger of increased Communist strength in the ranks, and of further deterioration of Serbo-Croatian relations at home. I also suggested that if the King gave us a few more days, we would find solutions to the problems that affected him.

I saw Šutej that evening, in the company of the three senior Serbian leaders, Jovanović, Grol, and Gavrilović. I was delighted to hear that negotiations had begun and that there had been no clash in front of the King.

The following day, Sunday, Vilder and I went to the country. We were sure that things were now moving in the right direction. On Monday, August 9, a strange calm hung over us. The only point of interest was that the day before, Šutej had told Jovanović and Grol that there could be no progress until Fotić was removed. Later, I learned that Šutej had said he would put his proposal to Krnjević categorically, and if rejected, he would join the government with me or with Martinović, his assistant. That evening, I had dinner with Major Boughey. He, too, came down heavily on Krnjević, saying, "We want a government that does its bit for the war effort, not one that squabbles all the time."

The next day, after seeing Grol, Vilder went to see Masaryk, hoping to get help in preventing the formation of a civil-service government. I went to see Šutej, who told me that the King's privy counselors wanted a government composed of several Serbian politicians and Croatian civil servants; this must not be allowed, he said. I then went to see Martinović, who had just been promised the finance ministry by Božidar Purić in his proposed government, and a post by Ćubrilović in his. Thus, behind the scenes a fierce battle was going on among the many contenders for the premiership in the King's personal government.

At 11:20 that morning, Howard had told me that the British were in no hurry to get a civil-service government and would still prefer to have the politicians come to an agreement. At 6:20, Vilder told me that Trifunović had tendered his resignation.

I went to see Šutej at 7:30. He asked me for the latest news. "Trifunović has resigned," I said.

"Didn't you know that?" he said. "The new government has already been sworn in. Here's the Reuters report of the list of ministers."

When I saw the list of ministers, I couldn't help laughing. Then Šutej told me the King had approached him on August 6, saying, "You are a trusted friend. Smooth the way for me to form a government of civil servants. I'm thinking of making Jukić foreign minister and Martinović finance minister. Don't stand in the way. I told the Serbs it was all finished with the political parties, but they wouldn't listen to me." Before we parted, he added, "There's no stopping the Kremna prophecy."

Božidar Purić had been placed at the head of the civil-service government. A former minister in Paris, he was well known to Eden. When the King had told Eden that the politicians could not settle their differences, he had presented a list of candidates for the premiership. Eden had said, "Take Purić. He's the man for the job. You have confidence in me, and Purić will do what I tell him."

What we did not know at the time was that Churchill had given his approval for a government of civil servants on July 31. When told by the King that the Yugoslav government had refused to go to Cairo, Churchill had become very angry. Eden tried to get a stay of Churchill's decision by making a last-minute appeal to the politicians to settle their differences.

But the party leaders were in no hurry to reach agreement. Meanwhile, the King rushed ahead to exploit Churchill's sanction and form a government that would approve his marriage as soon as possible.

When we learned the true circumstances under which the Purić government had been formed, my friends and I concluded that the people in Britain responsible for it had been misled in their assessment of the situation. The King was blamed, justly, for failing to carry out the customary consultations after the Premier's resignation; and Trifunović was blamed, also justly, for having submitted his resignation on the grounds of dissension within the cabinet. We realized that the fall of well-known political figures in London would cause bewilderment in Yugoslavia, further aggravate Serbo-Croatian relations, and strengthen the Communists, who declared that the new government was the best one for them. The Great Serb faction in exile was exultant. The Croats were represented in the cabinet only by Martinović, and even he was once nearly ousted. All power was in the hands of the Great Serb faction, while inside the country Mihailović held sway. The greatest mystery to me was that Mihailović was kept in a cabinet approved by Churchill and Eden, after they had criticized him so severely. Purić's government was not treated very favorably by the press in Britain, though Eden welcomed his advent and directed the press not to attack him. The German and German-satellite press, particularly Pavelić's, exploited the fall of the party government as proof that Croats and Serbs could not work together.

All this was grist to our mill in our battle to overthrow the Purić government and bring back a representative team. My friends pleaded with me to promote operations to this end. I accepted, but insisted that they all get to work on achieving a clear-cut understanding among as many politicians as possible. We agreed that any new government must make reconciliation, both at home and in exile, its top priority. This meant that Mihailović must cease to be armed forces minister, that Fotić must leave Washington, and that the King's marriage must be left to the King. The pivots of a new government coalition were to be the Croatian Peasant and Serbian Agrarian parties. Branko

Čubrilović, a Bosnian Serb and a member of the Serbian Agrarian party, was the favored choice for premier, for several reasons. He was on good terms with the King; Šutej had worked with him in Bosnia for a number of years and wanted to work with him now; and it would make a good impression in Bosnia and Herzegovina if we could announce that there was co-operation in the government between Serbs and Croats from that area, which had been the scene of some of the worst massacres. Čubrilović, a liberal-minded man, declared himself ready to enter a government formed by a Serbian Democrat.

The first step was to approach the King and try to determine what his reactions would be. I saw him on August 16, and explained that I had not been able to see him for political talks while Krnjević and Šutej were in the cabinet. Now I was free to do so. I then put forward the objections to the Purić government and the reasons why I would not be able to remain at my present post.

The King replied, "There will soon be an opportunity for changes. I hear I am accused by malcontents of walking in my father's footsteps and creating a new January 6."

"A British January 6," I said. Furthermore, I told him, the Croats could not go on being third-class citizens in his kingdom. Why could not a Croat be ambassador in Washington, I asked. I suggested that Fotić himself should request a transfer from Washington in order to ease the tension between Croats and Serbs. The King promised to get the Americans to propose this to Fotić.

Subsequently, I asked my friends to redouble their efforts to secure understanding among the politicians. I sought help from Steed and Seton-Watson, and I saw Masaryk and Beneš, who were astonished at what had happened to us. Masaryk promised to have a talk with Eden. On August 17, I saw Howard, who denied that the Purić government was the result of British maneuvering. I said that Purić represented nothing, and there was a danger that the Croats would say to the Serbs: "It is your inflexibility that has caused the downfall of party government, and we Croats have been thrown out by the King. So good-by to you and him."

"That would be fatal," Howard said, adding some disparaging remarks about our politicians. But he became attentive when I mentioned the Soviet ambassador. I said Bogomolov was delighted, because the Purić government was strengthening pro-Soviet forces in Yugoslavia.

I saw Biddle the following day, and told him that the Purić government should resign once it had gotten the King married, but at the moment he was exposed and everything would be blamed on him. A representative government, I maintained, could be formed quickly; I was working extremely hard on this problem. Biddle defended the King energetically, but was disturbed to hear that Bogomolov was so pleased with the Purić government.

On August 19, I was informed by the new British ambassador, R. C. Stevenson, that the civil-service government was now in a position to settle the problems still outstanding, because, unlike politicians, they had no fear of the consequences. It was understandable that I should raise the Fotić question, he said, as well as the question of my own position, now that Krnjević and Šutej were no longer in the cabinet. "The government will resign," he assured me, "as soon as it gets back to Yugoslavia." He then asked me about Mihailović, and about Purić, whom I knew well.

"Mihailović," I replied, "represents a large section of the Serbian community, particularly people on the right. But Serbian left-wingers, and all the Croats, are against him. Purić is superficial and reckless, anti-Croatian and antidemocratic. His behavior in the cabinet is that of a dictator. Any ship entrusted to his command will be steered onto the rocks."

I went to see Purić on August 21, at his request. I told him that the Croats could not accept the status of second-class citizens in Yugoslavia. "Offer Fotić a post in your government," I said. "That will settle one of the difficult problems that brought down the politicians' government."

"Well," he replied, "we hadn't thought of that. We can discuss the matter. But then you will have to come into the government, too."

"I would not refuse on principle," I said. "But first we shall have to see what effect your statement has had in the country."

I was referring to a statement Purić had broadcast over the BBC on August 12, in which he said that his government "would remain in charge until its return to the country." He had told me then that he had removed my name from the list of ministers given him by the King because I had ideas that were not in accord with his. Now he said he was dissatisfied with Martinović, and offered me his post. I refused.

"I understand," he said. "You don't want to serve under me."

"I can't sit still," I said. "I shall go and see His Majesty again."

"Well, don't tell him I've got to go at once. Give him at least two months. Otherwise we shall both look foolish, he and I." He said he would try to settle the Fotić question within the next couple of months; he liked my idea that Fotić himself should ask to be relieved of his duties in Washington or be given a post in the cabinet.

On August 31, I saw Stevenson. I told him that Churchill had been misguided in giving his blessing to the civil-service government, but Stevenson defended it on the grounds that even a party government would have to resign as soon as it returned to Yugoslavia.

"In the meantime," I said, "the civil-service government will be the cause of many evils, because it will strengthen the hands of the extremists. In Yugoslavia, only a fraction of the population is actually fighting . . . the majority are against chaos and in favor of a democratic system. . . . The government ought to be giving leadership to these people. . . . How can Purić's government give adequate guidance to people inside Yugoslavia when no one in this government is allowed to open his mouth? The danger is that the wrong interpretation of the Purić episode could lead to an aggravation of Serbo-Croatian differences, with the Serbs thinking that Yugoslavia has become Serbia, and the Ustashi starting up new massacres. . . . Who is going to take the responsibility for all this?"

He looked startled. "I hope you are being too pessimistic," he said.

"This is manifestly a Great Serb government," I said, "because ever since Yugoslavia came into being, the army and the diplomatic corps have been the cornerstone of Great Serb regimes. I myself would be in favor of a civil-service government, if 98 per cent of the army and diplomatic corps were Croats."

He admitted that I had a valid point. I told him I could understand the British position if the Purić government were a challenge to the Russians. Stevenson became embarrassed, and his fingers nervously tapped the papers on his desk. I said that I did not mind a blow being struck at the politicians who deserved it, but this blow had fallen on the whole Yugoslav nation. All this had happened, I added, when we were in a position to have a representative government, without Trifunović and Krnjević; in fact, we could form such a government immediately, within six hours.

Later that day, I urged Šutej to have a serious talk with the Democrats. "See if you can bring the Purić government down," I said. "Stop quibbling. I don't want to hear any more about whether or not the British are going to back us, until you senior politicians produce a basis for agreement among yourselves."

Late that evening, Vilder told me that Churchill had made an important statement from Quebec: he declared that he hoped to see the kings of Greece and Yugoslavia "restored to their thrones by the choice of their liberated peoples."

On September 3, Čubrilović had an audience with the King. He came to see me immediately afterward. He took an apple from his pocket, held it up, twirled it round, and sniffed it. "It's all settled," he said. "The King gave me this apple as a token of the agreement. I kissed it. I gave him my memorandum, which he read no less than three times. While reading the list of ministers, he paused at Kosanović's name. He won't have Stojan Pribićević, because he has taken American citizenship. Bora Mirković will have to be rehabilitated in Cairo. You and Šutej he welcomes with open arms. He'll take Simić to get him away from Moscow. The Draža question he'll settle with the British. The King said, 'Don't let me down by blabbing.' He paused a moment at Konstantinović's name, saying, 'Prince Paul's man.' The British didn't want the party leaders, he said. They've been keeping him informed about what both the Serbian and the Croatian party leaders have been saying against him. He has given an order for the Court Minister to precede him to Cairo."

Later in the day, Purić told me he had spoken to Eden about Churchill's Quebec statement. "The King will go back to the country immediately after the army goes in," Eden had said. "There's to be no Allied military government for you." The British were 100 per cent in favor of the Yugoslav state. "The King will enter Yugoslavia with a rifle in his hand, like his forefathers," Purić had said.

Three days later, Masaryk told me that Churchill had taken

the Mihailović-Tito issue into his own hands. "I've also heard that the view in some British military quarters is that the King's civil-service government is a great blessing for Yugoslavia," he said. I told him that Moscow radio had begun to attack Mihailović, and I was wondering whether we ought to persuade Mihailović to give up his post rather than be forced to leave under pressure.

I was ordered to appear before King Peter on September 10. He complained that he couldn't work with the politicians until they agreed among themselves, and I gave him a detailed account of the action taken to bring about such an agreement. I also showed him an article in the *Statesman and Nation* sharply attacking the Purić government. I said frankly that the Purić government was a disgrace to him, to the people of Yugoslavia, and to the Allies. The cabinet Čubrilović had proposed to him seemed sensible to me; I would back Čubrilović whether I was in the cabinet or not. The King said, "Čubrilović is the sort of man I want." I attacked Živković, who had said that he could hardly wait for the King to get to Cairo, where he would be under his thumb. This remark shocked the King, but I pressed on: "He bows and scrapes to you here, but I assure you that's what he's been saying. He was the same with your father: whatever was popular was his doing, whatever was unpopular was your father's fault. As for the Purić cabinet, they are already declaring that they are being dictated to, that they are ashamed to be ministers; and they are putting the responsibility on you. The cabinet's job is to shield and protect the King."

"You are right," he admitted. "I am exposed to a great deal of danger."

I suggested that the changes be effected before the departure for Cairo. The King said, "It would be a good idea if you went straight to Stevenson with your proposal."

It was my belief that the new government should be a government of reconciliation, including reconciliation between the King and the party leaders. I asked if I might present that interpretation to Stevenson and Masaryk.

"You may."

"If the changes cannot be effected here," I said, "ought we then to come to Cairo?"

"Most certainly," replied the King.

I saw Stevenson that same day. "We are backing the King," he said, "because he is one of the factors holding Yugoslavia together. I agree that this government is putting the King in a very vulnerable position, and it would be as well to give a political complexion to it. But it must be understood that any government will have to resign as soon as it sets foot on Yugoslav soil. It would be as well to have a government that will work for reconciliation."

I said, "We must have a positive policy toward Bulgaria, and close co-operation with Czechoslovakia, Britain, and the Soviet Union if we are to achieve reconciliation."

"What has been decided about Fotić?" he asked.

"He's to get another post; he, Kosanović, and Šubašić—it's for the best that all three leave the United States."

I mentioned Šutej and Simić, the ambassador in Moscow. When we came to the armed forces ministry, he said, "I have nothing against General Bora Mirković; but, as you know, he's in Africa."

"We want to settle that and the Mihailović question in agreement with you," I said. "We are prepared to accept the responsibility for easing relations, ours and yours, with Moscow." I explained that we wanted an improvement in relations with Moscow on terms acceptable to the British. He was glad to hear this. As for myself, I told him I was prepared to join this government for patriotic reasons, but I would back the government even if I were not in it. Had they any objections to me?

"That is a matter between you and the King," he replied. "In any case, we two know each other and will be able to work together well."

Next morning, Stevenson told me that he had talked with his people at the Foreign Office, and with the King. They found our proposal interesting, but it was too late to carry it out. He also told me that the King was prepared to put the government into the hands of younger people. Čubrilović was going to Cairo. "You, too," he said. "That's good. There things can get moving. . . . I advise you, as a friend, to get your proposals down on paper and submit them to the King, so that there are no misunderstandings later." He said that operations in Italy were not going to progress very quickly, and that he was pleased that we were going to get a government that would work to end the civil war in Yugoslavia.

I informed the U.S. naval attaché, Captain Callan, of my talk with Stevenson, and asked him to pass the information on to Biddle, whom I saw on September 13. Biddle was not altogether satisfied with our scheme, because he was so strongly tied up with Purić. In the end, however, he said, "What's good for you is good for us." He still seemed somewhat uncertain about Fotić, though. He was worried that the Americans might not agree to a new ambassador. When I told Šutej this, he said, "Don't worry. The Chargé d'Affaires can carry on in Washington. The main thing is for Fotić to go. You go to Cairo, if they will let you. I accept your scheme."

Vilder also agreed that the government I proposed was the only one with which the King could return to the country. When I outlined my scheme to Grol and Vlaić, I proposed that Vlaić or Knežević enter the new government. "We have our own line," said Grol, "and we will not depart from it for the sake of some technical government or other."

The King and cabinet left for Cairo on September 14. I saw Howard that day, and raised some rather thorny issues. I said we would take responsibility for removing Mihailović from the cabinet, provided the British did not say no. Regarding Bulgaria, we wanted to conduct a positive policy in line with British plans. I also asked him how we should respond to the Soviet offer to train a squadron of our airmen. He said he would let me know before my departure for Cairo.

On September 27, Howard informed me that the British could not discuss affairs with the opposition, because the Purić government was a legal one. I replied that this was understood, and that we were simply asking friendly questions. He also told me that in his private opinion, Mihailović should be excluded from the cabinet in order to make co-operation with Tito possible. Besides, Mihailović was in control of only one-third of the country; it was, therefore, "fallacious" to argue that he had to be minister of the armed forces. As for Bulgaria, the British were in favor of a federation, but how would the Greeks receive a close Yugoslav-Bulgarian association? So many grave problems were involved here. As for sending airmen to be trained in the Soviet

Union, he said that Mihailović would not approve of this. I took this to mean that his superiors were not in favor of it.

Seton-Watson expressed the fear that the proposed Ćubrilović government would not be strong enough. I acknowledged this possibility. He told me he had had a letter from Ivan Meštrović, the famous Croatian sculptor, saying that Milan Nedić and Mihailović were both in favor of a Great Serbia, and that the only solution was a Yugoslav federation.

At the beginning of October, I took leave of my British and Yugoslav friends. As Bogomolov was in Moscow, I was given a farewell dinner, on October 9, by his assistants, Volkov and Saharov. They listened carefully to my account of Yugoslavia's grave economic and social problems and talked about the aid the Soviet Union would be able to give us. I thanked them and said we must also count on Anglo-American aid.

I said good-by to Orme Sargent on October 11. He was extremely cordial and said that the British would be glad to see people from inside Yugoslavia given cabinet posts.

Purić tried to stop me from going to Cairo. He pensioned me off and instructed Bogoljub Jevtić, our ambassador to Great Britain, to see to it that I not be given priority for traveling to Egypt. But Jevtić had received other instructions from the King, and the British authorities were aware of the purpose of my visit, so Purić only discredited himself.

I arrived in Cairo on October 17. The first news was that my friend Martinović had been "dismissed" from his post as finance minister two days earlier and had been prevented by Purić from seeing the King for the official surrender of his office. This was the fate I had predicted for him in London.

Overlooking all the difficulties Purić had made for me, I went to see him. I had to find out whether he had obtained any secret pledges from Eden. I told him I could understand his anti-Partisan policy if he had Eden's promise of British backing to the bitter end. He replied, "I never mentioned the matter to Eden. He merely said that Draža was 'all right.' " Ćubrilović informed me the next day that Purić was telling his friends that he and the King would be going back to Yugoslavia in British tanks.

CHAPTER 15

In a memorandum dated July 6, 1943, the British embassy in Washington informed the State Department that the British government's policy regarding resistance in Yugoslavia was: to continue to support Mihailović, provided he accepted certain conditions; to supply the Partisans as well, provided they pledged themselves not to attack Mihailović; and to continue efforts to unify all resistance movements. Churchill was particularly insistent that all resistance forces in the Balkans accept British guidance. If Mihailović consented to this, Tito would eventually have to do the same.

The Yugoslav cabinet was busy settling an internal crisis when it should have been making every effort to bring about an understanding between Mihailović and the British government and between Mihailović and Tito. The government simply ignored Eden's proposal to make Mihailović's forces an integral part of the British army. Major Kenneth Greenless, a member of the British mission to Mihailović, wrote about him after the war: "His predicament became still worse when in spite of the demands of the British mission his government did not consent under any circumstances to put him under the immediate command of the Allied General Headquarters. This meant that the wishes of the Allied General Headquarters were always sent to him more as beggings than as orders. In connection with this, his responsibility grew from day to day and the chasm between Allied and Yugoslav strategy became deeper and deeper."

Tito's men were at pains to brand Mihailović a collaborator. On April 23, 1943, Partisan headquarters for Croatia gave Major William Jones, a British liaison officer, some documents on

Chetnik-Italian co-operation, which he passed on to his head-quarters in Cairo. Dedijer has related that, on July 31, Deakin was handed the captured records of a Chetnik contingent, which showed it was guarding a railway line by agreement with the Germans. (Deakin, who shared Tito's grimmest days of battle against the Germans, was full of admiration for Partisan heroism. His description of their epic battles fired Churchill's imagination and marked the beginning of Churchill's sympathy for Tito's struggle.) When Brigadier Fitzroy Maclean, a career diplomat with experience of Russian Communism and a knowledge of the Russian language, was parachuted to Tito's headquarters in mid-September to head the British military mission, he was swamped with documents showing collaboration by one or another of Mihailović's commanders. These papers, which Deakin examined, translated, classified, and annotated, eventually did great damage to Mihailović's reputation. Their impact was reinforced by reports given by Italian generals to British military authorities after the fall of Italy.

There were two factions among Mihailović's military commanders: one was anti-British; the other favored co-operation. According to Jasper Rootham, the officer in charge of the British military mission in eastern Serbia, the Chetnik commander there strongly recommended in August, 1943, that Mihailović take military action against the Germans. One of Yugoslavia's many tragedies was that the London *émigré* government paid no attention to this all-important matter. Whereas Jovanović had, at least in principle, accepted British policy regarding Mihailović and Tito, Purić remained evasive while he was in London and threw his support completely to Mihailović when he arrived in Cairo. Until the fall of Italy, Tito showed moderation in his dealings with the British, because he was delighted to have contact with them.

Split was liberated for seventeen days. The *émigré* government never appeared on the scene, nor did the British land on the Dalmatian coast. Tito's troops obtained large supplies of Italian arms in Croatia and Slovenia. Mihailović gained little in the way of Italian arms; he was in Serbia, where there were no Italians, and British officers had been advising Italian commanders to surrender their arms to Partisan units rather than to Mihailović's.

The Italian commander in Gorizia gave help to the Partisans there, and in Montenegro a "Garibaldi" division of Italian prisoners of war was formed under Tito's leadership. In Dalmatia and the Croatian littoral, people came crowding to join Tito. Within two weeks, Partisan ranks swelled from 20,000 to 140,000.

This tremendous growth, coupled with the absence of British troops, put the Partisans in a position of great strength, and in a number of places they began settling accounts with their adversaries in a drastic fashion. In Slovenia, the anti-Communist forces, some eight thousand strong, had occupied the most important strategic points in anticipation of the Allies' arrival. They were under orders not to attack the Partisans. It was these men, not the Germans, whom the Partisans attacked when they obtained arms from the Italians. From September 9 to September 16, many of them were ruthlessly slaughtered. Similarly, in Montenegro, some Chetnik leaders were slaughtered in the monastery at Ostrog on October 19.

While these tragic events were unfolding, the Yugoslav civil-service government was on the high seas, bound for Egypt, and the politicians sat in London raking over the reasons for their downfall. On August 3, Eden had said that it was "in their own interests that they go as soon as possible to Cairo." If they had done so, the Croatian ministers at least could have been in Split immediately after the fall of Italy; they would have been in contact with their own people for the first time in two and a half years. I believed such contact invaluable, and I was determined to keep the government together until it occurred. I realized that the Italian surrender would greatly strengthen the Partisans; this meant that it was essential to establish a combined resistance while their forces were still weak. Unfortunately, this never came to pass. Growing from strength to strength, the Partisans showed little inclination to negotiate with other resistance groups. Instead, they began to demand their submission.

The German army swiftly recaptured many areas of liberated territory from the Partisans. The island of Vis remained free, thanks to the British navy. If the London *émigré* government had listened to Eden's advice and conducted a policy of reconciliation, it could have gone to Vis to direct the struggle against the Germans and deal with the other important issues. Instead, the professional politicians had no influence on the course of events. Nor did Purić's government, which also rejected Britain's policy of reconciliation among the resistance groups.

Britain was finally able to render large-scale assistance to the resistance in Yugoslavia. Between June, 1941, and June, 1943, she had dropped only twenty-three tons of war materials to Mihailović and six and a half tons to Tito. In June, 1943, Churchill ordered thirty-two aircraft placed at the disposal of the SOE in the Mediterranean; these were used to drop 150 tons of arms and supplies into Yugoslavia every month. By the end of September, the figure had risen to five hundred tons per month. At the beginning of July, Mihailović and Tito had pledged not to attack each other, and from July to September, British policy was one of "equal assistance" to Mihailović and Tito. However, attacks and reprisals followed, and the British reverted to their earlier plan: to partition the country into separate zones for Mihailović and Tito. Mihailović rejected the plan out of hand. Major Novaković, who parachuted to Mihailović from Cairo, barely escaped with his life when he advocated the plan. The Foreign Office finally came up with the idea of replacing Mihailović with, as Llewellyn Woodward put it, a commander "of more moderate views who might reconcile Cetniks and Partisans in common resistance to the Germans." The British were faced with a dilemma: they had to either replace Mihailović or cease supporting the Chetniks altogether and assist only the Partisans.

In those fateful days, the government was headed by a Great Serb extremist, Purić, who continued to lead Mihailović astray with optimistic messages, such as the one sent on December 31, 1943: "There is a good chance that things are going to improve for us soon." Ilija Šumenković, then Yugoslav ambassador in Ankara, told me that Purić had sent similar messages through him. Fotić was also full of optimism. British analysts have since shown that the successive Yugoslav governments bore the major responsibility for bringing British policy to the point where a break with Mihailović would necessitate a break with the Chetniks themselves. General Wilson wrote in a letter on October 15, 1945: "The worst people I had to deal with were those with the Yugoslav government in exile who came to Cairo in 1943."

Purić believed he would succeed in imposing upon Churchill and Eden the policy which his predecessors, "senile incompetents," as he called them, had failed to impose. He also believed that he and the King, without Mihailović, would be able to play a great political role. And so he isolated the King from everyone. When I arrived in Cairo, I was able to see the King only for a few minutes to hand him a letter from Princess Alexandra. He promised to give me an audience, but the royal summons never came.

I immediately got in touch with Čubrilović and Mihailo Konstantinović, who was being considered for a post in our proposed government. I soon became acquainted with Bora Mirković, who was being considered for the post of armed forces minister. He claimed to know Mihailović well, and he was sure he could influence him. That pleased me. I talked with Stevenson about this, but he said that any decision concerning another government rested with the King. Purić's assistant, V. Saponjić, told me of a meeting in Cairo attended by the King, Purić, and Eden. When Eden spoke of the need to remove Mihailović from the cabinet, Purić lost his temper and shouted: "If that's what you want, we shall start direct talks with the Russians." Eden replied cynically, "Go ahead!" King Peter related in his memoirs that Purić asked Eden what his own views on Yugoslavia were. " 'A completely free Yugoslavia,' replied Eden, 'and to return him,' pointing to me, 'to the throne.' . . . I rebuked my minister," continued the King, "for losing his temper with Eden." It was only then that Eden realized that he had recommended an extremist to King Peter.

Eden was very anxious to come to an agreement with Hull and Molotov on a common policy in the Balkans. On October 23, he proposed that resistance fighters in Yugoslavia "be advised to avoid conflict with each other." But Hull did not support him, and Molotov expressed no views on the matter, so Eden dropped the issue for several days. A week later, when he discussed the Yugoslav question with Molotov again, he got a somewhat more favorable reaction: "We discussed General Mihailović, his Četniks and the Partisans. I told him that we were pressing the Četniks to take action against the Germans and asked him to advise the Partisans not to take action against the Četniks. Molotov said that his Government had little contact with the Partisans and would like to send a mission to them. . . . I welcomed this idea." Eden proposed that Moscow exert its influence to bring about an accord between Tito and Mihailović, and he outlined for Molotov a plan whereby the two factions would be united but still free to operate in separate areas.

The first conference between Roosevelt, Churchill, and Stalin took place in Teheran at the end of November, 1943. The topic of discussion at the Big Three meeting on November 29 was Yugoslavia. Churchill proposed that assistance be transferred from Mihailović to Tito. According to William Hardy McNeill, author of *America, Britain and Russia,* this was in part an attempt by Churchill to head off possible conflict with Russia over British activities in the Balkans. Eden arranged with the Soviets to send a military mission to Tito. When Molotov said that they wanted to send half of the delegation to Mihailović, Eden replied that difficulties had arisen with Mihailović, and the British were going to withdraw their own mission from him.

Churchill viewed Turkey's entry into the war as essential to the Allies, and one of his main objectives at the meeting was to bring Roosevelt and Stalin around to his point of view. He also hoped to get them to agree to the opening of a Balkan front once Turkey did join the Allies. Stalin, however, was primarily concerned with planning a landing in northern France; the entry of Turkey into the war, aid to Yugoslavia, the capture of Rome, were relatively unimportant to him. Roosevelt, anxious to accommodate Stalin, agreed that the main invasion should take place in northern France, with a smaller-scale landing in the south of France. Since Stalin did not want a Balkan front, he supported Roosevelt's proposal, and it was incorporated into clause 4 of the Teheran agreement. Clause 2 stated the desirability of Turkey's entry into the war, but in fact the American chiefs of staff were opposed to it, and it did not happen until the war was nearly over. Churchill's displeasure was evident; some years later, he wrote: "I regard the failure to use otherwise unemployable forces to bring Turkey into the war and dominate the Aegean as an error in war direction which cannot be excused by the fact that in spite of it victory was won."

The first clause of the Teheran agreement stated that "the Partisans in Yugoslavia should be supported by supplies and equipment to the greatest possible extent, and also by Commando operations." The single most important factor leading to this decision was the report brought to Churchill and Eden by Fitzroy Maclean at the beginning of November. The report, in Maclean's words, "caused something of a stir." Many of my British friends have told me that this report brought about the break with Mihailović. But even after the report and the Teheran decision, the Mihailović problem remained unsettled.

I saw William J. Donovan in Cairo on November 20, and pleaded with him to do everything in his power to bring the Chetnik-Partisan civil war to an end. My friends and I sent a memorandum to the Big Three appealing for efforts to reconcile the resistance forces in Yugoslavia and asking that aid be withheld from any group fighting solely to seize power and establish a dictatorship in Yugoslavia after the war. On December 4, I learned that several wounded Communist leaders had arrived in Cairo—Milentije Popović, Vladimir Dedijer, and General Miloje Milojević. In Jajce, on November 29, Tito had proclaimed his own government and forbade the return of the King until a plebiscite had been held to determine whether the Yugoslav people wanted a kingdom or a republic. On the following day, I was summoned to an audience with the King. As I entered his villa, I had the feeling that I was in a fortress. The door beyond the hallway was blocked by the King's Yugoslav and British adjutants. I stayed with the King for about fifty minutes. He immediately asked me for the meaning of the Jajce announcement, and whether I knew anyone in Tito's so-called government. I told him that he must begin talks at once with the exiled politicians and take into the government those who were likely to come to an agreement. He was rather unsure of himself at first, but later he gained confidence. I pledged my support but told him he had to follow the advice of Churchill and Roosevelt. He said that Roosevelt had promised there would be zones of partition between Mihailović and Tito, and that both would come under American command.

I learned later that on November 24, Roosevelt, citing the example of the reconciliation between Generals Charles de Gaulle and Henri Giraud, had told the King and Purić that he would do everything possible for Mihailović, that he could effect a reconciliation with Tito as he had between the Frenchmen when he sent a message to De Gaulle saying: "No coming, no money."

After his return from Teheran, Roosevelt did not see either the King or Purić in Cairo. How can this be explained? On the eve of the Teheran conference, Roosevelt had read a report, made by Major Linn Farish, the OSS delegate to Tito, eulogizing Tito and his Partisans. Walter Roberts maintains that this report "dramatically changed FDR's view of the Yugoslav situation." (Farish later modified considerably his opinions on Tito.) After Teheran, Roosevelt would not see Fotić either. Earlier, he had accepted Fotić's suggestion that four American bombers be given to the Yugoslav air force crews training in America; he had handed these over on October 16, making a speech in which he emphasized American interest in Yugoslavia. Fotić told me in 1946 that when he asked him a number of questions relating to Allied strategy, Roosevelt said, "You can be sure I will never consent to the division of Europe into spheres." But Fotić persisted: "Perhaps it would be rude to remind you that military operations may lead to that." Roosevelt replied, "You are asking that because you know I cannot escape from this car."

Robert Murphy has related in his book *Diplomat Among Warriors* that he tried to explain the Tito-Mihailović situation to the President, "in the hope of getting some definite policy directive. But Roosevelt was not interested." According to Murphy, the President suggested that " 'we should build a wall around those two fellows and let them fight it out. Then we could do business with the winner.' Neither then nor later did Roosevelt ever have any consistent policy toward Yugoslavia." In a description of a November 15 conference aboard the warship *Iowa,* which was taking Roosevelt to the Cairo conference, Maurice Matloff recalled the President saying that "he would not want to use U.S. troops to settle local squabbles in such places as Yugoslavia. Instead, the Army and Navy could be used to enforce an economic blockade and seal off trouble spots." On February 21, 1944, in line with this view, Roosevelt rejected Churchill's proposal "for an expedition composed of British troops under an American commanding General," and, says Matloff, he "would not even consider a 'token' U.S. force for such a project."

After my audience with the King, I asked Donovan to arrange for Roosevelt to see the King and advise him in his tragically complex situation. One reason for my appeal was that high-level political and military talks were in progress regarding Mihailović.

It had been suggested that an Anglo-American commission be sent to Yugoslavia; a reply was being awaited from the Russians as to whether they wanted to join. Donovan had submitted to the Cairo conference a plan for ending the civil war in Yugoslavia by subordinating both Mihailović and Tito to Allied Middle East command, with a threat of boycott if they failed to obey its orders. Donovan volunteered to visit Yugoslavia in order to help implement this plan. However, the plan was not adopted. The Americans succeeded only in insuring that Mihailović would be given a last chance to prove he was prepared to battle the Germans.

On December 5, after the Partisan Anti-Fascist Council's announcement in Jajce, Purić issued a government statement that was full of crude abuse of the Partisans. The following day, Eden told him that the British would continue to recognize the royal government but would assist the Partisans. On December 7, Purić said to the American ambassador, Lincoln MacVeagh, apropros of Eden's statement, "I can't declare war on the British Empire and so I must swallow it." The following day, Cabinet Minister Richard Law made a statement in the House of Commons on the Teheran decision to give aid to the Partisans, and on December 9, Hull told a press conference: "It is our intention to assist in every possible way the resistance of the Yugoslav people, and to deal with the resistance forces from the point of view of their military effectiveness, without, during the fighting, entering into discussions . . . which may have arisen among them, and which tend to divert the national energies from the main objective of expelling the Nazis from their country. In line with our consistent policy we consider that political arrangements are primarily a matter for the future choice of the Yugoslav people."

On December 10, Churchill told King Peter that he had been enormously impressed by reports on the scope and strength of the Partisan movement. He also told Purić that the British had evidence of Mihailović's collaboration with the enemy, and because of this, the British government might cease supporting him. Hugh K. Grey, in a long report to the Foreign Office, said that Mihailović's policy "involved certain contacts and collaboration with the occupying forces, and once proof of this was forthcoming His Majesty's Government would have been placed in an impossible position vis-à-vis their Soviet ally had they continued to support him." He maintained that this was "the deciding factor" for Churchill's withdrawal of support to Mihailović.

Purić reportedly refused to accept Churchill's allegations concerning Mihailović's collaboration, and he demanded to see the evidence. Churchill replied that it was a "British state secret." Purić then warned Churchill of the great responsibility he was taking in adopting a policy that would lead to a Communist regime in Yugoslavia, and disputed the accuracy of Churchill's information about the strength of the Partisans. Relations between the British government and Purić became very strained.

Purić hoped for American backing in his attempt to change the British attitude toward Mihailović. The Foreign Office, however, had, on December 7, made an effort to explain to Washington the reasons for its demand that Mihailović be removed from his position as armed forces minister. Stevenson told MacVeagh on December 16 that "the Foreign Office states that it has under reconsideration its whole policy toward resistance movements in Yugoslavia as a result of a report from the British liaison officer with the Partisans, a copy of which has been sent to the Embassy in Washington for transmission to the State Department. . . . On the basis of this information . . . the British Foreign Office is considering the possibility of suggesting to King Peter that Mihailovitch be summoned to Cairo and replaced by a commander who would cooperate with the Partisans." Stevenson went on to say that on December 12, he himself had proposed to the Foreign Office that if Mihailović were to undertake a certain operation, "consideration should be given to the question of continuing to support him militarily but his removal from the Cabinet in any case should be sought"; and that, if he failed to carry out that operation, the King should be requested to remove him not only from the cabinet but from his military position as well. Further, "Commander-in-Chief Middle East should advise Tito of the decision and inform him that the King orders him to collaborate with the Chetniks against the enemy."

When I spoke with Stevenson that same day, he assured me that the British would not allow Yugoslavia to come under exclusive Russian influence. "Jesus Christ himself couldn't settle your crisis if we fail," he said. According to MacVeagh, Stevenson had said that he was going to inform Purić that the British government was withdrawing its military mission from Mihailović and ceasing to send him aid; this, he claimed, would lead to Purić's resignation. Stevenson felt that the new government, which he expected to be headed by Čubrilović, with me as foreign minister, would attempt some sort of *rapprochement* with the Partisans.

Churchill explained his policy this way: "It was important that no irrevocable political decisions about the future régime in Yugoslavia should be made in the atmosphere of occupation, civil war, and *émigré* politics. The tragic figure of Mihailovic had become the major obstacle. We had to maintain close military contact with the partisans, and therefore to persuade the King to dismiss Mihailovic from his post as Minister of War. . . . The only hope which the King possessed of returning to his country would be, with our mediation, to reach some provisional arrangement with Tito without delay and before the partisans further extended their hold upon the country."

The new hand of the British military mission to Mihailović, Brigadier Charles D. Armstrong, requested Mihailović to blow up two bridges in Serbia by December 29. Mihailović sent the following telegram to Purić: "This attempt to get us to destroy major targets on the railway lines at this time means that the British want us to draw upon ourselves the strong German forces now operating in the Sandžak; this means they want us to assist the Communists, who would then thrust straight away into Serbia, the mainstay of our resistance, which would then be destroyed." On December 24, Mihailović informed Purić that he had had a conference with Armstrong and had asked for an extension of the time limit. Mihailović had suggested that, in order to end the civil war, a meeting should be arranged between Yugoslav army representatives and Tito's representatives, with British "delegates" as intermediaries. Mihailović urged Purić to follow up on Armstrong's proposal as soon as possible. Any other Yugoslav premier would have taken heed of Mihailović's desire to do everything possible to end the civil war and would have opened negotiations immediately. Colonel Bailey said that Mihailović had consented to negotiations with the Communists because he had come to realize that he would not be able to crush them. How then was Purić going to crush them? On January 7, 1944, he told Mihailović that he only had to make sure that he was stronger than the Partisans at the time of the German withdrawal; then he would be able to seize power before they did. Purić was carried away by the insane hope that he could improve Mihailović's position by offering Stalin an alliance, using Beneš as an intermediary. If he had given Mihailović's entreaties the attention they deserved, he would have been able to keep the British links with Mihailović alive. Donovan's plan could have been of crucial importance here; every effort should have been made to get London and Washington to adopt it.

Tito's Anti-Fascist Council had passed resolutions on November 29 at Jajce proclaiming its executive committee as the government for the duration of the war, condemning Mihailović and Purić as traitors, and declaring that King Peter would not be allowed to return to Yugoslavia. These resolutions, broadcast two and a half weeks later over Radio Free Yugoslavia, prevented the implementation of Stevenson's plan for the King to remove Mihailović from the cabinet, and put an end to the cabinet composition for which I had worked so hard since August. On December 23, the Foreign Office informed the American ambassador in London that "its previous exploration of the idea of persuading King Peter to get rid of Mihailović is now defunct as a result of Tito's recent declaration." The Foreign Office was also of the opinion that joint Anglo-American-Russian action might be necessary to persuade Tito to co-operate with the King, because "the King resisted the Germans and, although ill-advised, he has done his best and we cannot throw him overboard." Referring to Radio Free Yugoslavia's attacks on the King and his government, Eden wrote in his memoirs: "This made me increasingly reluctant to advise the King to dismiss General Mihailović and risk alienating his only supporters in the country." So Eden advised Churchill that the dismissal of Mihailović "can now be only a quid pro quo for Tito's willingness to come to terms with the King." He instructed Stevenson that "no further steps towards dismissal of Mihailović" should be taken. On December 20 he sent Churchill a telegram: "The moment seems to have come when we ought ourselves to make a direct proposal to Tito in order to bring matters to a head." Eden proposed either that the King go to Tito (Maclean was opposed to this), or that a preliminary Churchill-Tito meeting be held, followed by a meeting between the King and Tito in Churchill's presence. After the exchange of many telegrams between Churchill, Eden, Stevenson, and Maclean, it was left to Churchill to raise this delicate question with Tito.

On December 16, Hull told Fotić that he would not be a party to any pressure exerted on the Yugoslav government to abandon Mihailović and shift its support to Tito. This must have contributed to Purić's failure to treat Mihailović's message as a matter of the highest priority. Jasper Rootham has described this in his book *Miss Fire*. Once Rootham felt he could trust Mihailović's commander, Colonel Petrović, he confided to him that, as far as he could see, "unless Mihailovich gave orders to his commanders . . . to intensify activity against the Germans, it would be all up with the movement as far as the British were concerned." Petrović then showed him copies of the telegrams he had been sending to Mihailović since August, recommending precisely this. "We gradually began to understand," wrote Rootham, "that Petrovich thought that Mihailovich, by his policy of pursuing Serbian interests at the cost of alienating the British, was in fact signing the death-warrant of the Serbian people, and perhaps also of the Monarchy of which he was the loyal servant." Petrović told him early in 1944 that the best solution would be for the Partisans and the Chetniks to be placed under the direct orders of the Allied supreme commander in the Mediterranean, and that Mihailović and Tito should have an Anglo-American-Russian commission at their headquarters to make certain that the orders of the supreme commander were carried out. Rootham sent Petrović's proposals to his headquarters, because he felt they represented a "spirit of compromise which we had not met before." Rootham learned later that the "pro-English and 'action' party at Mihailovich's own headquarters were at the same time, and independently, putting forward somewhat similar proposals to one of the British officers there." My colleagues and I had foreseen this sort of attitude among Mihailović's officers; that was why we had been considering Bora Mirković for the post of armed forces minister.

On December 31, MacVeagh informed Washington that Stevenson had shown him the Foreign Office's telegram turning down Mihailović's request for mediation between Tito and himself. The Foreign Office maintained that the request was merely an act of "deathbed repentance" on Mihailović's part, and suggested that he make his offer directly to Tito. Stevenson explained that he could not do that, because unless he had an intermediary, the Partisans would cut his throat. MacVeagh concluded his telegram to Washington by stating that although the British were giving Mihailović a few more weeks before making a final decision regarding their position toward him, they were giving him virtually no practical assistance. General Wilson, however, was opposed to a complete break with Mihailović, asserting that his forces were holding down at least two Bulgarian divisions; and Armstrong made a fervent plea that links with Mihailović not be completely severed now, when he was showing greater willingness to co-operate than ever before.

Rootham has related that he requested his headquarters to send additional weapons to Mihailović's men so that they could blow up at least one of the bridges assigned to them. His request was denied, "on the grounds that no more arms of any kind could be dropped to Mihailovich's forces until they had proved their honorable intentions by actually carrying out some operations instead of talking about them. . . . Whether or not Mihailovich himself understood that it was meant to be his final opportunity to redeem himself is one of the things that we shall probably never know. However that may be, neither operation was ever carried out."

In a lecture in London, on July 23, 1961, Armstrong described the normal course of his talks with Mihailović: "Allied Middle East command has ordered me to ask you to undertake some operations," he would say. And Mihailović would reply, "Certainly, if you provide the arms." But the reply from Cairo was always, "No action—no arms!" And Mihailović would say, "There can't be any action if there are no arms." "The situation was discouraging, to say the least," the Brigadier told his audience, "but I did not know the way out."

CHAPTER 16

For us, one of the great puzzles of the war was Churchill's policy toward Tito. We tried to comprehend it but finally realized that none of our explanations was satisfactory. Our allies were equally puzzled; Louis Joxe, the general secretary of the French National Liberation Committee, said that the British policy toward Tito was "completely incomprehensible to the French." Hamilton Fish Armstrong told me on November 22, 1944, "We are not bound by this policy of Churchill's. We have never understood his enthusiasm for Tito and his conviction that he could get Tito away from the Russians. How could he have been so naive? How could his judgment have been based on the opinions of incompetents?" And Churchill himself, speaking in Brussels in 1945, admitted that his policy toward Tito had been "one of the biggest mistakes of the war." When Djilas reminded him of that remark six years later, Churchill replied, "I don't remember having used those words, but I was so angry at all of you that I could have said something worse." It is in Churchill's character that we find the explanation for his great blunder that cost Yugoslavia hundreds of thousands of lives and brought Communism to the country.

In an interview on BBC television, Clement Attlee once explained that Churchill "always required some strong people round him saying, 'Don't fool over this.' He has big ideas, and every now and again perfectly futile ones; he doesn't always know. I remember Lloyd George saying to me once, 'There's Winston there, Winston—he's got ten ideas on this, one of them is right, but he never knows which it is.' A certain amount of truth in that." On one occasion, Harold Nicolson said to me,

"Winston is not always wise. He likes Tito as he likes all adventurers." And Lord Moran has written, "Winston . . . dislikes people who are for ever making trouble. 'Anyone can do that,' he snorts impatiently." All the Yugoslav governments, of course, made trouble, and thus lost any chance of restraining Churchill from the fatal move that affected their country.

According to John Colville, Churchill's secretary during the war, "His sympathy for people in distress was immediate." Thus, it was with a man of fine sensibilities that the successive Yugoslav governments in London failed to establish genuine contact; they were unable to explain to him all the facets of their nation's appalling sufferings. Instead, they irritated him to such a degree that his impulsiveness led him to back Tito. His entire personality was brought into play here. As a born fighter himself, he was filled with admiration for Tito's resistance. His emotional reaction to the heroic Partisan struggle blinded him to the price of that struggle for the people of Yugoslavia.

But Churchill and Eden both felt great sympathy for King Peter as well, because of his difficult position. They thought that through him they would best be able to reconcile Serbs and Croats and insure that a constitutional system guaranteeing basic political freedoms would prevail in postwar Yugoslavia. When they decided to attempt to bring Tito closer to the King, they were certain that British troops would be going into Yugoslavia and would, by their presence, help bring the civil war to an end and establish a constitutional monarchy. They rejected Mihailović's appeal for mediation between him and Tito probably because they thought it would delay, and possibly completely undermine, their mediation between the King and Tito. There is no doubt that Tito, in order to get as much help from Churchill as possible, dangled far greater prospects before Maclean than he had any intention of fulfilling. The same game was played later by his envoy in London, Velebit, who said to R. Bruce Lockhart, "You've got to help us, so that we don't fall completely under Soviet control."

In a letter delivered by Maclean in late January, 1944, Churchill told Tito he would not be sending any further military assistance to Mihailović, and would be glad to see him eliminated from the cabinet. But he also said, "It would not be chivalrous or honourable for Great Britain to cast [King Peter] aside. Nor can we ask him to cut all his existing contacts with his country. I hope therefore that you will understand we shall in any case remain in official relations with him, while at the same time giving you all possible military support." Tito's reply of February 3 was polite but noncommittal. Churchill wrote him again on February 5, repeating that he felt a "personal responsibility" toward King Peter. He asked Tito if the King's dismissal of Mihailović "would pave the way for friendly relations with you and your Movement, and, later on, for his joining you in the field, it being understood that the future question of the Monarchy is reserved until Yugoslavia has been entirely liberated. . . . I much hope that you will feel able to give me the answer you can see I want." Tito replied four days later, demanding the dissolution of the government in Cairo, Mihailović's dismissal, recognition for his own government, and the King's submission to the resolutions passed by the Anti-Fascist Council on November 29, 1943. Churchill, encouraged by favorable reports from Maclean, sent Tito a friendly reply. In a major speech in the House of Commons on February 22, he eulogized Tito and his movement. Maclean's advice was that the King should accept Tito's demands; the Foreign Office, however, was unwilling to give the King the same advice.

But neither by writing to Tito nor by sending his son Randolph as a member of the military mission to Tito was Churchill able to achieve the results he expected. He wrote to Tito on February 25, asking for assurance that "if King Peter frees himself from Mihailovic and other bad advisers, he will be invited by you to join his countrymen in the field. . . . I cannot press him to dismiss Mihailovic, throw over his Government, and cut off all contact with Serbia before knowing whether he can count on your support and co-operation." He expressed the hope that Tito might modify his demands, and he informed him that he had ordered the withdrawal of the British military mission to Mihailović. "The problem," wrote Llewellyn Woodward, "was how to get rid of General Mihailovic without giving Marshal Tito, indirectly, a complete victory in [the] civil war. [Churchill] had not made a solution of this problem easier by entering into direct correspondence with Marshal Tito, and thereby increasing his status." Woodward also described the Foreign Office's proposal for the King to return to the country, for Tito to be appointed premier, and for other anti-German elements, both in exile and within the country, to be co-opted to his council. Tito replied on March 27 that his National Council would not permit the King's return.

After this uncompromising reply from Tito, Eden wrote to Churchill that King Peter should now try to raise himself above the internal dissensions of his country "by making a suitable public declaration to the effect that his only desire is to unite his people in the face of the invader, and that all internal political issues should be postponed until after the enemy has been driven from the country." This was the advice I myself gave the King at all my audiences with him. "You must raise youself above everyone," I told him. "Say that you will submit to the will of the people on whether you will be their king or not, but demand firm guarantees from Churchill and Roosevelt that the people will be able to express their will freely. They are certain to vote for you. Your reputation will be enhanced, as will the reputation of the government formed on this program."

Eden's proposal was eight months late. We could have had this sort of government if Churchill had not permitted the King to form a civil-service government, and if Eden had not welcomed Purić with open arms.

During the three months that Churchill and Eden were haggling with Tito for the King's recognition, the Purić government was in a vacuum. In a memorandum to the State Department on the Yugoslav crisis, Carl F. Norden pointed out that some of our people were proposing a government "on a truly national basis," that is, including people from within Yugoslavia. "This would be difficult to bring about," he wrote, "but it would have the great advantage of placing Tito in a defensive position where he would have to show his colors, and would give the Government a chance to take the political initiative from him." My colleagues and I had worked unceasingly for a government composed of politicians prepared to accept a program similar to the one laid down by Eden.

Purić was apprehensive; but I was surprised at Fotić. I asked him why, when Roosevelt refused to see him any more, he had not warned the other members of the government of what he must have known was about to happen. He replied that he had still hoped the Americans would prevent Churchill from recognizing Tito as the only resistance leader in Yugoslavia. Because of this, he had even led Mihailović astray; at the end of February, Colonel Bailey informed Stevenson that "Michailovitch thinks he can play off the United States against the British and that he has been encouraged in this thought by Mr. Fotich in Washington."

Just after Christmas, 1943, I saw Nikolai V. Novikov, Soviet ambassador to Egypt and Yugoslavia. He received me courteously. In the course of our discussion on the Yugoslav government crisis, I noted that he spoke with considerable moderation about Mihailović. He told me that he personally had drafted the Soviet government's policy statement on Tito and Mihailović, issued on December 15. We did not know at the time that Stalin had considered Tito's Jajce resolutions "a stab in the back." We had heard that the Soviet government wished to send a military mission to Mihailović; that was an enigma to us.

Novikov was a representative of the Soviet Union's overt policy, and, in that capacity, he behaved correctly. When Stevenson asked him about the Soviet government's attitude toward King Peter, Novikov replied, "Its attitude is shown by the fact that I am accredited to him." In late December, I saw Beneš, who had stopped at Cairo on his way from Moscow. He told me that his talks with Stalin had led him to believe that Stalin was not against the King but was against the Purić government. He felt it was high time the King improved his standing with Stalin by dissolving the Purić government. Beneš had told Purić this and wanted to tell the King as well; but Purić made that impossible. Beneš also told me that Molotov had shown no reaction when he mentioned Purić's proposal for a Soviet-Yugoslav alliance. On December 20, United States Ambassador W. Averell Harriman informed Hull that "Stalin had told Beneš that he believed in a continuation of the Yugoslav federation. He was not averse to the king but did not like the present government. He was sympathetic with Tito . . . but was open minded and would not interfere in the natural development of internal politics with the present government."

Solod, the Soviet embassy counselor, who was frequently in our company, told us in January, 1944, that one part of their military mission to Yugoslavia would go to Mihailović and one part to Tito. The Soviet government was not going to grant Tito the recognition he requested.

I had another talk with Novikov on March 24. He was well informed about our problems, so our conversation proceeded smoothly. I told him that since August, my colleagues and I had been prepared to take the responsibility for removing Mihailović from the cabinet. He told me that before his departure for London, Stevenson had spoken of my colleagues as possible members of a new government. But he went on to say, "We don't meddle in government reshuffles. The important thing for us is the situation inside the country."

"But the tragic muddle here has to be cleared up," I said. "A lot of people around Mihailović are counting on a falling-out between the Soviet Union and Britain. It's a matter of the greatest urgency to get a reconciliation government formed."

He was skeptical. "We have faith in your good will and good intentions, but you are not the government," he said.

"And if we were?"

"If a government were formed here that would recognize Tito as the champion of resistance, that would be fine; but I do not believe this will happen." He repeated for the third time that circumstances would compel the Western Allies to recognize Tito. I promised I would talk with my colleagues and let him know.

Later, when I went over this conversation in my mind, I realized that Novikov must have been instructed to persuade me to side with Tito. When he saw that he was not going to succeed, he came out with his proposal for a government that would recognize Tito.

I had dinner that evening with the people I had suggested as members of the new government, and I told them what Novikov had proposed. They all refused to go along with it. Two days later, I told Novikov of their reactions. We did not see each other again. Two weeks later, Tito's first delegation passed through Cairo on its way to Moscow. The titular head of the delegation was Velimir Terzić, but the man really in charge was Milovan Djilas. Djilas and I conferred many hours on April 7–9 and threshed out the whole of our nation's tragedy. I stressed the need for reconciliation between the Partisans and the other resistance groups, but Djilas said this was not possible; the other groups should enter the ranks of the National Liberation army. He also said that from the Partisan point of view, the Purić government was "the most suitable." When I defended Maček, who had been the object of hostile Partisan criticism, Djilas exclaimed, "We may have to conduct negotiations over the King, but we do not have to include Maček and the rest in this." He acknowledged that the question of the recognition they were seeking would not be easy to settle, although I gathered it was of the greatest importance and urgency to them—in fact, I felt that the main purpose behind Djilas's visit to Stalin was to obtain that recognition. In *Conversations with Stalin*, Djilas has related that at their first meeting, on June 5, Stalin said to Molotov, "Couldn't we somehow trick the English into recognizing Tito, who alone is fighting the Germans?"

My talks with Novikov and Djilas confirmed my presentiment that after the war Yugoslavia was going to be governed by a most extreme Communist regime. Needless to say, this greatly disturbed me. The civil war had fanned the flames of hatred into a conflagration; by now the vast majority of the population was firmly opposed to the Communists because of the huge sacrifices they demanded of the people. Novikov and Djilas were both demanding unconditional surrender from the entire Yugoslav nation. The Yugoslav Communists had planned to reach Trieste at all costs, which led me to believe that they were an important link in a vast Communist conspiracy to conquer Europe. To achieve this aim, the Communists were prepared to hurl the Yugoslav people into a fateful conflict with the Western world.

General Korneev, head of the Soviet military mission to Tito, escorted the delegation to Moscow. Some Czech officers I knew well in Cairo told me how scornfully Korneev had spoken of Tito's Partisans. He said they were not an army at all and were unable to carry out real military operations, and he disputed the British figures regarding the actual strength of the Partisans. We were astonished to hear this. I realized now that Stalin was playing a diabolical game, which the Yugoslav Partisans were incapable of understanding. Hamilton Fish Armstrong has written that "when Eden voiced disappointment over Mihailovich's recent role, Molotov reminded him that the Chetnik leader represented the majority of the Serbian population and could not be ignored." Stalin's game was to pressure Churchill over Yugoslavia in order to gain concessions from him on territories closer to the Soviet Union. Negotiations on this went on from the beginning of May until the end of June.

I said good-by to Stevenson on March 7, before his departure for London with the King and Purić. I told him that British policy was a complete mystery as far as the Yugoslavs were concerned, and I strongly advised that Mirković and Konstantinović be considered for senior posts in a new cabinet. On March 10, I sent him a message through his deputy, Philip Broad, saying that Konstantinović would make the best premier and Mirković the best armed forces minister. Like Mihailović, they were both Serbs, and it was more fitting that Mihailović be dismissed by a Serb than by a Croat like Ivan Šubašić, the former ban of Croatia, who was being considered for the premiership. When R. Joyce, OSS chief in Cairo, told me this, I could not believe that Šubašić would accept so unpleasant an assignment.

On March 5, I saw a letter from L. Tomašić, a Croatian deputy in the National Assembly, addressed to Krnjević and Šubašić: "Let us know whose sphere of interest we are in. If we are in the Russian, then we shall make some arrangements with the Partisans. . . . If we are in the British sphere, we can liquidate them. . . . If we get no reply, we shall make arrangements with the Germans . . . so that this terrible toll of life among our people doesn't go on." I realized, after reading this message, how much confusion there was in the minds of people at home, even the best among them, and how much fear there was of the unknown. That same day I had a talk with Miho Krek, who had stopped off on his way to Italy. He spoke with great sadness about the Partisan massacre of Slovenian youth, and told me of his party's decision following this tragedy: "We have followed your advice. We tried to come to terms with the Partisans, and we forbade our lads to attack them. Now we have lost the cream of our youth. . . . From now on we have to go our own way. An agreement with the Partisans is no longer possible." A member of the Djilas delegation, the sculptor Anton Augustinčić, told me that when the collapse came, there was going to be a lot of bloodshed. Because he could not bear to witness "score sheets being written in human blood," he said, he would try to stay in Moscow for at least a year after the end of the war.

At the beginning of April, I saw two of Mihailović's field commanders, Major Baćović and Major Lukačević, who had come out to attend King Peter's wedding. They still believed Mihailović would defeat the Partisans, in spite of the help being given them by the British. Mihailović had hidden caches of 150,000 rifles, and he would use them when the time came for a national uprising. They believed that there was going to be a landing of British troops in Yugoslavia, and when that happened, they said, 70 per cent of the Partisans would desert Tito, because at least that number still favored the King.

Baćović was insistent on the need for measures to prevent new massacres between Serbs and Croats. He said there would be two hundred Fočas (the town of Foča had become synonymous with massacre after the slaughter of Moslems there) unless there were agreements between Mihailović and the Croatian Peasant party, between the Chetniks and the Croatian Domobrans. He said, "We shall have to send the refugees from Bosnia and Herzegovina and from Croatia northward through Serbia, because they are seething with revenge." He spoke of his close ties with many Croatian army officers and offered to put me in touch with the Croatian chiefs of staff in Sarajevo and Mostar. He could do this, he said, through the Yugoslav military headquarters in Cairo, which, unknown to the British, was keeping in touch with Mihailović. I could not accept his offer, both because British policy had turned against the Chetniks and because I was not prepared to issue instructions to officers in Croatia without the sanction of the Croatian Peasant party.

In the House of Commons, on April 6, Eden said that the British government would welcome co-operation between the Croatian Peasant party and "the liberation forces under Marshal Tito." However, he made it clear that the British regarded this as "necessarily a matter for the two parties to arrange between themselves." Perhaps this was the British reply to Tomašić's questions.

On April 14, I asked MacVeagh how the Croatian Peasant party could co-operate with the Partisans when the Partisan leadership had launched a smear campaign against Maček, whom the Ustashi were holding under house arrest. He replied that "the British are looking after your affairs. Churchill has invited the King and Purić to London. There may be prospects for some sort of solution. . . . We are also aware that the best way to stop the civil war would be with American troops," he continued, "but where are these troops? In Italy, as you can see, we're bogged down. What American is going to approve of sending troops to Yugoslavia because of a civil war?"

"They would be going for purely military reasons," I said. "Helping to stop the civil war would be incidental."

"We need our troops," said MacVeagh, "for the second front, for Burma, for Italy, and elsewhere. Responsibilities cannot be accepted without force. Now that Churchill has some resources, we shall see the results."

He then asked the reasons for the long delay in settling the Yugoslav crisis. I said that, in my opinion, Churchill was trying to persuade Stalin to accept a settlement, but Stalin was holding back because he believed the tide was running in favor of "his man." He then told me that there had been a huge reaction against Tito in Serbia. "One has only to talk to a Serb to realize that. The trouble is, we have only been listening to Tito's and Mihailović's propagandists. . . . The Partisans have already Sovietized all the people in the camps." (He was referring to the refugees from Dalmatia who were brought to camps in Egypt because of the military operations in the areas where they lived.) "We can also see the Soviet finger in the Greek pie," he said, referring to a mutiny in the Greek army.

"Eden," I told him, "has now proposed that the Croatian Peasant party throw in its lot with Tito. But how can the party do that when Tito is demanding Maček's head? Maček is a martyr in the country, and his men in exile are excluded from the cabinet, while the British are backing the King, Mihailović, Purić, and Tito all at the same time. What can our people be expected to make of all this? The Partisans have told me that the Purić government has enabled them to double their ranks; so they want him to stay. . . . Why haven't the British backed the moderate people?"

"The King would then be without support from either Tito or Mihailović."

"But he would raise himself above everyone," I said. "And it wouldn't be easy for Tito to argue that he was associated with Mihailović."

He asked whether the King would lose his throne if he recognized Tito, because he would certainly lose Serbia.

"He need not," I replied. "His salvation could be to demand freedom for his people without being committed to one side or the other."

He accepted that.

After this meeting, I sent the following message to Šutej in London: "The politicians may be given a chance to form a government. The offer should be accepted immediately. Do not make any conditions. Summon me to London immediately, to inform you about some important talks."

But, for reasons of his own, Šutej gave diametrically opposed advice to Šubašić when the latter was appointed premier. Even King Peter forgot his promise to summon me to London for negotiations concerning a new government. In the meantime, I received another message from Tomašić. It was addressed to Šubašić, advising him "on no account to come to any agreement with the Partisans."

Early in 1944, Mihailović finally realized that the time for playing the fool was over. Late in January, as a countermove to Tito's Jajce congress of the previous November, he held a congress in the village of Ba. His intention was to provide his movement with a democratic program and to show it in a democratic light. In April, he sent a message to Maček expressing his willingness to co-operate with the Croatian Peasant party and the Croatian army. Maček told me after the war that he had favored negotiations with Mihailović, because he was "defending Serbian interests" in the same way that Maček was "defending Croatian interests," while Tito's interests were "the whole world." In June, Mihailović reported to Cairo that he had good contacts with the Croats in Maček's party.

The King arrived in London on March 9. On March 15, Eden requested the dismissal of the Purić government and of Mihailović as armed forces minister, and three days later, Churchill repeated the request. On March 20, King Peter and Princess Alexandra were married. At this point, Churchill and Roosevelt were experiencing difficulties with Stalin, who wanted a multilateral settlement in western Europe but a unilateral settlement in eastern Europe. Churchill tried to arrange a meeting with Roosevelt to discuss the problem; but instead of going to London himself, Roosevelt sent Under Secretary of State Edward Stettinius. The Soviet ambassador, Ivan Maisky, was brought into the talks, which concluded with an agreement that the Purić government had to be dismissed and a new government, acceptable to Tito, had to be formed. The pressure on the King continued for a fortnight after his wedding, with the Serbs in London exerting counterpressures. Every possible scheme was suggested: a new government under Simović; a committee of three, not a government, to conduct talks with Tito; direct talks between the King and Tito; and the King's appointment of Tito as armed forces minister.

Simović was Churchill's first choice, which explains why, on February 20, Simović called upon all Serbs to enter Tito's ranks. It was the King, not Tito, who rejected Simović. Churchill warned the King that unless Mihailović were replaced soon, he himself would publicly accuse Mihailović of collaboration with the Germans, and the King and his government would be treated in accordance with this. King Peter appealed to President Roosevelt for help: "In these times so difficult for my people, and me being fatherless, I address myself to you, Mr. President, as to a trusted friend, asking you to be good enough and send me, without delay, your advice and opinion." Stettinius informed Hull on April 21 that Mihailović would relinquish his ministerial post but was to remain chief of staff of the high command. The American liaison officers with Mihailović protested, and as a result of their influence, it was decided early in April to guarantee aid for Mihailović. However, this plan was squashed by Roosevelt, under pressure from Churchill. Donovan was busy behind the scenes trying to arrange for Šubašić, the man who had been saying for a year in New York that he would be able to "reconcile the King, Tito, Maček, and Draža," to be made premier. At the end of April, in response to Churchill's prompting, the King summoned Šubašić for consultation.

Šubašić arrived early in May. He was introduced to the King by Donovan, who said, "This man is the most faithful of Your Majesty's subjects in exile. My people have been watching him for over a year, and that is what they have established. He ought to be your premier." And Šubašić said to the King, "You and the government here are the important people. Tito and Mihailović are nothing." The King summoned the senior Yugoslav politicians to a joint meeting with Šubašić, over which he himself presided. On behalf of the Croatian Peasant party, Krnjević declared that he had complete confidence in Šubašić, that he would approve any measures taken by him in agreement with the King, and that there was no need for the King to summon him for further consultation. On May 12, John Winant informed Hull that the Foreign Office's view was that Šubašić did not want to be premier. On the same day, Roosevelt replied to King Peter's appeal, saying that it would be in the best interests of Yugoslavia to use Mihailović's "excellent talents in the field but relieve him of government responsibility." On the matter of the government reshuffle, Roosevelt said: "This is a question on which you will now have the wise counsel of Ban Subasic. I was pleased to learn of your decision to call him to London."

On May 9, Churchill informed Tito that Šubašić was to be appointed premier; on May 24, he told him that the King had "sacked Purić and Company." That same day, he stated in the House of Commons that Purić had resigned. By refusing to offer Tito large-scale aid, Churchill had induced him to agree to negotiate with the new government. In their negotiations with Šubašić and Stevenson, Jovanović and Grol demanded a promise of supplies for Mihailović as well, in return for which they would agree to Mihailović's dismissal from the post of armed forces minister. Their demand was rejected. None of the Serbs wanted the premiership, but they were all against Šubašić, and they would not enter his government. A deadlock ensued—the King refused to dismiss the Purić government, and Churchill would not accept this refusal. Finally, Churchill called on Donovan for assistance.

Donovan was staying at Claridge's, the same hotel where the King and Šubašić were staying. There he saw the King at 10:30 P.M. on May 31. He had telephoned Šubašić at 10:15, telling him to inform the King that he was coming down to his suite in about fifteen minutes. He said he wanted to see the King alone, because he had something very important to say to him. It was embarrassing for Šubašić to have to disturb the King, who had already begun preparing for bed.

After exchanging the initial courtesies with the King and Šubašić,

Donovan said to the King, "Tonight I am not General Donovan. I am President Roosevelt's plenipotentiary, and I say to you: a harsh war is in progress. We cannot allow anyone to upset the war effort. Yugoslavia must have a government. You have here the Ban of Croatia. He has got to be premier by noon tomorrow. If he is not, the consequences will be very serious." He got up to leave, saying, "Good night, Your Majesty."

At ten o'clock next morning, Šubašić was sworn in as premier. The old government learned about it an hour later from the priest who had administered the oath.

Šubašić was sworn in separately for each ministry. At the start, then, this was a government of one man in charge of fourteen ministries.

CHAPTER 17

O n the same day, the King broadcast a message to the country over the BBC. He stated that his new government would devote itself "to the high purpose of working with all those elements in our country who are actively resisting the enemy." He called for unity, condemned those collaborating with the enemy, and proposed that all political questions be deferred until the liberation, when the people would be free to declare their will. Afterward, he stated to newspapermen, "I believe Mihailović will agree. If he does not, then his value to the country is finished." This was interpreted as a condemnation of Mihailović.

Now the paramount task was to open negotiations with Tito. If Purić had been the worst possible choice to head a government of civil servants entrusted with mediating between Mihailović and Tito, Šubašić was the worst possible choice to conduct negotiations with Tito. Purić was reckless; Šubašić was the living embodiment of ingenuousness and vanity. Subject to sudden mood swings and deep depressions because of a severe diabetic condition, he was unsuited to conducting high-level political negotiations.

I knew Šubašić well over a long period of time. A good-hearted, pleasant man, he was politically superficial and occasionally devious. In 1941, Maček wanted to remove him from his position as ban of Croatia because he was making a mess of things, but the war intervened. He liked to mingle with political bigwigs and enjoyed the reflected glory, but he had no understanding of political or international problems. When Churchill introduced Maclean to him, he had no idea that he was Churchill's delegate to Tito. Before the war, he had been a messenger for Maček, running errands to King Alexander and Prince Paul. Now he had taken upon himself the role of mediator between King Peter and Tito; but in effect he was still a messenger—between Churchill and Tito. "Šubašić is all right when he's working under instructions," Maček once said to me, "but he is incapable of conducting anything political on his own."

Tito approved Šubašić's appointment because he knew the man he would be dealing with. He would have accepted Simović, too, because he was in a position to blackmail him over a telegram he had sent instructing Mihailović to liquidate him. Šubašić was also vulnerable—at the outbreak of the war, he had failed to release a group of Croatian Communist leaders from a camp near Zagreb, and they were murdered by the Ustashi in July, 1941. The main factor in Šubašić's favor was that, with the King, he, as ban of Croatia, represented the legitimacy of the old Yugoslav state.

Tito narrowly escaped being taken prisoner or killed in the German parachute attack on his headquarters at Drvar on May 25, 1944. He was pulled up by a rope to an exit that had not been sealed off by the Germans. After several days on the run in wild country, an Allied aircraft picked him up and took him to Bari. From there he was taken on a British destroyer to the island of Vis, which was controlled by the British. Šubašić was to go to Vis later, for talks with Tito.

Ten days before his appointment as premier, Šubašić was given a briefing by Churchill on the future program of his government. The main points were the formation of a government with a good Serbo-Croatian-Slovenian political balance; exclusion of Mihailović; recognition of Tito; and a start to the unification of resistance forces and all political elements in Yugoslavia. Churchill put special emphasis on Yugoslavia as a constitutional monarchy in which the King's constitutional position would not impede the development of democratic principles. Churchill informed Šubašić that the new government would be given material, moral, and political backing by Great Britain and the United States, and he expected the Soviet Union to follow suit. Churchill believed that during his period of weakness Tito would be more willing to come to terms with King Peter.

Tito was now practically in British hands, so Churchill wanted the King to go immediately to Vis with Šubašić and establish his headquarters. He told them they had a "godsent opportunity and one that could scarcely have been dreamt of a few weeks ago."

Because Šubašić wanted to get all the credit for reaching agreement with Tito, he did not form his government according to Churchill's plan. He did not even consult with his political leader, Krnjević, before leaving to negotiate with Tito. Tito had his executive committee and his Anti-Fascist Council behind him, and he fell back on them when there was anything he did not want to accept. Šubašić had no one to fall back on except the King, who was too young and still under Churchill's tutelage.

King Peter, Šubašić, and Stevenson left London for Malta in Churchill's private plane on June 10. Šubašić and Stevenson went on to Bari on June 12, leaving the King on Malta waiting for an invitation from Vis to come and meet Tito. In Bari, Šubašić saw Živko Topalović, leader of the Yugoslav Socialist party, who had joined Mihailović's movement.

Šubašić and Stevenson arrived at Vis on June 14. Tito misled them in conversation after the dinner in their honor. He said that Maček's deputy, A. Košutić, was expected shortly in the liberated territory and that he would reach complete understanding with him regarding the Croatian Peasant party, and that he disapproved of anti-Maček propaganda. Tito also told Stevenson that he did not exclude the possibility "of meeting a little later on with King Peter, provided that an agreement were reached with the Royal Yugoslav Government," and that he did not plan to introduce Communism in Yugoslavia. On the basis of these promises Stevenson encouraged Šubašić to make ready for concessions to Tito. Molotov sent a telegram to Šubašić the same evening promising Soviet *rapprochement* provided Šubašić "came to a satisfactory agreement with Marshal Tito." On June 15, Šubašić opened negotiations with the question of unification of the resistance forces. There was surely no need to wrangle over the constitutional question, he said, as long as both parties agreed to defer making a decision until after the liberation. He then raised the matter of co-operation with the resistance groups in Serbia. Tito sat surrounded by his chief associates, while Šubašić was alone, like a condemned man. Tito said that co-operation with the Chetniks was impossible, and that granting even provisional recognition to King Peter would be very difficult and would mean departing from the resolutions adopted at Jajce.

Šubašić returned to his villa completely thwarted. Stevenson persuaded him not to send a telegram to the King, but otherwise he seemed disinterested and spoke of returning to London. Šubašić, afraid that British policy toward Tito might change if the negotiations were broken off, decided to draft some concrete proposals overnight. The next day, there was a long discussion of these proposals. Tito's associates subtly hinted at the possibility of co-operating with the royal government at some time in the future, when the government might serve as the channel for large-scale aid. Then they might be more favorably inclined toward the King and more willing to shift the blame for earlier events onto the King's advisers. They submitted their counterproposals, and Šubašić accepted them promptly, with minor amendments. He recognized Tito as marshal, but Tito refused to recognize the King as commander in chief.

The Tito-Šubašić agreement was signed on June 17. The Šubašić government, to be composed of men not compromised in the fighting against the Partisans, was to issue a declaration recognizing the achievements of the Partisan war; recognizing Tito's forces and condemning those who collaborated with the enemy; and calling on the whole nation to support Tito's movement. Tito merely accepted the obligation not to raise the question of the legitimacy of the monarchy for the duration of the war, and to provide two members for Šubašić's cabinet, adherents of his movement but not representatives of it. He refused to meet the King. In a telegram to Stevenson on June 21, Eden expressed his strong dissatisfaction that "Tito should have avoided a meeting with the King" and that the Tito-Šubašić agreement did "not seem to make any provision for bringing about a union or at any rate some *modus vivendi* between the Partisan forces on the one hand and on the other [the] Serbs. . . . I feel that this matter is of such importance . . . that it ought to be cleared at once."

On June 25, when he returned to London, Šubašić gave Eden a long report on the agreement. His small cabinet was finally formed on July 6. Eden was displeased that Šubašić had failed to get a single Serb from Serbia to co-operate with him. The

Foreign Office lost no time in following up its contact with Tito in order to settle the questions of the organization of the Yugoslav army, the position of Mihailović's forces, the high command, and Tito's meeting with the King. A conference, to be attended by Tito and Šubašić, was arranged for July 12 at Caserta, general headquarters of General Wilson, supreme commander in the Mediterranean. The King was to fly to Caserta as soon as Tito consented to meet him. The Foreign Office also wanted talks to be held in Caserta with Mihailović's representatives in Italy, so that some *modus vivendi* could be worked out between the Partisans and Chetniks after Mihailović's removal from the cabinet. The British were hoping to send Topalović, General Janković, and General Glišić to Mihailović with an escort of British officers and orders for him to leave the country immediately. Eden was informed earlier about the dissensions in Mihailović's ranks and wished strongly to save those who were willing to fight the Germans.

On March 14, the Foreign Office received a report from Bailey which said: "There already exists within Mihailović's organisation a well crystallised nucleus of dissidence. The officers concerned realise that Mihailović's mistaken policy has cost them Allied support, and involved their country in an unnecessary civil war. They are in touch with British officers with Mihailović's forces to whom they have declared that they are prepared 1) to cease fighting Partisans and come to a territorial agreement with Tito; 2) to initiate anti-German activity forthwith; 3) to abstain from political activity." It was said also that prior to the withdrawal of British officers "dissident officers be unofficially encouraged to take the law into their own hands, remove Mihailović, his immediate staff and political advisers, and put the policy" outlined above "into immediate effect. All this should be carried out before the withdrawal of Bulgarian troops from Serbia because Mihailović could exploit that to reinforce his position in Serbia. . . . It was pressure from this group that compelled him in December 1943 to ask H. M. Government to mediate between him and Tito. . . . It must be emphasised that at the moment there is practically no chance of getting any Mihailović forces to accept Tito's command."

The Foreign Office was already in possession of a telegram from Stevenson of February 28 stating that the "opposition group at General Mihailović's H.Q. . . . holds that the solution for Serbia is a new leader to replace Mihailović." These reports were examined at a high-level Foreign Office meeting on March 14. "It was agreed that there is no chance of bringing hostilities between the Partisans and Mihailović to a close or of turning Mihailović's forces to our advantage so long as Mihailović retains control. . . ." Bailey maintained that Mihailović would probably refuse to obey the King's orders and would make his successor a virtual prisoner. "No possibility exists of either King or H. M. Government imposing a new C. in C. by force from outside. Possibility of utilising the dissident officers in Mihailović's forces to effect a change of leadership and policy on their own initiative was then examined."

Churchill ordered that information be obtained from the British officers at Mihailović's headquarters as to whether there was a dissident group capable of removing Mihailović and assuming control of his organization without disrupting it or impairing its efficiency, willing to institute immediate anti-Axis activity, and ready to cease hostilities against Partisan forces everywhere. "If dissidents succeed in removing Mihailović without bloodshed and he could subsequently be evacuated from the country, H. M. Government is prepared to offer him asylum and treatment appropriate to his status and past services to the Allied cause."

British officers in Yugoslavia answered on March 26 that dissidents were unable to overthrow Mihailović, and said that the King, as the cornerstone of the structure, should make the dismissal. Mihailović would not stage a revolt against the King.

Šubašić, Stevenson, and their entourage flew to an airfield near Naples on July 11. On the following day, Stevenson was informed that Tito refused to attend the conference because there was dissatisfaction in his ranks over the agreement with Šubašić. Tito apparently regarded it as "beneath his dignity to meet the Ban of Croatia." Tito said he would come to the conference later, to discuss military questions with Wilson, and that he would arrange a meeting with Šubašić through General Velebit. Wilson demanded that Tito come immediately, but to no avail. An exceedingly awkward situation had now arisen. Stevenson announced that the Foreign Office and Wilson were annoyed at Tito's conduct, and had decided "to let him stew in his own juice" for the time being. Šubašić defended Tito to Wilson and his political adviser, Harold Macmillan. "It is just a little cloud," he said; "it will pass." According to Macmillan, Šubašić said he would return to London to put pressure on the King and the "old Serb party," and then "perhaps pay a visit to Moscow and, with the blessing of Stalin and the merit of having made a pilgrimage to the Holy Places of Marxism, suggest another meeting with Tito. This . . . will ease Tito's position, who is clearly suspect by the extremists in his own party."

Šubašić met with Topalović, Janković, and Glišić on July 13. Topalović said that the people in Serbia loved the King and regarded Mihailović as his viceroy, but that it was not essential for Mihailović to be armed forces minister. The Domobran army in Croatia could play an important role, because they were not the Ustashi. "We are convinced," he said, "that the Domobrans are Croatia's national army, sharing the feelings of the Croatian people." Šubašić's reply was highly inappropriate. "In Croatia," he said, "the highest authority is the Croatian Peasant party, and all the peasants are behind Maček. So what you are saying is that you believe that the Croatian people ought to use the Domobran army and the Croatian Peasant party organizations to fight the Partisans, while you calmly look on, sparing your own people."

"Every day," replied Topalović, "we come closer to the Croatian people in our sentiments, because we see that the situation in Croatia is worse than anywhere else in Yugoslavia, and we want to help the Croatian people in a real spirit of brotherhood."

"But we have not settled the Partisan problem," said Šubašić. "What are your thoughts on this?"

"We are prepared to co-operate with Tito on condition that the King remains commander in chief."

"But are you prepared to sacrifice Mihailović as deputy commander in chief?"

"I think we are," replied Topalović.

Topalović proposed two operational armies, one in Serbia and one in Croatia, completely co-ordinated under the King's command. In order to prevent Serbian revenge after the war, no Serbian soldier would be allowed to go to Croatia. He was prepared to enter the Šubašić government, provided Tito recognized the King as the legitimate authority and as commander in chief, with the understanding that after the liberation the people would decide whether they wanted a monarchy or a republic.

On July 7, Tito had informed Šubašić that the removal of Mihailović from the cabinet was no solution in itself, for the question of the high command in Serbia depended on who was still fighting the occupier there and on the relative strengths of the fighting forces. He had also stated his opposition to Topalović's entry into the government.

In every respect, Šubašić acted as Tito's advocate. He submitted a memorandum to General Wilson requesting proclamation of Tito's military units as the only armed forces of Yugoslavia, and subordination, by royal decree, of all forces to Tito. Wilson replied that it would be difficult to transform Tito's forces into a regular army, and he proposed that they be recognized as a "military force separate from the regular army." He pointed out that one of the advantages of having resistance units separate from the regular army was that they could be joined by Chetniks and Croatian Domobrans who wanted to fight the Germans.

Šubašić brushed Wilson's suggestion aside, and in so doing, he missed the last opportunity to create a non-Communist resistance that might have prevented the rise of Tito's dictatorship. The proposal he rejected would have enabled the Croatian Domobrans to go over to the Allies and thus fulfill the age-old desire of the Croatian people to have their own independent army. Šubašić should have indulged in some brinkmanship with Tito on this matter when the British first made their dissatisfaction known. Tito himself feared that Šubašić might do this to make up for the humiliation he had suffered as a result of Tito's refusal to attend the Caserta conference, and he quickly sent Šubašić the people he had chosen for the cabinet.

The Russians knew Šubašić's weakness, and they played on it. Molotov invited Šubašić to Moscow, and he was desperately eager to go. He quite forgot that he had been brought into the government to defend the King, the democratic system, and the Western cause. When he told Stevenson that he wanted to visit Moscow, Eden asked him why. Šubašić was at a loss. "You can go to Moscow if you like," Eden told him, "but you'll be followed by an Anglo-American joint declaration that will make you change your tune." Like Purić before him, Šubašić thought all his difficulties could be solved if he made an agreement with Stalin.

Šubašić was very neglectful of the Americans, considering that they were the ones who had actually maneuvered him into the premiership. At the time, I defended him against charges of treachery and duplicity, but later I came to the conclusion that his actions had been plain chicanery. The Americans believed that Šubašić was going to work for a genuine compromise between the contentious camps in Yugoslavia, and that he would make it possible for other resistance fighters, apart from Tito's, to come to the fore and receive Allied aid. They never imagined that he would assent to a complete capitulation to Tito, thus consigning to oblivion all the other political elements and resistance forces in Yugoslavia. Earlier, he had said to the Americans, "The King has to be in the center, between Tito and Mihailović. The guerrilla forces have to be taken out of politics." On July 7, in a telegram to Robert Murphy, then an adviser attached to Wilson in Caserta, Hull said: "Available information indicates that the accord is not a compromise between Yugoslav political groups but essentially an arrangement between the British and Tito, representing an almost unconditional acceptance of the Partisan demands." He asked how the civil war would end if "open and unconditional support is given one faction." In American diplomatic documents of this period, there are repeated cautionary reminders that Chetniks not collaborating with the Germans were not to be attacked, and that arms were being given to Tito not to be used to settle old scores, but for use against the Germans.

But who was in a position to keep a check on this?

The idea of grouping the Balkan countries into separate spheres of action was broached for the first time by Eden to Molotov on October 25, 1943, after Molotov's refusal to accept the British plan for a confederation of those countries. When the Tito-Šubašić agreement was signed, Roosevelt had already agreed to Churchill's proposal that within three months Yugoslavia and Greece should come into the sphere of British war operations and Bulgaria and Rumania into the Russian sphere. However, Stalin wanted a fuller measure of agreement than Roosevelt's assent seemed to imply. He wanted a real, permanent partition of spheres of interest; and he continued to encourage Churchill in his plans for Yugoslavia and Greece in order to obtain his agreement to a partition scheme. Churchill was hoping that by indulging Tito, he might more easily obtain Stalin's assent for Yugoslavia to enter the British sphere of influence and Tito's acceptance of a British landing in Yugoslavia. After that, Churchill would be able to take the reins in his own hands and, to use Eden's word, "correct" what was wrong with Britain's short-term policy toward Yugoslavia. Dedijer has described how Randolph Churchill threatened the Partisans with this in the summer of 1944, saying that his father had made an agreement with Stalin, and "now we'll show you partisans a thing or two." The idea was a good one; but where were the troops for a landing in Yugoslavia to be found? All that could be considered were the ten divisions earmarked for the landing in southern France that had been decided on at Teheran. The Normandy landings had taken place on June 6, and with the breakthrough in northern France, the operation in the south was no longer necessary. Churchill and his commanders in Italy therefore decided that the ten divisions should be used to accelerate the defeat of the German army in Italy and then sent through Yugoslavia into the Danube valley toward Budapest and Vienna. The American chiefs of staff, however, still insisted that the landing in southern France should go ahead. On June 28, Churchill sent Roosevelt a telegram stating that a landing in southern France would bring with it "the complete ruin of all our great affairs in the Mediterranean. . . . Let us resolve not to wreck one great campaign for the sake of another," he concluded. "Both can be won."

Roosevelt's reply was negative. On July 1, Churchill sent him a final appeal: "We are deeply grieved by your telegram. . . . The splitting up of the campaign in the Mediterranean into two operations neither of which can do anything decisive, is, in my humble and respectful opinion, the first major strategic and political error for which we two have to be responsible." In conclusion, he said he was sending instructions to Wilson to dispatch troops to southern France, but, on the advice of his own chiefs of staff, he had to "enter a solemn protest." Roosevelt replied on July 2 that the orders could not be changed. It was a bitter blow to Churchill. Why was Roosevelt so stubborn in backing the views of his chiefs of staff? Harold Macmillan has interpreted it thus: "Apart from Roosevelt's desire, at that time, to please Stalin at almost any cost, nothing could overcome the almost pathological suspicions of British policy, especially in the Balkans." Admiral William D. Leahy, who was very close to Roosevelt, said that he "knew all the time that Roosevelt would be opposed to any diversion of force to the Balkans." And Wilson has written in his memoirs of the "consistent policy of the United States to avoid the Balkans as if it was a pest house" and of the "Balkan-phobia policy of the U.S.A." It is a pity that no one reminded Roosevelt at that time that Yugoslavia had not been considered a pesthouse by his government in the spring of 1941, when it had done its best to push Yugoslavia prematurely into the war. Lord Alanbrooke vented all his rage on the American strategy when he wrote: "History will never forgive them for bargaining equipment against strategy and for trying to blackmail us into agreeing with them by holding the pistol of withdrawing craft at our heads."

General Harold Alexander had worked out a plan for a landing in Yugoslavia and further advance up into Europe, and Harold Macmillan was assigned the task of securing American acceptance of this plan. Macmillan thought that General George C. Marshall would agree to it once he understood that a thrust through the Ljubljana Gap was really as much an Austrian operation as a Balkan one; and, indeed, Marshall "seemed relieved" when this was pointed out to him. Alexander asked Macmillan to present his plan to Churchill personally. He explained that he would be able to split the German forces in Italy in two, provided the divisions that had been earmarked for southern France were not taken away. Unless the Germans put up ten fresh divisions against him, nothing could stop him from reaching Vienna, and this would be the best possible contribution to an Allied victory in northern France. He concluded, Macmillan recalled, by saying that "here was an opportunity of inflicting such a defeat on the German Army as might have unpredictable results, and . . . such a chance must not be missed."

Impressed by Alexander's plan, Churchill refused to accept Roosevelt's decision to stay out of the Balkans. He thought it might be easier to change Roosevelt's mind if he could bring General Eisenhower, with whom he had a number of talks regarding the wisdom of the landing in southern France, around to his point of view. According to Harry C. Butcher, Churchill told Eisenhower that Alexander's army in Italy was being wasted; the men should be used as reinforcements for a thrust through the Ljubljana Gap into Austria. But Eisenhower only told him that if he wanted this operation for political reasons, he would have to deal with Roosevelt. With tears in his eyes, Churchill reportedly accused the Americans of "bullying" the British over matters of high strategy.

Šubašić made no progress in forming a coalition government with the Partisans or in settling any other questions, so Churchill decided to negotiate directly with Tito. The two met in Caserta on August 12. Also present for the conference were General Wilson and Ambassador Stevenson, as well as Šubašić and Savica Kosanović, one of his ministers. That morning, Tito saw Churchill alone. Churchill first talked about Allied war strategy, then questioned Tito about various Yugoslav problems. When the discussion turned to Yugoslavia's future, Tito was quick to assure Churchill that "he had no desire to introduce the Communist system into Yugoslavia. . . . I asked Tito if he would reaffirm his statement about Communism in public," Churchill wrote, "but he did not wish to do this as it might seem to have been forced on him." Earlier that day, Wilson had given Tito a memorandum informing him that the Allied armies would be establishing military governments in the areas occupied by them that had previously belonged to Italy; should they occupy Austria and Hungary, they would count on the co-operation of the Yugoslav authorities in securing the ports and the lines of communication with these two countries. Tito expressed his objections to this in a letter to Churchill, and they discussed the matter at a meeting on August 13, this time with Šubašić and Stevenson present. Churchill promised to help with arms as much as he could, but he warned that deliveries would be stopped if the arms were used in the civil war.

Tito and Šubašić had separate discussions on the question of a joint declaration. In further discussions with Churchill, Tito refused to countenance the idea that the Partisan movement did not have the support of the Serbs. "I did not press this point," Churchill wrote, "particularly as Tito had said that he was prepared later on to make a public statement about not introducing Communism into Yugoslavia after the war." Churchill had also requested an assurance that Tito would "not use the armed strength of the Movement to influence the free expression of the will of the people on the future régime of the country." He pointed out that "democracy had flowered in England under constitutional monarchy, and . . . Yugoslavia's international position would be stronger under a king than as a republic." Tito replied that the King's ties with Mihailović had been very damaging to him. He was willing to meet with the King, but not at this time.

The Yugoslav participants at the Caserta conference, accompanied by Stevenson, flew back to Vis on August 14. On the following day, they opened negotiations with representatives of Tito's National Committee. On August 17, Šubašić and Tito delivered to Churchill the promised public statement, in which Tito declared that his movement was not out to establish Communism, "as the enemy alleges." To mark the occasion of his agreement with Šubašić, Tito called upon his numerous adversaries in Yugoslavia to "join the National Liberation army." On his return to London, Šubašić dismissed Mihailović from his post as chief of staff of the high command. But Tito still would not assent to the formation of a coalition government.

Soon after his meeting with Tito, Churchill began to have doubts about the wisdom of having accepted Tito so warmly. Eden has described Churchill's second thoughts thus: "On August 31st Mr. Churchill, somewhat disenchanted by his meeting with Tito, sent me a minute remarking upon our responsibility for supplying Tito with arms with which he could subjugate Yugoslavia. In view of the minutes I had been sending him for many months, I commented to the Foreign Office that we hardly needed this reminder. The Prime Minister had indeed persistently championed Tito despite our warnings." Lord Moran has provided an excellent description of Churchill's mood at this time. In a diary entry from around the time when Churchill came to realize that Roosevelt was not going to assent to a landing in Yugoslavia, he wrote: "He is no longer in good heart about the general situation. . . . I tried to comfort him. . . . He burst out: 'Good God, can't you see that the Russians are spreading across Europe like a tide; they have invaded Poland, and there

is nothing to prevent them marching into Turkey and Greece!'
. . . The American landings in the south of France are the last
straw. He can see 'no earthly purpose' in them: 'Sheer folly,' he
calls them. He had fought tooth and nail, he said, to prevent
them. If only those ten divisions could have landed in the
Balkans . . . but the Americans would not listen to him: it was
settled, they said. . . . He has got it into his head that Alex
might be able to solve this problem by breaking into the
Balkans."

Churchill had pinned his last hopes on the offensive launched
against the Germans by General Alexander on August 26. He
told Roosevelt about it on August 28, expressing the hope that, if
Alexander succeeded, they might have another opportunity to
discuss the possibility of a thrust through Istria, a matter raised
by Roosevelt on his own initiative at Teheran. Alexander would
have succeeded if he had had only slightly stronger forces.
Churchill has commented lugubriously in his history of the war:
"The army which we had landed on the Riviera at such painful
cost to our operations in Italy arrived too late to help Eisenhower's first main struggle in the north, while Alexander's offensive failed, by the barest of margins, to achieve the success it
deserved and we so badly needed. Italy was not to be wholly free
for another eight months; the right-handed drive to Vienna was
denied to us; and, except in Greece, our military power to
influence the liberation of Southeastern Europe was gone."

The door was now wide open for a terrible and vindictive
Communist regime in Yugoslavia.

CHAPTER 18

The people of Yugoslavia were bewildered by the change in Churchill's policy toward Tito after the fall of Italy. As Tito's forces grew stronger, recruiting people by force and thrusting them into battle against the Germans, the Chetniks, and the Ustashi, the people grew increasingly anti-Communist.

The Germans carried out ruthless reprisals against the local population by burning down villages and rounding up men, women, and children and burning them alive. Protests against these atrocities were made even by the German minister and the Wehrmacht representative in Zagreb. In addition, units of a Cossack division, brought in by the Germans to help keep order, scoured the Croatian countryside with fire and the sword. Glaise-Horstenau urgently requested that they be withdrawn. The Partisans were requisitioning everything they could lay their hands on in villages that had been stripped almost bare by the Germans. All able-bodied people were forced either to join the Communists or to seek refuge in anti-Communist bands. A middle course was no longer possible.

After the Tito-Šubašić agreement, there was great apprehension among the political groups in Yugoslavia. The Slovenian leaders in exile sent a former minister, Franc Snoj, back to Slovenia to try to persuade the anti-Communist groups to work out a reconciliation with the Communists. At the beginning of August, Mihailović sent a letter to Maček, along with orders to be signed by the King, appointing certain Croats to specific posts in the Croatian army. Once these men were installed, he said, the Croatian army would co-operate with his army. Košutić was also exchanging letters with Tito's military headquarters in Croatia, which held out prospects for an agreement under favorable terms. M. Lorković, Pavelić's foreign minister, and A. Vokić, his armed forces minister, were trying to arrange for Pavelić's retirement and the establishment of a Croatian government consisting of Croatian Peasant party members and moderate adherents of Pavelić's movement, so that Croatia could go over to the Western Allies. Deakin told me that Tito had said that he no longer feared the Chetniks, because they were compromised, but that he did fear the Croatian Peasant party.

When King Michael of Rumania overthrew Ion Antonescu on August 23, 1944, and broke with Germany, excitement in Croatia reached a pitch. Vokić and Lorković were supposed to be making similar arrangements. Pavelić knew what was going on among his ministers, and presumably had given his consent; but when he realized what had happened to Antonescu, he called Kasche back from Germany, alleging that Glaise-Horstenau was behind the conspiracy. He made the same allegations to Himmler on August 29. After a cabinet meeting on August 30, Vokić and Lorković were arrested. Košutić managed to hide for a week before going to the Partisans. He met with Partisan delegates in Topusko and attempted to get them to agree to put Šubašić in charge of the Croatian army. His efforts failed, and despite a written guarantee of complete freedom from the Communist negotiators, Košutić was soon arrested.

There had been great turmoil in Mihailović's camp after his commanders Lukačević and Baćović came back from Cairo. Lukačević, backed by most of the other commanders, proposed that they start operations against the Germans. Mihailović thought the suggestion was premature. Throughout the summer, Lukačević kept away from Mihailović. The arrival, in early August, of an OSS mission at Mihailović's headquarters strengthened his position somewhat.

Meanwhile, Tito was hurrying along his plans for getting his troops into Serbia. The Foreign Office was annoyed with Maclean because, according to Llewellyn Woodward, he had apparently told Tito that the British wanted him to "extend the scope of his Movement in Serbia. . . . Mr. Eden telegraphed to Brigadier Maclean that our policy was not to help Marshal Tito to impose his Movement on Serbia, but to promote cooperation between him and the Serbs." Eden was even more direct in his memoirs: "Mr. Churchill and I were agreed that we must prevent the Partisans' major effort being directed against the Serbs, even if they be Mihailović Serbs." They were unable to prevent this, however, with the policy they were conducting, nor could they keep a check on the use of the weapons they supplied to Tito.

Entering Serbia was Tito's main objective after his abortive attempt to cross the Ibar in the early spring of 1944. At the beginning of September, his forces won a major victory in a three-pronged attack. Wherever possible, the Partisans avoided direct confrontations with the Germans, striking only at their internal enemies. The anti-Communist forces in Serbia, with weak German reinforcements, fought shoulder to shoulder against Tito's drive, but they were unable to stem his advance. Well equipped with Allied arms, the Partisans were now driving forward to make contact with the Soviet forces that had fought their way through Rumania and Bulgaria to the frontiers of Serbia. Mihailović ordered a general mobilization. There was a good response, but it was to no purpose because he had no arms; the Germans preferred to blow up their ammunition dumps rather than hand them over to Mihailović. King Peter's BBC broadcast of September 12, calling on all Serbs, Croats, and Slovenes to "join the National Liberation army under the leadership of Marshal Tito," did not help at all. As a result of the broadcast, Mihailović's units lost as much as half their strength in some areas. Tito thanked the King for the speech, assuring him that he would never forget it because of its assuaging effect on the civil war.

On August 31, Šubašić wrote to Tito, asking for his co-operation in setting up a coalition government. Tito sent a negative reply. Eden then wrote to Tito, urging him to support Šubašić's efforts. Tito again refused. The time was not yet ripe for a coalition government, he told Eden. His own National Committee had complete authority within the country and was capable of bringing the war of liberation to its conclusion. Grinding his teeth, Eden said to Šubašić, "We would not have abandoned Mihailović if we had known Tito was going to behave like this." Šubašić told Jančiković, the Croatian Peasant party representative, that he had been so upset by Eden's outburst that on leaving him he did not know where to go.

On September 19, Tito flew secretly to Marshal Tolbukhin's headquarters in Rumania, and from there to Moscow. The British were not informed of this trip. Tito's representatives, who, according to Molotov, were well aware that his destination was Moscow, said he had gone off to Serbia. This move so angered Churchill and Eden that Churchill called Tito "a snake in the grass."

In Moscow, Tito consented to the temporary entry of Soviet troops into Yugoslavia. Stalin obliged Tito with that formula in order to facilitate Tito's later insistence that the British should also ask his permission to enter Yugoslavia. But the political aspects of the Stalin-Tito talks were equally important. Stalin, concerned about the slow advance of his troops toward Berlin, and anxious for German troops to be drawn away from the Berlin sector, had been pressing Churchill to open a front in Yugoslavia. Now, in a cautious attempt to prepare Tito for this possibility, Stalin asked him what his attitude would be if the British were to land in Yugoslavia. When Tito objected even to the suggestion, Stalin became angry. In April, 1952, Tito told the French Socialist leader Guy Mollet that in late September, 1944, Stalin had strongly urged him, Tito, to accept King Peter's return to the throne, hinting that the British and Americans would land in Yugoslavia. In his biography of Tito, Dedijer has related that Stalin said to Tito, "You need not restore him forever. Take him back temporarily, and then you can slip a knife into his back at a suitable moment."

In the spirit of the tentative agreement reached at the end of June, Churchill and Roosevelt gave Stalin their backing with regard to Rumania and Bulgaria. When these two countries approached Britain and the United States for peace terms, they were referred to the Soviet Union. Now it remained to be seen whether Stalin would reciprocate by respecting British and American interests in Yugoslavia and Greece. Churchill proposed another Big Three meeting, but Roosevelt rejected it because of the presidential election. According to Lord Moran, Churchill felt that "the Red Army . . . would not stand still awaiting the result of the election. . . . 'I am going to Moscow,'" he declared.

Churchill felt, now that Allied troops were approaching the

German frontier, that the West was in a strong bargaining position vis à vis Stalin. He and Eden were warmly welcomed in Moscow on October 9. That evening, in a relaxed atmosphere, Churchill turned to Stalin and said, "Let us settle about our affairs in the Balkans. Your armies are in Rumania and Bulgaria. We have interests, missions, and agents there. Don't let us get at cross-purposes in small ways. So far as Britain and Russia are concerned, how would it do for you to have ninety per cent predominance in Rumania, for us to have ninety per cent of the say in Greece, and go fifty-fifty about Yugoslavia?" While the interpreter was translating for Stalin, Churchill jotted down the percentages, adding Hungary, which was to be fifty-fifty, and Bulgaria, which was to be 75 per cent for Russia and 25 per cent for Britain and the other Western countries. He handed Stalin the piece of paper. Stalin looked at it thoughtfully for a moment, then "took his blue pencil and made a large tick upon it, and passed it back to us. It was all settled in no more time than it takes to set down." Thus Churchill has described the scene. In a message to his colleagues in London, he explained that "the numerical symbol 50-50 is intended to be the foundation of joint action and an agreed policy between the two Powers now closely involved, so as to favour the creation of a united Yugoslavia after all elements there have been joined together to the utmost in driving out the Nazi invaders. It is intended to prevent, for instance, armed strife between Croats and Slovenes on the one side and powerful and numerous elements in Serbia on the other, and also to produce a joint and friendly policy towards Marshal Tito, while ensuring that weapons furnished to him are used against the common Nazi foe rather than for internal purposes." He concluded by saying that the agreement was "only an interim guide for the immediate war-time future, and will be surveyed by the Great Powers when they meet at the armistice or peace table to make a general settlement of Europe." This was done at Yalta in early February, 1945, when the principle of "joint responsibility" for eastern and southeastern Europe was adopted to replace the percentages system of influence. Churchill's hope that Tito's forces would not use Anglo-American arms against their internal adversaries remained wishful thinking.

It was agreed in Moscow that Bulgarian troops should be withdrawn from Yugoslavia and Greece, and that Tito and

Šubašić should be called upon to come to terms regarding a coalition government. Eden accused Tito of accepting generous aid in arms from the British and then hiding from them on Vis. There were long discussions concerning King Peter. At a British embassy dinner in Moscow on October 11, Stalin said that in Tito's view, the Croats and Slovenes would refuse to join any government under King Peter, and that in his own view King Peter was "ineffective." Eden, according to his own account of the evening, replied that the King was courageous and intelligent, and Churchill pointed out that the King was very young. " 'How old is he?' asked Stalin. 'Twenty-one,' I [Eden] answered. 'Twenty-one!' exclaimed Stalin with a burst of pride, 'Peter the Great was ruler of Russia at seventeen.' " Churchill told King Peter about the Moscow talks and reported that Stalin would prefer a monarchy in Yugoslavia to "a makeshift republic"; the King, however, would have to hold a plebiscite to allow the people to decide what kind of government they wanted. Churchill added, "When [the] time comes I shall see to it that [a] plebiscite is conducted under British, Russian, and American supervision," and he promised to conduct an election campaign on the King's behalf. In April, 1963, Colonel Robert McDowell informed me that, at their first meeting, he had told Mihailović that "the United States would take no part in military operations or occupations in southeastern Europe, but that the United States would participate with the other Allies in a guarantee of free elections in that region after an armistice."

Stalin had made a fervent plea to the Americans and British to remove five to six divisions from the Italian front for a landing in Yugoslavia and a drive into Hungary. Somewhere near Vienna, these troops were to join the Russian army, which was then in Rumania and poised to attack Budapest. Why did Stalin, who had for so long been opposed to an Allied landing in Yugoslavia, suddenly make this proposal to Churchill? Chester Wilmot has explained this change of heart as resulting from Stalin's fears that the German troops withdrawing from Greece might reinforce the German-Hungarian defense forces, and his fears of a halt to the Russian offensive on the Vistula. Wilmot has related that after the war Marshal Zhukov confessed that "when we reached Warsaw, we could not see how we could get beyond the Vistula unless the German forces on our front were considerably weakened." Stalin may have hoped that an Anglo-American drive toward Hungary would compel Hitler to withdraw several divisions from the Vistula to meet the threat. Stalin repeated his proposal to Ambassador Harriman on December 14. This time he spoke of a landing in Dalmatia and an advance to Zagreb, and from there a drive into Hungary and Austria. This time, his request was prompted by the slowdown of the Russian advance on Budapest.

When Stalin first proposed a landing in Yugoslavia, Churchill hoped to obtain Roosevelt's assent. Thus, on October 10, he appealed to Roosevelt to agree to a transfer of two, or preferably three, American divisions to Italy. Roosevelt refused.

I expected Šubašić to summon me from Cairo as soon as he had formed his government. We had been good friends for many years; we had become very close indeed during my stay in New York in 1942 and during his stay in London in 1943. But it was not until the middle of September that he finally sent me a message, through his assistant, Stojan Gavrilović, that I was to come to London immediately. Gavrilović told me in confidence that Šubašić intended to appoint me ambassador in Paris. Other sources said that I was to get the embassy in London.

I arrived in London on September 28 and saw Šubašić the following day. We greeted each other with the greatest cordiality. I did not wish to break with him before he answered two questions for me: why had he capitulated to Tito on every issue, and why had he not called me to London when he took over the premiership? The explanation he offered was no answer. I told him, in peasant idiom, that he had sold the freedom of Croatia for a pipeful of tobacco, the freedom that it had taken twenty years of harsh struggle to achieve. I asked him how he expected to establish a democratic system without even a single policeman under his control, while Tito was absolute master not only of his party's army, now recognized by Šubašić as the national army, but also of the state machinery and the secret police, OZNA, which had begun to operate on a large scale abroad as well as in Yugoslavia. I told Šubašić that he had handed the entire sovereignty of the Yugoslav state to some anonymous committee, and that he was erroneously leading many people in Yugoslavia to believe that if Tito came to power, he, Šubašić, would save them;

255

whereas, in truth, he would save no one, and vast numbers of people would lose their lives. All this stung Šubašić to the quick. (Later my words were proved entirely true, when Šubašić was powerless to save even his former *chef de cabinet*, Šipuš, from being killed in a most terrible fashion: he was fastened by a rope to the back of a cart and dragged by galloping horses until he was torn to pieces.) Finally, I asked him why he had waited nearly four months before calling me to London when he knew that I had a great deal of important information for him. He said he was unable to answer this question. I demanded an answer, threatening that I would have nothing to do with him unless I got one. He still refused. I then said, "I spurn your brotherly embrace, and from now on you are a stranger to me," and left immediately. He stayed there, deeply troubled. He told my friend Tomo Jančiković that he did not sleep for two nights after that.

I realized at once that Šubašić's government had a full-scale crisis on its hands. Churchill had made a speech in the House of Commons on September 28 in which he had made no reference to his meeting with Tito or Šubašić; whereas in all his earlier speeches he had praised Tito to the skies. Savica Kosanović, the senior minister in Šubašić's government, told me that this omission was disastrous for Šubašić as well as for Tito. He told me that the Americans had also lost confidence in Tito, and that Šubašić had deceived both King Peter and Churchill by giving them exaggeratedly optimistic reports about his talks with Tito on Vis. Kosanović wanted me to make peace with Šubašić, and he offered me the pick of any embassy I wanted. On the same day, Jančiković told me that there had been messages from people in Croatia asking us why we were having political dealings with Tito when everyone at home was solidly behind Maček and opposed to the Partisans. Tito waited until October 9, after Churchill and Eden had asked Stalin to apply some pressure, to invite Šubašić to participate in negotiations on a coalition government. Churchill saw the King before his departure for Moscow and promised to defend his cause as though it were his own. He also managed to persuade the King not to dismiss Šubašić until he returned from the talks with Stalin. After his return, Churchill said to the King that Šubašić "has sold out on pretty cheap terms to Tito."

I was very curious to know why the Americans had sent the OSS mission to Mihailović after the British had broken off relations with him. In mid-September, after making inquiries among my American and British friends, I learned a great secret: the German army in Serbia had made an offer to surrender to McDowell and Mihailović. We know now that, at the end of August, an offer was made by H. Neubacher, German minister for the Balkans, "whereby all German troops would withdraw in Balkans approximately up to Danube-Sava line without any interference on part of Allies in return for German promise to employ these troops against Russians." McDowell had replied that no offer aimed at dividing the Allies could be entertained. I learned further that Mihailović had been advised by certain American authorities to keep his forces strong at all costs and to withdraw to the northwest corner of Yugoslavia, where he would have the best chance of contacting the Allied forces fighting in Italy.

The Soviet Union declared war on Bulgaria on September 5, and concluded a peace on September 9. This led to a government of "Fatherland Front" and Communist party members. The Russian army crossed into Bulgaria when war was declared and, on entering Sofia, placed the Bulgarian army under its command; but Bulgarian troops in Greek Thrace and Yugoslav Macedonia were not withdrawn. Stalin wanted parts of these territories for Bulgaria. Churchill put a stop to that in Moscow. At one time, Hitler had expected the Russian advance to reach as far as Greece, and, expecting the British to react unfavorably to a Russian entry into Greece, he kept his troops there to prevent a British landing. Hitler was still maintaining that the British would prefer the Germans to the Russians in Greece, because they had not made any attacks on his troops there. But when the British started sea and air bombardments, and Russian troops entered Yugoslavia and joined some of Tito's forces on October 1, Hitler ordered the withdrawal of his armies from Greece, southern Albania, and southern Macedonia. In all, 350,000 German troops were withdrawn from Greece.

While these troops were retreating over the difficult terrain of the Yugoslav countryside, relations between Tito and Wilson became strained. Wilson was planning to have troops land in

Yugoslavia and set up their headquarters near Sarajevo, in Bosnia. When he proposed that the first small-scale landing serve as a preliminary to larger landings later, Tito delivered a tirade about the American mission attached to Mihailović. When Wilson submitted a proposal for a large-scale landing, Tito rejected it and put in a request for arms to equip 300,000 men. Wilson informed Churchill that Tito seemed to be employing "blackmail methods to hasten his recognition." Nevertheless, Wilson recommended to Churchill that "nothing should prevent the immediate introduction of British forces into Yugoslavia to ensure the isolation and destruction of the retreating Germans."

Tito's attitude toward the British and the Americans became apparent immediately after he installed himself in Belgrade on October 20, with the strong help of Russian troops. The British and Americans were told not to send any more troops to the islands or to Dalmatia. At the end of October, the Partisans refused to allow a British destroyer to enter Dubrovnik harbor. The captain asked permission to be allowed to open fire, but his superiors replied, "That is just what Tito wants." In November, three hundred commandos under Colonel MacAlpine were prevented from disembarking at Vis by Partisans standing on the quay with fixed bayonets. Churchill telegraphed to Wilson on November 20: "My confidence in Tito has been destroyed by his levanting from Vis in all the circumstances which attended his departure. We have agreed with the Russians to pursue a joint policy towards him and Yugoslavia fifty-fifty. There is nothing in this to prevent the landing of the British forces you mention."

In November, the German intelligence service arranged for a Montenegrin delegation to cross to Italy to try to persuade Anglo-American troops to land on the Dalmatian coast. Once they got to Italy, however, all the delegates were interned in a camp. The Germans deliberately evacuated several ports to entice the British to land there. A British landing, they hoped, might lead to clashes between the British and the Partisans, and ultimately to a British-Soviet conflict. In addition, the Germans made a truce with the Partisans in the Trieste area. A few months later, they tried to expand this arrangement into an agreement for joint resistance against attempts by the Western Allies to land anywhere in that area. It later became apparent that the German intention behind the secret negotiations held in Zurich in

March, 1945, between General Karl Wolff and Allen Dulles was to bring Anglo-American troops into conflict with Tito's forces, in the hope that this would lead to an Anglo-American conflict with Russia. It was being said in Berlin at that time: "A desperate military situation demands a desperate foreign policy. . . . We can ourselves decide who will occupy Europe after us." A little later, the threat was made in Berlin that with "one single stroke all British and American hopes" would be destroyed, and their conflict with Russia would "hold back Germany's collapse."

Soviet troops, supported by Bulgarian troops and local Partisans, captured Niš on October 15. Five days later, Soviet troops, supported by Partisans, captured Belgrade. Mihailović's commanders offered to co-operate with the Russians in the captured areas, but the Russians refused. Mihailović himself was in Bosnia with the American mission.

This mission was a thorn in Tito's side, and every possible obstacle was placed in the way of American officials in Belgrade. Tito protested to Churchill; his subordinates lodged a protest with Colonel Charles W. Thayer, head of the American mission to Tito. Thayer has related that Arso Jovanović, Tito's chief of general staff, demanded that McDowell be withdrawn "on the ground that he was giving the Chetniks political prestige they didn't deserve." The Partisans were afraid of any independent observer; three months later, they were even protracting negotiations over the UNRRA observers, at a time when they could get no other food supplies and the people in Dalmatia were dying in great numbers. Churchill exploded, and wrote to Eden on December 19: "I have come to the conclusion that in Tito we have nursed a viper."

Finally, in mid-November, McDowell was withdrawn. I talked with him in Washington two years later, in December, 1946. He told me how astonished he had been to find such understanding among Serbs, Moslems, and Croats. People had had enough of civil war, and were anti-Communist. "Your people in exile were proclaiming loudly the whole time that understanding among Serbs, Moslems, and Croats was impossible," he said; "and this led the Western Allies to support Tito, who maintained that he would establish that understanding. . . . If ever I'm asked, I shall tell our authorities never again to pay attention to *émigré* assertions. If only I had been able to get to Draža by June, the course of events in Yugoslavia would have been different. If Draža had come out with me, as I urged him to, and had had a talk with General Wilson, a lot of things would have been put right."

McDowell's report when he returned to Bari may have influenced Wilson's decision to revive the plan for a landing in Yugoslavia; but now there were new stumbling blocks: a shortage of landing craft, stagnation of the offensive in Italy, and Tito's opposition to a landing. In one of his better moods, Tito had asked Wilson to send him "some field artillery for operations in Montenegro." Wilson granted his request immediately. "Since the Partisans had no experience of handling the weapons," wrote John Ehrman in *Grand Strategy*, "a small British force, known as Floyd Force . . . landed at Dubrovnik on 28th October to operate under the orders of the local Partisan commander. For the first few weeks, all went well. Floyd Force carried out a successful operation against the Germans early in November, which earned the thanks of the Yugoslavs. But in the second half of the month, the atmosphere suddenly changed. The British artillery, which by then was operating inland, was ordered to withdraw at once to the neighbourhood of Dubrovnik, on the patently artificial excuse that the Germans were threatening to attack the town; and on the 25th, the Partisans stated . . . that no agreement had been signed authorizing the entry of British or American troops into Yugoslavia, 'such as has been signed between Yugoslavia and the Soviet High Command.' "

The British said to Tito, in effect: "You have neither the knowledge nor the capability to carry out conventional operations against the German army. Leave that to us!" But Tito rejected British offers of help. People with the Partisans have told me they would often point out German troops passing by, and the Partisans would reply, "Why attack them and make useless sacrifices?" Their main objective was to prevent the British from landing in Yugoslavia. Stalin's fears that the German army, in its retreat from Greece, would reinforce the German front against him in Hungary became a reality, and he entreated Churchill to land British troops in Yugoslavia.

German experts who have made a study of the German retreat through Yugoslavia are astonished that the British army did not land in Albania and Yugoslavia and destroy the German army, which had to move, for the most part, along two narrow, impassable roads. Some columns were fifty miles or more in length. The Germans, almost completely lacking in antiaircraft defense, were an ideal target for guerrilla attack backed up by conventional well-equipped ground and air forces. In the view of German experts, their army would have been demolished if a combined attack of this kind had been mounted.

CHAPTER 19

Stojan Pribićević told me late in 1944 that Communist leaders in Belgrade panicked when they heard that Soviet divisions were going to evacuate Serbia and move up the Danube to fight the Germans on the Hungarian front. They were wondering how they would be able, on their own, to drive out the Germans and take care of all of their internal adversaries as well. Russian and Bulgarian troops had taken the Vojvodina and parts of Croatia for them, but the task of liberating the rest of the country was now theirs alone. They ordered a general mobilization of all age groups. The first proper front was opened in the Srem, and here young, untrained, and ill-equipped troops were sent into the front ranks of the battle. In January, 1945, the well-armed German soldiers allowed the untrained Partisan army to advance up to their fortified positions on a line between Sremska Mitrovica and Fruška Gora. Then they raked them with machine-gun fire and attacked with armored cars, pushing the Partisan army a long way back. It is estimated that some sixty thousand young men, sixteen to twenty years of age, mainly from Serbia, were killed. Suddenly, the whole of Serbia was in mourning.

Mihailović sent a moving appeal to Wilson, begging for British troops. He refused Wilson's invitation to come to Italy, for this would have meant abandoning his men to their fate in order to save himself. But what was he to do? He has been blamed for ordering mobilization on September 6 and then taking so many unarmed men with him on his retreat. He still believed the Allies would land, bringing arms with which he could equip his men. Hence his call to his followers in Serbia and Montenegro to come

262

to Bosnia, from where they would go to Dalmatia to meet the Allies. Although a large proportion of his men in Montenegro wanted to withdraw into Albania and from there move into Greece, they finally obeyed his summons and came to Bosnia. They brought with them some thirty thousand noncombatants, including elderly and infirm people of both sexes, fleeing the vengeance of the Communists. At the head of the refugee column came the Orthodox bishop of Montenegro and a large number of priests.

On December 10, Mihailović sent a message to General Alexander, repeating his earlier proposal that he be put under Alexander's command. The assumption was still that British troops would be landing, and Mihailović wanted to be in the British army when that happened. He received no reply to any of his messages, but he never gave up hope.

The shortage of provisions and medical supplies was becoming more acute by the day. Typhus was decimating his people; the Partisans were ruthlessly pursuing them; they had to be on the alert day and night. Ill-clad and ill-shod, they trudged over the Bosnian mountains. At night, they would hear the shouting of orders: "Liquidation squad, forward march!" and they would crouch in terror, expecting to be butchered. Finally, Mihailović sent an agonized appeal to his former government colleagues abroad: "The Serbian people are at this moment suffering the greatest affliction in their history. The Partisans have instituted a ruthless terror, in which the best among the leaders of the community and the heads of old, established families are being indiscriminately killed. Concentration camps are being set up and filled with the flower of the Serbian people. In the hope of bare survival, people are fleeing to the mountains like animals. There they are exposed to cold and hunger. We entreat you to bring a delegation out of the country to inform the Allies of our tragic situation. Our appeal is urgent, for tomorrow may be too late. Help us to find a way out of this hell. If you do not, the curse of the people will haunt you and all those in exile who have done nothing to help us. If you are not in a position to secure help for us, then do all in your power to come and join us so that we may perish together."

In areas where Partisans and Chetniks were locked in mortal

combat, the scenes were unspeakably horrifying. An account of such a battle, fought in Dalmatia on December 3, 1944, concludes thus: "Sometimes they have no time to reload, so they use their rifles as clubs, beating the enemy over the head, on the body, anywhere. . . . And when the rifle no longer suits their purpose, they seize each other by the throat, biting and punching each other to death, finally lying with broken bones, still locked in their deadly embrace. There is no shouting, no screaming. All that can be heard is a hollow rattle in the throat, a strangled groan, the dull cracking of bones. Now and again, the sound of shooting, sporadic, infrequent. The five Savić brothers . . . all killed, side by side."

During these tragic days, Šubašić was in Belgrade negotiating with Tito over the formation of a coalition government. The agreement, signed on November 1, provided for the establishment of a democratic system in a federal Yugoslavia. A regency council was to represent the King until the electorate decided what form of government it wanted. The government was to consist of twenty-eight members, only six of whom were not Communists. After signing, Šubašić fulfilled his long-cherished ambition and went to Moscow. The King and Churchill were both displeased that Šubašić had not informed them of the trip beforehand and had sought Stalin's approval of the agreement before he had asked for theirs. Churchill asked Stalin not to approve the agreement, and, in front of the King, accused the Premier of treachery.

On returning to Belgrade from Moscow, Šubašić learned that trouble was awaiting him in London. With this in mind, on December 7, he and Tito signed a supplementary clause to the November 1 agreement, providing for elections to be held for a constituent assembly three months after the country was liberated, and guaranteeing full political rights for all who had not collaborated with the enemy.

During the time that Šubašić was in Belgrade, Tito's London delegate, Velebit, took him out hunting whenever he was free, so that he would see as few local people as possible. In spite of this, several people did get to see him, at the risk of their lives, and informed him that mass executions were taking place in and around Belgrade, by the slit-trenches that had been dug by the

Germans. The victims were being brought to the firing squads without trial or investigation. Instead of hastening back to London to inform Churchill, Šubašić wasted nearly three weeks going to Moscow, and then concealing the information upon his return to London. He extolled the Communist regime as the most democratic Yugoslavia had ever had, and among the most democratic in the world. That is what the wretched man actually wrote to the Foreign Office a few days after his return to London.

When I came back to London, I saw all my acquaintances—Yugoslav, British, American, and Czech—as well as King Peter. R. Bruce Lockhart informed me that, at the beginning of July, the Americans had blocked the proposal for a landing in Yugoslavia. On October 25, King Peter told me that before going to Moscow, Churchill had promised him that he would defend him to the last in his talks with Stalin, and that the premier of the coalition government, no matter who he was, would be a royal premier. The King had a great many complaints about Šubašić; he wanted to be rid of him at all costs, and he asked me to think about the best way of accomplishing this.

One of the most interesting talks I had in London was with Hamilton Fish Armstrong. Obviously annoyed with Šubašić, he emphasized that "he was not brought in just to capitulate to Tito." He was surprised that Šubašić had not formed a strong cabinet before starting negotiations. When he asked me about the mood in the country, I replied that in any free elections the voting would be as follows: in Croatia, 90 per cent of the votes would go to Maček; in Serbia, about 75 per cent would go to the King and the existing political parties; in Slovenia, about 70 per cent would go to the Christian Social party and other democratic parties; and in Macedonia, the Communists might get 50 per cent of the votes.

"So that means," he said, "that Tito may be imposed on the country by the Russian army with British arms."

"That is the position," I replied. "Tito must be made to declare that he accepts the will of the nation."

"Which means that an interim regime must be installed, so that all the political forces can make themselves felt as soon as possible."

Then he asked me about Šubašić's trip to Moscow.

"Šubašić," I said, "felt that his position with the British and Americans was weakening; that's why he went there."

"I see, trying to get backing from that quarter."

My talk with Armstrong convinced me that I had a good plan to submit to the King when he summoned me, as he had promised to do. The summons, however, never came.

My talks with the King and with Yugoslav politicians had made me realize that a crisis was bound to arise as soon as Šubašić returned to London; and I knew that our politicians were not capable of offering the King an alternative government. It occurred to me that it might be in the national interest if, when offering an alternative to Šubašić, we reminded our Western allies that they were considerably in debt to the Yugoslav people for the events of March 27, 1941. Thus I came to the conclusion that Mirković would make the best premier. He would provide stronger safeguards for the people's freedom than Šubašić, and if we put him forward, we would have the first resistance leader face to face with the second resistance leader. I felt that it would be as well for the cabinet to remain with the King, in case Mirković and Tito did not reach an accord over a revision of the Tito-Šubašić agreement. Mirković had to come to London and regularize his status, because he was still in the British army. I intended this to be my first advice to the King when he called me for consultation.

The King saw Šubašić when he returned from Moscow and Belgrade. He was not satisfied with Šubašić's report, and the crisis I had foreseen now began. On December 4, Stevenson told me that five army corps would be needed for Yugoslavia; if a smaller force were sent and became heavily involved, it would have to be either reinforced or withdrawn. The German experience had shown that guerrilla bands could not be destroyed without a large army. Stevenson attached particular importance to Stalin's pledge not to use Yugoslavia for his own ends. When I said that the political consequences were bound to be far-reaching, no matter where in Yugoslavia the British landed, he held out the prospect that British troops might land in Istria and go on to Zagreb. On December 18, Harvie-Watt told me that British troops would be going to Yugoslavia after all. On the following day, I was told by Harold Nicolson that the Big Three would meet in six to eight weeks and that one of their tasks would be to settle the Yugoslav question. D. H. Carr, then deputy editor of the *Times* of London, told me a few weeks later that this meeting was going to be held in the Crimea in early February.

I saw Douglas Howard on January 1, 1945. He had a number of objections to my plan. "It might provide an opening," he said, "for people in Yugoslavia who want to go their own way. . . . What would the King get out of that?"

"If the King is to give way on everything," I replied, "then he must firmly insist on guarantees of democratic rights and freedoms for the people. Otherwise even those who have supported him all along will now abandon him."

"That's true," he said. "But who are the people who could be sent to Yugoslavia?"

"Some of the party leaders," I said. "Those who have come to their senses."

"They've missed the boat," he said.

"There are others who are eligible—General Mirković, Izidor Cankar, Mihailo Konstantinović, and possibly myself, if that would do any good. Mirković has one good card to play with Tito—March 27."

Howard pricked up his ears.

"They could only accept responsibility," I continued, "if the Western powers gave them wholehearted support at the conference with the Russians. It's a terrible thing for Šubašić to have driven us into such a position. He was the worst possible choice. Why didn't you take Šumenković instead of Purić, and Konstantinović-Mirković instead of Šubašić?"

"The King wouldn't accept them," he said. "They were on our list; so were you. We were told you had been summoned, but you never turned up. Who blocked that?"

"It must have been Purić."

"We didn't know that. And we felt we hadn't a minute to lose—we had become so impatient as a result of past experience with your people never being able to agree about anything. The situation now would be laughable if it weren't so serious."

"The King's in a dilemma," I said. "If he doesn't sign, he stays in the frying pan; if he signs, he's in the fire."

"That seems to be the position," he said.

Once again I tried to explain the purpose behind the new government. The best solution would be for the British to take the whole of Yugoslavia "in trust."

"Greece," Howard said, "has shown us the meaning of that. Once bitten twice shy."

I asked him whether the King and Šubašić had seen Churchill yet.

"Churchill has seen the King twice," he replied. "The King promised to send him a memorandum by yesterday at the latest. He still hasn't received it. He'll be seeing Šubašić after he has studied the memorandum."

On December 29, I sent a long memorandum to Richard C. Patterson, the American ambassador to Yugoslavia, warning that acceptance of the Tito-Šubašić agreement might be tantamount to approving a Communist regime. Acceptance would also do great injustice to the hundreds of thousands of prisoners of war and inmates of camps, all of whom were now exiles from their country. These same thoughts actually found their way into President Roosevelt's message to Congress on January 6. And on December 5, Churchill had said in the House of Commons: "No government can have a sure foundation so long as there are private armies owing allegiance to a group, a party, or an ideology instead of to the State and the nation."

As I had received no summons to an audience with the King, I tried to think of another way to make my advice to him known. There was no alternative but to launch Mirković as candidate for premier. I chose the *Daily Herald,* organ of the British Labour party, for making his candidacy public. I knew the paper's diplomatic correspondent, W. N. Ewer, well. I saw him on January 9 and filled him in on the latest developments. Next day the *Daily Herald* published an article by Ewer stating that King Peter was about to summon Mirković from Cairo to become premier and open negotiations with Tito for a revision of the Tito-Šubašić agreement. The article created a sensation in Yugoslav circles. Šubašić declared that he was finished as premier.

The spirit of conciliation in Ewer's article was singled out for praise—the desire to see all the resistance groups in Yugoslavia united against the German army, and rights and freedoms for all Yugoslavia's national communities firmly guaranteed. In spite of all the trouble that the Communist revolt in Greece had been causing Churchill, he was nevertheless willing to earmark some British forces to help insure a happier political outcome in Yugoslavia. As soon as he had returned from his historic Christmas Day flight to Athens, he took the Yugoslav problem into his own hands.

In his memoranda to Churchill, the King referred to the "unconstitutionality of the proposed regency" and to the unacceptability of the "interim legislative power of AVNOJ" (the Anti-Fascist Council for the National Liberation of Yugoslavia). Churchill saw Šubašić on January 8, and the King on January 9. These meetings were also attended by Eden and Stevenson. When Eden remarked that the King had some justification for his grievances, Šubašić promised to try to get the base of AVNOJ broadened. After that, Churchill asked Šubašić a crucial question: "Would it help you politically if we were to send two divisions of our troops into Yugoslavia?" After consulting Tito, who had strong objections to the proposal, Šubašić turned down the offer. He explained the rejection thus: "I rejected it because I did not wish to fan the flames of civil war in Croatia between Croatian Domobrans and Tito's forces. I did not wish it to be said that, while one Croat had ordered the killing of Serbs, another Croat was handing Serbs over to the Communists in order to save the Croats. We must stick together and share what fortune brings." By rejecting Churchill's offer, Šubašić destroyed the last chance to save a large number of Croatian army troops and Serbian and Slovenian resistance fighters by bringing them over to the Allied side. Many, including Mihailović and the Croatian Domobrans, were desperately anxious for the British to begin operations anywhere in Yugoslavia, so that they could join them. But Tito had spurned Churchill's offer of two divisions and also asked for the withdrawal of Floyd Force, which was effected in mid-January.

In early January, Churchill obtained approval from the war cabinet to propose to King Peter that he accept the Tito-Šubašić agreement. "The three Great Powers will not lift a finger nor sacrifice one man to put any king back on the throne in Europe," he warned the King. If he signed, he would "retain his constitutional position," but if he did not, he would be "by-passed and left isolated and impotent." Patterson informed the State Department that whether Šubašić returned to Belgrade to continue as premier or resigned would depend on the manner in which the King expressed his rejection of the agreement.

On January 11, the King's chancellery issued a communiqué stating that the King accepted the general provisions of the Tito-Šubašić agreement, but not without reservations: "As constitutional monarch it is his sacred duty to see to it that the people are consulted and their freely expressed will given full respect. . . . His Majesty has raised two essential objections. . . . The first concerns the suggested form of the regency, and the second the provisions of article 2 of the amendment by which the Anti-Fascist Council for National Liberation would wield unrestricted legislative power until the Constituent Assembly had finished its work. This suggests transfer of power in Yugoslavia to a single political group."

Churchill informed Stalin the same day that King Peter had issued his declaration without consulting the British government or his own premier. The declaration could not be considered "an act of state," because it had been "delivered without advice from any Prime Minister." Churchill suggested that they "simply by-pass King Peter" and accept the Tito-Šubašić agreement as valid. He asked Stalin to hold off his decision until Roosevelt gave his opinion, and Stalin agreed to do so. On January 17, he informed Stalin that Šubašić was still pressing the King to discharge his constitutional duties. If he succeeded, Churchill said, "it [would] make matters easier for us and, I feel sure, for the Americans also." Churchill was very anxious for the Americans to adopt his position regarding the King and Tito. The following day, Churchill made a speech in the House of Commons. "It is a matter of days within which a decision must be reached," he said, "and if we were so unfortunate as not to be able to obtain the consent of King Peter, the matter would have, in fact, to go ahead, his assent being presumed." On January 20, the King wrote to Churchill that he did not feel it was just to make such a presumption. Although, as he had said before, he approved of the agreement in principle, his two earlier objections still held. Churchill instructed Stevenson to go directly to the King and tell him that if he did not sign immediately, the agreement would be brought into effect without him. The King refused to see Stevenson. He summoned the members of his government and read them his reply to a letter Šubašić had sent on January 20. He accused Šubašić of having acted without consulting him and of having brought him and the government into a "difficult and uncalled-for situation," and he said that Šubašić should never have requested Allied endorsement of the agreement before seeking the approval of his own king and government. That evening, he sent Šubašić a second letter, demanding his resignation by nine o'clock the following morning, and he informed the press of his move.

The King's dismissal of Šubašić was influenced in large part by persistent prodding from General Donovan. Donovan had been working for Šubašić's downfall since autumn, when he had realized that Šubašić had put himself completely in Tito's power. By January, Šubašić's actions seemed to him to be pure treason. When Churchill's pressure on the King was at its most intense, Donovan flew to London from the Far East to offer the King encouragement. "The sooner you dismiss that traitor, the better," he told him. I was told this by the King himself.

On January 23, Churchill told Stalin that the King had dismissed Šubašić without consulting the British government. He proposed that the Big Three begin putting the Tito-Šubašić agreement into effect, and in the meantime grant no recognition to any new government, whether appointed by the King or by Tito. He told Stalin that he had been in touch with the United States government, and he suggested that it might be a good idea for Stalin to "say a word to them" as well.

The King was unable to form another government to help him fight the Tito-Šubašić agreement and Churchill. He gave audiences to a number of politicians after Šubačić's dismissal. It was not until the crisis reached its climax that the cabinet, in agreement with Tito, offered to change the King's eleven million dinars into dollars at a favorable rate, which made it easier to obtain his assent to the agreement. It would have been better for his prestige if he had refused to sign, even though Churchill might then have carried out his threat that "if [the King] continued his obstruction, we should ask him to leave the country."

On January 29, the dispute between the King and Šubašić was smoothed over. After Šubašić tendered his resignation, the King entrusted him with the task of forming a new government. Šubašić agreed to try to get Tito to accept the King's two main objections to the agreement. Difficulties then arose over the candidates for the regency. Meanwhile, the Big Three had met at Yalta, and had adopted, along with the general Declaration on Liberated Europe, separate resolutions proposing that the Tito-Šubašić agreement be put into effect with additional provisions for broadening the base of AVNOJ, and that the acts of AVNOJ be submitted for approval to a constituent assembly. The King and the cabinet accepted the Yalta resolutions on February 12, and Tito accepted them on February 13. Šubašić went to Belgrade with his cabinet on February 15 to open negotiations with Tito for the appointment of the regents. Two days later, they were followed by Srdjan Budisavljević and Grol, who had agreed to accept posts in the first coalition government. The King instructed Šubašić to try to secure the appointment of Grol, Šutej, and D. Sernec as regents, and to see to it that as many political parties as possible were represented in the government. Šubašić promised the King that he would do so. Negotiations over the regents went on for more than two weeks. Finally, on March 3, the King, under British pressure, accepted Tito's candidates. The regency was formed and sworn in on March 5, and the coalition government on March 7. On its first day in office, the government issued a declaration promising full political freedom to the people. Then the Allied ambassadors were sent to Belgrade.

After the war, I was told by Dennis Healey, who had been on the planning staff of the supreme command in the Mediterranean, that he had worked on a plan for a landing in Yugoslavia in 1945. Churchill tried to get American assent to a landing in Yugoslavia both at the Malta conference and at Yalta, but he was unsuccessful both times. He still had hopes, however, that a quick German collapse in Italy would enable him to send troops to Vienna before the arrival of the Russians. On February 4, the day after his arrival in Yalta, Stalin suggested to Churchill during an informal visit that, since the Germans were unlikely to attack the British in Italy, it should be possible to "leave a few British divisions on the front and transfer the rest to Yugoslavia and Hungary and direct them against Vienna. Here they could join the Red Army and outflank the Germans who were south of the Alps." The last we were to hear of the possibility of a British landing in Yugoslavia was when Eden, on March 3, urged the King to accept the regency: "We shall assist you once we have made our landings—around Rijeka certainly, and probably also in Split." It occurred to me that Turkey, which had declared war on Germany on March 1, would be sending several divisions to the Italian front, so that Churchill would now be able to take a few of his divisions out of Italy and use them for a landing in Yugoslavia. Unfortunately, these hopes proved vain. According to General Alexander, in an interview published in the *Times* on September 29, 1945, the main obstacle to a landing in northern Yugoslavia was shortage of landing craft. They had been taken from him first for the Pacific in 1944, and then for the Rhine crossing in 1945.

Why did Stalin want Churchill to send forces through Yugoslavia to Hungary and Austria? First of all, he wanted relief on that front so that he would be able to make a rapid advance along the front leading to Berlin. Second, he wanted to provoke a dispute between Churchill and Tito; this would enable him to force Churchill to accept a definite demarcation of spheres in the Balkans and perhaps even a carving up of Yugoslavia itself. Stalin was well aware that Roosevelt's objective was to make all the liberated countries in eastern and southeastern Europe the joint responsibility of the Big Three. Although Stalin did not like this, he had assented to it at Yalta to appease Roosevelt, and it had been agreed that the ambassadors of the Big Three should form a commission to settle any differences arising in this area. But Stalin's heart was still set on a distribution of spheres of influence, whereby each partner would be absolute master of his own sphere.

CHAPTER 20

Some of the Yugoslav trade-union delegates who came to London in February, 1945, to attend the congress of the World Federation of Trade Unions told us of the wild enthusiasm throughout Serbia over the news that the King had dismissed Šubašić and was demanding freedom for the people. They spoke of the reign of terror at home and asked us to put them in touch with the Americans. This I was glad to do. They wanted the King to stand firm on the question of the regents, whatever the consequences. They were prepared to put up with even greater hardships, if only recognition could be withheld from Tito's terrorist regime. Most distressing to them was the wholesale mobilization, patricularly of young people, who had been sent off to fight the Croatian army; this created further antagonism in Croatia against the Serbs. They reported that the Partisans had said to them: "If what is happening in Belgrade makes you shudder, just wait and see what's in store for Croatia and Zagreb." Refugees from Croatia and Bosnia were asked for the names of people who had wronged them; they were promised that the score would be settled. The whole of Belgrade was in the grip of mortal terror. The police force was virtually liquidated. Grol, who had become vice-premier, remarked shortly after his return to Belgrade: "This is a slaughterhouse, not a state." Patterson reported to his government that Grol told him that "his [Grol's] influence is nil. Subasic is a prisoner in [the] Foreign Office and powerless. . . . Terrorism and executions are increasing. Belgrade is a fortress occupied by Tito's best troops while ill equipped boys are sent to the fronts." A few days later, Patterson reported, Grol said that "Communists are ruthlessly eliminating their op-

ponents; men who were with Mihailovich or gave him funds are
. . . being tried and executed." He added that Mihailović had
told his supporters "to keep out of politics since he cannot protect
them from reprisals."

In the autumn of 1944, a combined force of Dimitrije Ljotić's
anti-Communists and Chetniks from Dalmatia and the Lika had
been dispatched, with German assistance, to the front in Istria.
The greater part of Milan Nedić's forces had joined with Mihailović's and were in retreat through Bosnia, where they were
joined by anti-Communist forces from Montenegro and Herzegovina along with a large number of refugees. Some hundred
thousand people trudged through the snow in the worst of
winter. There was a shortage of food, medical supplies, and
clothing, and there was no shelter. Some of them retreated
northward under the protection of the Germans; others drove
themselves on as best they could. The Croatian Domobrans did
their best for these people, but the Ustashi forces attacked them.
The Chetniks retaliated, of course. Seeing the ring closing
around them from the south, the east, and the west, Pavelić and
his associates sought a way out of the morass into which they
were sinking. Early in November, 1944, they tried to contact the
Anglo-American command in Italy with a proposition to join a
bloc of anti-Communist fighting forces regardless of whether
they were Serbs, Montenegrins, or Slovenes. Several of Pavelić's
senior associates drew up a memorandum, which stated: "The
emergency . . . calls for some new military and political combination within the framework of the old Yugoslav idea. . . .
We would therefore recommend the formation of an anti-
Communist bloc based on some project for a federal reconstruction of Yugoslavia which would command the sympathy of the
Western Allies."

In mid-March, the bulk of Mihailović's forces was scattered
along the lower reaches of the Bosna River. General Alexander
Löhr, commander in chief of German troops in Yugoslavia, sent
a message to Mihailović stating that he was prepared to surrender
his army to the Allies and to proclaim the independence of
Austria. General Alexander rejected the offer. Mihailović was
bitterly disappointed, for he had hoped that acceptance would
also provide him with a life line. John Toland has given us a
different version of this episode. He maintains that Hitler him-

self sent an emissary to Mihailović, asking him to inform Alexander that "the Führer promised to withdraw all troops from the Balkans, provided that England and the United States agreed to start occupying the abandoned area in twenty-four hours; after the Balkans had been completely occupied by the West, Hitler would pull out of Hungary and Czechoslovakia." At the same time, SS General Karl Wolff was meeting with Allen Dulles in Switzerland, in an attempt to negotiate the surrender of the German army in Italy. Both moves were aimed at provoking a dispute among Britain, America, and Russia, in the hope of averting Germany's total defeat.

Mihailović was now faced with his last crucial decision: whether to remain in Bosnia or withdraw to the northwest, where the first units of the Anglo-American army would be arriving. Ljotić and the other anti-Communists already in Istria called upon him to join them. There were differences of opinion at Mihailović's headquarters over which direction to take. According to Dedijer, Tito's agents at Mihailović's headquarters urged him to return to Serbia. The Montenegrin and Herzegovinian Chetnik commanders, supported by a few Serbs and the commanders of the forces from eastern Bosnia, were in favor of continuing the withdrawal to the northwest. Mihailović himself favored remaining in Bosnia and returning to Serbia later. These two camps had almost reached the point of armed conflict when the Partisans suddenly launched an attack, sparing neither the wounded nor the sick. They had to keep moving to find hiding places from the vengeful Partisans on the one hand and the Ustashi on the other. Alone and abandoned, they endured unimaginable hardships and suffering. Emissaries were sent to Pavelić in an attempt to save twelve hundred wounded at the mouth of the Bosna and to obtain medical supplies for one thousand cases of typhus. The medical supplies were sent through the town of Slavonski Brod.

Sekula Drljević, a political leader who had been driven out of Montenegro in July, 1941, when he tried to proclaim its independence, was staying with Pavelić in Zagreb. Drljević, realizing how desperate the Montenegrins were, wanted to exploit their plight for his own political ends. He promised that he would obtain safe passage through Croatia for them if they would proclaim their military forces "the Montenegrin army," and him their political leader. An agreement was concluded on this basis. It was arranged that these forces should move out of Slavonski Brod, along the left bank of the Sava, in the direction of Zagreb. Although Mihailović had not approved of their decision, he bade farewell to the main body of the forces in an exceedingly moving ceremony. Mihailović rode on a white horse, escorted by two other riders. He said that he wished them well on their thorny path ahead, and that he was going to remain with the down-trodden people there. When he told them that he and they had been abandoned by their allies and by their king, his voice was choked with sobs. He saluted them, spurred his horse, and galloped back to his headquarters.

As the Partisans, in their advance behind the retreating German and Croatian armies, captured one town after another, one region after another, they started large-scale liquidation of their enemies. It is said that they murdered fourteen of the sixteen friars in a Franciscan monastery in Herzegovina. In Mostar, hundreds were massacred on the day the city was captured. In Travnik, eight hundred Domobrans were driven into a tunnel, which was then sealed up at both ends. And the infamous Ustashi criminal Max Luburić had sixty men and women hanged before evacuating Sarajevo. When the Partisans entered the town, an eyewitness told me, "the victims of the Ustashi were taken down from the gallows, and Communist victims took their place."

In the early spring, the Germans began pulling out of the Srem and Slavonia. They had been holding that front in order to protect the right flank of their army in Hungary and to cover the withdrawal of their army from Greece. The towns and villages of the area that fell into Communist hands suffered the same fate as those elsewhere. The lamentations could be heard on all sides. The Croatian Communist leader, Andrija Hebrang, went behind the front lines and into the Srem and lower Slavonia to investi-gate this heart-rending situation. When he saw the full horror, he made a vehement protest to Tito. T. Babić, an elder statesman of the Croatian Peasant party, who had represented the area for many years and was now a leading member of Tito's Anti-Fascist Council, fell on his knees before Tito and implored him to take these unfortunate people under his protection. Tito's political organizations were handing over to the execution squads people who were not Ustashi and had never done any harm to the Serbs.

Reputable members of the Croatian Peasant party were killed, because the Communists considered members of that party their most dangerous political opponents.

Reports of the Partisans' brutal treatment of the civilian population spread quickly, and there was a great exodus in front of the advancing Partisans. People loaded whatever they could onto their carts, took their cows along with them, and set out into the unknown, leaving behind them hearth and home. All the roads to Zagreb were choked with refugees. It has been estimated that at the end of April there were about half a million refugees outside the gates of Zagreb.

The country was racked by the malignant forces of diverse hatreds. Svetozar Vukmanović-Tempo's mother suffered unbearable anguish all through the war because she knew she was bound to lose one of her sons—either Tempo, the Communist, or his brother, a priest and a rabid anti-Communist. The brother was taken prisoner in Slovenia as he was fleeing the Communists, just before the end of the war. When asked what was to be done with him, Tempo is said to have replied, "Kill him!"

Just before the collapse, the most hardened of the Ustashi criminals set about exterminating their enemies in the prisons and concentration camps. They destroyed buildings as well as people; they set fire to railway cars filled with prisoners and left them burning. Max Luburić and his gang liquidated many thousands in this way. The men who had tried to get Croatia away from Nazi Germany—Lorković, Vokić, Tomašić, Farolfi, and several colonels in the Croatian army—were murdered by Luburić and his men. And in Stara Gradiška and Jasenovac, they murdered those who had left Mihailović and set out for Zagreb under Sekula Drljević's guarantee of safe passage. Major Djurišić had been leading these troops in the direction of Istria, where they hoped to form a strong anti-Communist front. Mihailović also had his eyes on Istria as a possible destination. Their plan was to set up a little Yugoslavia in Istria and the major part of Slovenia, where they could carry on an effective resistance against the Communists. Drljević and the Ustashi did not like this plan, so Pavelić sent Luburić to intercept the Djurišić forces. Reinforcements were brought in, and the battle began on April 2. After five days of fierce fighting, Djurišić's resistance was crushed, and he withdrew in the direction of Banja Luka with a few of his men. The bulk of his forces was taken to Stara Gradiška, where some were imprisoned and the rest were sent on to Zagreb. A few days later, Djurišić and his associates surrendered to Croatian Domobran officers. Subsequently, however—it has still not been satisfactorily explained how—they fell once more into Luburić's hands. He liquidated all of them, along with those jailed in Stara Gradiška—a total of some 150 officers and a few political people from Mihailović's movement. Among those killed was Dragiša Vasić, onetime chief political adviser to Mihailović.

Just before the collapse, Mihailović sent two Croats, Predavec and Parac, to Zagreb to make an agreement with Maček for political and military collaboration along the lines recommended by Colonel McDowell. By the time the two emissaries arrived in Zagreb, on April 16, they had fallen into the hands of the Ustashi. Thus, by April 22, they had had three meetings with Pavelić instead. Pavelić said he was the only authority in Croatia in the war against the Communists, and Mihailović should therefore conclude a military and political agreement with him. Predavec had no choice but to send this proposal to Mihailović. He signed his message "Predavec," which was a code to Mihailović that he was under duress. Mihailović never replied, and Pavelić finally permitted Predavec and Parac to leave for Ljubljana. Predavec was also permitted to leave a memorandum for Maček, asking if he would be willing to see emissaries from Mihailović. Maček refused, believing it to be an Ustashi trick.

The Croatian Domobrans and the Ustashi had become totally dependent on the German army. The Germans demanded the evacuation of all towns along the railway line in order to secure the passage of trains carrying the retreating German army. If this demand was not met, they warned, there would be no supplies. Pavelić accepted this with good grace. Croatian army officers received written orders, which they had to accept under pain of severe penalties, to remain with their commander in chief to the last in order to join the British troops. It was a time of great perplexity. I had been aware that this sort of situation was inevitable, and I also knew that the British army would hasten to occupy Trieste before the Partisans got there. I sent a message through A. Juretić, who was then in Switzerland, for the Croatian army to move toward Trieste. My message was passed on to Archbishop Stepinac, in Zagreb. I believed that the

Croatian army would be able, with Slovenian support, to hold on to at least their own territory, and that Mihailović would be able to hold out until the Allies finally intervened to put an end to the civil war. We in London had no idea that Serbian forces had already reached Istria. I expected the Croatian army to overthrow Pavelić and install Maček as Croatia's leader, but this did not happen. Only the Ustashi forces were properly equipped with arms and ammunition, and Pavelić refused to step down until the last moment. Anti-Communist feeling ran high in all parts of Yugoslavia, but there was no unity in the anti-Communist ranks. A U.S. State Department pamphlet referred to the Communist takeover in Yugoslavia as "a story of the weakness and disunity of many and of the strength and unity of a few."

Tito was well aware of Churchill's desire to land troops in the area that, at their first meeting, he had called the "German armpit." The British air force refrained from bombing the broad belt between Rijeka and Zagreb because the British would be crossing this territory and it was essential not to have important railway junctions destroyed. An extraordinarily interesting situation would have developed if in fact the British army had landed in that area. On its left flank would have been the Serbian and Slovenian anti-Communist forces; in the middle, Croats; on its right, Mihailović. The German army would have surrendered to the British immediately, leaving the entry to Austria wide open. Tito greatly feared such a situation; it was therefore in his interests to offer to help the Germans put up a stiff resistance to any British landing. In addition, an earlier agreement not to attack each other was still in effect between the Germans and the Partisans in the region. Tito now issued orders for his tanks and best units, armed and equipped by the British, to move posthaste in the direction of Trieste without engaging the Germans in battle. The objective was to get to Trieste before the British. Foreign Office experts had entertained great hopes that "anti-Partisan forces in northwest Yugoslavia might . . . prevent Tito's troops from entering . . . Trieste in advance of British" forces.

Hundreds of thousands of refugees from all parts of Croatia had swarmed into Zagreb in the last days of the Ustashi state, which had now dwindled to a very small territory. Day and night, the agents of Ustashi terror abducted young people and pressed them into the army, to create a buffer ahead of them in their retreat. Large numbers of refugees continued to retreat with the Croatian army. It was May 3 before Pavelić remembered Maček. He asked Archbishop Stepinac to urge Maček to see him. Maček agreed to do so, for fear that the Ustashi would murder him if he refused. The Archbishop also urged him to go abroad, where he would be able to carry on his struggle for the freedom of his people. "I shall remain in the country," the Archbishop told him, "and defend them here to the best of my ability. But you certainly ought to leave." Maček was unwilling to take such an important step without consulting his closest followers, whom he was now able to see for the first time in four years. He knew that the Ustashi took a dim view of the fact that two of his closest friends, Šubašić and Šutej, were in Tito's government. He was also being attacked by the Communists as a "traitor" and "enemy of the people." He thought it possible that they might murder him and put the blame for it on the Ustashi; or that the Ustashi might do the same thing, and blame the Communists.

The day after Stepinac saw Maček, Father Škrabec, of the Slovenian National Committee in Ljubljana, told Maček that a free Slovenia had been proclaimed as an integral part of federal Yugoslavia. The Slovenes wanted to know what the Croats intended to do. They believed that British troops would soon be in Slovenia, and Stepinac believed these troops would reach Zagreb before the Partisans. The Slovenes had asked the Serbian anti-Communist forces to come to Slovenia immediately. Hitler and Mussolini were both dead; the surrender of the German army was expected at any moment. Mihailović and the remnants of his forces, about thirty thousand strong, were making a drive through central and western Bosnia, moving in a semicircle in an attempt to reach the Srem and Serbia. The Partisans tracked their movements from the air. Mihailović's last radio contact with London had been on April 14.

Maček left Zagreb with his family and a few close friends on May 6. He made contact with the advance units of the Seventh American Army outside Salzburg on May 8, and was immediately taken under their protection. Shortly afterward, Pavelić and his government set out in the direction of Austria. On May 7, Löhr surrendered to him the command of the Croatian army. The last units of the Croatian army left Zagreb on May 8. Several Ustashi units followed. The first Partisan units entered Zagreb on May 9. Ill-clad and ill-shod, they marched into the city in single file. Very few people came out to the streets to greet them. It was a beautiful day—but gloom was in the hearts of the people of Zagreb.

The Domobrans were in a state of panic. The army and refugee columns were forced to make a slight detour to the west, because Partisans and Bulgarians, coming from the east, had taken Maribor. Ten trains had come into the Maribor station, each composed of sixty boxcars crammed with men, women, and children. The Partisans had stopped the trains and ejected the people, who numberèd approximately fifty thousand. The long army and refugee column tried to make for Dravograd instead, but the Partisans pounced on its left and right flanks. Because of the many civilians among them, the Croatian army troops were unable to engage in battle, so they attempted to negotiate with the Partisans. The Partisans protracted the talks, waiting for the arrival of reinforcements so that they could cut off the line of retreat in front of this enormous multitude. The Croatian troops finally broke through the Partisan cordon and crossed the Austrian frontier. Not very many of the refugees managed to follow them. Some fled to the hills and returned to Zagreb along various mountain tracks. Whole columns were captured and sent to neighboring centers to be sorted out. In Maribor, it was reported, mass executions, without trial or investigation, were in full swing by May 10.

On May 14, the bulk of the Croatian army reached Bleiburg, a few miles from the Yugoslav border on the Austrian side of the Drava basin. The entire plain was covered with troops and civilians erecting tents. Although they lacked many necessities, they were happy in the belief that they had escaped the lurking jaws of death. They took comfort in the fact that they had escaped under the protection of the British army.

There is no doubt that among this great multitude were people who had violated the laws of humanity and the rules of war. They should have been screened out and dealt with according to international law. Pavelić and his government cared nothing about the Croatian army or the civilians, whom they had taken with them only to convince the British that they enjoyed these people's support. As soon as he reached Austria, Pavelić changed into civilian clothes, had his bushy eyebrows clipped, and set out for the Alps. He destroyed all documents except the Argentinian passport, in the name of Ramirez, that he had procured for himself in Berlin in the summer of 1943.

The British army ostensibly conducted negotiations with delegates of the Croatian army. The last stage of the negotiations was attended by Partisan representatives, who demanded that the Croatian troops be returned to Yugoslavia. They promised that they would be treated in accordance with the provisions of the Geneva convention. The British demanded that they be disarmed first. This condition was met on May 15, backed up by a show of force, with guns bristling from tanks and warplanes droning overhead. Many refused to surrender and fled to the adjacent Alpine forests; some committed suicide. In addition to the Croats, some nine thousand Slovenian Domobrans, five thousand Montenegrin Chetniks, and three battalions of Ljotić's volunteers were also handed over by the British on the Bleiburg plain. Tito's people claim that about 120,000 Croatian Domobrans and civilians were handed over. Croatian sources put the figures higher, while the figure given by the British to the Americans was much lower.

It is said that scarcely 5 per cent of those handed over survived. Some managed to break away and return to Austria, where they told tales of the horrors they had experienced. A train of Ustashi children aged ten to twelve was stopped at Jesenice, the frontier post. The children were taken off the train and murdered. Even people who had never stirred far from their homes were not spared the terror by their new masters. The prisons of Zagreb were crammed full, and there was a concentration camp in the city itself. In some streets the cellars were packed with prisoners. For two months, there were nightly executions of people taken from these cellars, which were continually being filled with new victims. A number of outstanding university professors were liquidated. The possibilities for personal revenge during this period were unlimited. Even the members of the Soviet missions were shocked. "We too once committed senseless acts like these, killing off important specialists, only to regret it later," they warned. In the villages, screams of agony could be heard every night. The whole of Yugoslavia, sealed off from the world, was gripped by fear. A member of the French military mission, on a visit to London, said to me: "Moša Pijade told me that they had no lists of the people they had liquidated, so he was unable to say whether the man I was interested in had been killed or not."

My birthplace, in the triangle formed by Mount Vučjak and the confluence of the Bosna and Sava rivers, suffered tremendously. A contingent of Croatian troops and some Ustashi got trapped there and continued fighting after the war had ended. The Partisans attacked with a force of untrained youths from the Vojvodina and Serbia, and they met with disaster. Some were driven to the Sava and drowned. A truce was arranged, but it was broken by the Partisans, and the battle started up again. The Partisans finally overwhelmed the defenders, went in with their knives, and killed the entire male population over sixteen. The local militia, who had protected their towns and villages from Ustashi, Chetniks, and Partisans alike, were disarmed, and many of them were executed. The total number massacred has been estimated at five thousand. After a time, the survivors were unable even to weep; all their tears had dried up.

Mihailović's forces were cornered in the same defiles where Tito's forces had been caught in the German offensive of spring, 1943; and there they were decimated. The Drina and its tributaries were filled with the corpses of Mihailović's army. Mihailović himself, along with a few of his closest associates, managed to escape through the Partisan ring. He remained in hiding in eastern Bosnia and western Serbia until early March, 1946. He was being pursued with extreme caution because Tito wanted to capture him alive at all costs. The Communists wanted to stage a big trial to impress people at home and abroad. First they caught up with his most distinguished commander, Major Nikola Kalabić, who had led the "Royal Guard" contingent until the collapse. They duped him into sending Mihailović a message that British officers would be arriving at his headquarters to discuss plans for further action. Kalabić, accompanied by several members of the secret police dressed in British uniforms, arrived during the night at Mihailović's hide-out, located between Višegrad and Užice, and called to him to come out. He was seized the moment he stepped outside. Mihailović's two escorts and Kalabić were killed in the ensuing scuffle. The trial for Mihailović and his surviving associates lasted from June 10 until July 15, 1946. He concluded his defense with these words: "I believed I was on the right road. But a merciless fate swept me into this maelstrom.

. . . I wanted to do many things, I started many things; but the hurricane of the world blew, and I and my work were carried away." Mihailović was condemned to death and shot in the early hours of July 17, on Topčider Hill, overlooking Belgrade.

Bloodshed continued in Yugoslavia for a long time after the war ended. The secret police and the People's Courts worked overtime. People were sentenced for war crimes, for collaboration with the enemy, for "betrayal of the people," and, under various headings, for opposition to the Communists. They were sentenced to loss of status and confiscation of property. The whole system of the rule of law had broken down; the terror continued to rage. C. L. Sulzberger quoted Moša Pijade as having declared, "The altar lamp of the terror must never be extinguished. The people must have fear." The exact number of people who lost their lives during the collapse and in the months immediately following will never be known. The people of Yugoslavia had been able to endure the horrors of war because there was always the hope that an Allied victory would put an end to it all. But the victory came, and the horrors continued. For Yugoslavia, victory meant defeat, for the killings went on with no end in sight. A prominent Croat wrote to us at that time that "the people of Croatia have shed more tears in the last months and undergone more sorrows than they have done during the two hundred years of their existence." The tragic fate of the Yugoslav people pointed up the stark truth of the words of Clement Attlee: "Evil principles employed in the fight for power are not laid aside when victory is won."

Yugoslavia's allies were unable to change the ghastly situation. They protested against Tito's failure to implement the decisions of the Yalta conference. Eden asked Šubašić at the San Francisco conference why he did not bang the table with his fist in disapproval. Šubašić, Grol, and Šutej appealed to the Western powers in the hope that they might induce Stalin to try to persuade Tito to honor his agreement with Šubašić. The American chargé d'affaires in Belgrade, Harold Shantz, reported on July 7 to President Truman: "Šubašić expressed hope that Big Three will make a public reference to this and remind Yugoslav Government that [Tito-Šubašić] agreement must be carried out. . . . Stevenson and I believe such action desirable." But Roosevelt, the man with the greatest influence on Stalin, was dead, and

Churchill was out of power at the point when he was ready to do battle with Stalin over the implementation of the Declaration on Liberated Europe.

The British ambassador in Belgrade, Stevenson, was very optimistic that the Potsdam conference would result in considerable changes for the better in Yugoslavia. In the early stages of the conference, Churchill had had fierce altercations with Stalin over Tito's infringement of his agreement with Šubašić. Stalin had refused to discuss the matter unless Tito and Šubašić were present. Truman, who was in a hurry to return to the United States, would not invite them because he thought they would protract the conference. When the conference was resumed, after the British elections had brought Attlee and Ernest Bevin to power, Yugoslavia was simply wiped off the agenda. James F. Byrnes has given us this account: "The Soviet Union had placed on the table a second series of charges against Greece in obvious retaliation for a British paper directed against Yugoslavia. . . . Mr. Bevin pointed out that the agenda carried two papers against Greece and one against Yugoslavia. He proposed that all three be dropped. Stalin quickly replied 'Yes, welcome.' " Truman indicated that he was satisfied.

In a speech in Belgrade on August 7, Tito said that the monarchy was an "outmoded, tyrannical institution, incompatible with democracy." The former American ambassador in Moscow, Joseph Davies, visited King Peter the following day with an official message suggesting that he repudiate the Tito-Šubašić agreement and withdraw his mandate from the regents. He did so immediately.

The hopes of the Yugoslav people were then transferred to the forthcoming meeting of the Big Three foreign ministers in London. Shantz informed his government that Šubašić had acknowledged that "his policies had betrayed all Croatia." Grol, unable to endure the tyranny any longer, tendered his resignation to Tito on August 18. On September 27, Shantz reported to Washington: "A relatively small group of Communists, inspired and directed by Moscow, has succeeded in foisting a ruthless totalitarian police regime on the Yugoslavs. For this state of affairs we, and to a greater degree the British, are partially responsible. . . . We are convinced of our obligation to make our position clear to [the] world and to attempt to redress [the] harm we have done . . . in establishing Tito in power. . . . We owe it to ourselves and the Yugoslav people to state plainly that we do not consider conditions envisioned at Yalta and elsewhere to have been met."

To prevent Šubašić from meeting Maček in Paris, Tito refused him permission to attend the London conference in early September. On October 12, in response to pressure from the surviving members of the Croatian Peasant party, and in protest against the "terrible situation in [the] country and reign of terror that has been brought upon the people," Šubašić tendered his resignation. He was a bitterly disappointed man. When he settled in Zagreb as a private citizen, he is reported to have said to one of his relatives, "Tito's Yugoslavia is the last Yugoslavia." Just before his death, he wrote to Maček asking his forgiveness for all the evil he had brought upon the Croatian people. Yet, after leaving office, he had told his secretary that if Tito had asked him, he would have gladly gone to Moscow as ambassador. That was the man upon whom Churchill had rested his hopes for British influence in Yugoslavia.

On October 17, Byrnes reminded London and Moscow that, according to the Tito-Šubašić agreement, the coalition government must remain in power until the constitution had been voted on. Moscow refused to comply. On November 6, London and Washington sent identical notes to Tito, containing a mild reminder about the commitments he had made regarding democratic freedoms. Tito held the elections on November 11 with a single list of candidates, while the secret police and the Communist party organizations exerted extreme pressures to get as many people as possible to the polls. In accordance with the established Communist pattern, Tito received 99 per cent of the votes. The Constituent Assembly proclaimed Yugoslavia a republic on November 29. Patterson informed Washington on that day: "Our efforts to help create [a] democratic government in Yugo[slavia] broadly representative of the people have failed and we are of [the] opinion [that the] US should not recognize [the] new Government which is now being formed." Talks between London and Washington got under way immediately in an attempt to find a solution to this development.

While London and Washington were working on the problem, Stalin suggested that his plan for dividing southeastern Europe into spheres of influence might provide them with a means for dealing with Tito. The Yugoslav authorities seized a Moscow newspaper in late August because it contained the following brief comment on the Yugoslav situation: "Is it really fair to blame the Soviet government for the work of some Trotskyists in Yugoslavia?" Stalin's diplomats in Belgrade responded to their Western colleagues' complaints about the excesses of the regime with their own ominous comments. "These people are of no importance," they said. "What is important is your country and our country. They have to agree."

London and Washington agreed to accept the new state of affairs in order to make it possible for their ambassadors to remain in Belgrade. The decision was made public on December 25, while Byrnes and Bevin were in Moscow trying to establish contact with Molotov. In an article published in 1955, Professor Philip Mosely had this to say of the Moscow conference: "At the Moscow conference of Foreign Ministers, in December 1945, the United States received Soviet acquiescence in the substance of its claims to sole control over occupied Japan, and the Soviet Government gained the substance of American acquiescence in the policies which it was following in East Central Europe."

In special editions, Belgrade newspapers reported on May 2 the news that the Yugoslav troops had entered Trieste, Monfalcone, and Gorizia on May 1. On the same day, Churchill ordered the cessation of all aid to Tito. The relations between Great Britain and the United States and Tito became very tense. Alexander had assumed that he had Tito's verbal agreement to the occupation of that region by Anglo-American troops following his conferences with him in Belgrade on February 21 and 24. At the end of March, the Foreign Office decided not to grant to Tito additional arms, to prevent his troops from entering Trieste and Austria before the British. However, Alexander had already delivered forty tanks and 106 field guns. The Foreign Office comment was: "It seems fairly clear that in recent months F. M. Alexander has been pursuing a policy of generosity and consideration to Tito which is quite out of keeping with the Prime Minister's and our own present ideas."

The Trieste crisis produced some dramatic turns. Churchill was eager to eject Tito's troops from the Trieste-Gorizia region by force. President Truman wired Churchill on May 15: "Unless Tito's forces should attack, it is impossible for me to involve this country in another war." Stalin also withheld his support from Tito. As a result, an agreement on the division of the Trieste-Gorizia region into zones A and B was signed on June 9. Tito was allowed to station some of his troops in zone A only.

CHAPTER 21

F. W. Deakin, whose knowledge of the Yugoslav tragedy is firsthand, has told me more than once that Tito's uprising might have been crushed by the end of 1941 if there had been no Ustashi massacres of Serbs. Chetnik reprisals against innocent Croats, and the Communist uprising, brought further convulsions to the tragic situation; but there is no doubt that the bestial Ustashi massacres were the chief cause of the terrible events leading to the final catastrophe. The successive Yugoslav governments bear a large responsibility for the worst aspects of the outcome. George W. Rendel, with whom I have discussed this several times since the war, has said: "The Yugoslav government was greatly at fault for having lost its reputation in the eyes of the British as a result of its internal dissensions. The problems, it is true, were terrible. The government just didn't realize that, in the situation such as it was during the war, the problem of Serbia and Croatia was of secondary importance. In 1943 we were still not certain that we were going to win the war; we just knew we should not be beaten. Our own government made great mistakes—the unconditional support to Tito, for instance. Your government did not have sufficient prestige to be able, with support from certain official quarters in Britain, including my own, to prevent Churchill from rushing in with unconditional support for Tito." On the rift between the Serbs and the Croats after the news of the massacres reached London, he noted in his memoirs that "the Serbian and Croat members would hardly meet. I begged the Croat members to issue some clear and unequivocal statement condemning and repudiating the atrocities perpetrated by the Ustashi. But, with what seemed typically short-sighted obstinacy, they refused to be either wise or generous, and continued to flog the dead horse of Croat grievances. . . . By this time both parties had lost sight of the facts that the world war was at its crisis; that, whatever its issue, a totally new world was likely to emerge; and that these internal feuds and ancient griev-ances had now about as much relation to present reality as the disputes of archaeologists about Nineveh or Tyre." After describ-ing how he came to resign when his government changed its policy toward Mihailović, he wrote: "As for the unfortunate Yugoslav exiles, their ultimate fate, mainly through their own fault, was what was to be expected. Under American pressure, our schemes for an advance through the Balkans were abandoned. We were thus obliged to rely more and more on Tito to harass the German flank."

In an attempt to get news of Maček, who was in the care of Eisenhower's general headquarters, near Reims, I went to see Douglas Howard at the Foreign Office on June 27, 1945. I was very upset by the developments at home, and I told him that Yugoslavia would have fared better if she had declared war on Britain in 1941 rather than joining her. "If we had," I said, "it would have been the British, at least, who occupied us." He reminded me of the role our own politicians had played in bringing about the present situation: "It's your people who are to blame," he said. "They sickened everyone with their quarrels. . . . Our people here came to the conclusion that it would be no good sending the members of your government back to Yugo-slavia, because they would have only carried on their squabbling there. . . . If only three of them could have agreed just once on something!" There was nothing I could say in reply, because he was right. Sargent wrote, on March 23, 1943: "I still feel that in our own interests we shall sooner or later have to rid ourselves of this hopeless—and indeed dangerous because so hopeless—Yugo-slav Government."

The worst dereliction on the part of the government was the politicians' failure to grasp the thin lifeline provided by Eden's March 7 proposals for a reconciliation between Chetniks and Partisans. If they had been able to reach agreement with Eden on resistance in Yugoslavia, they would have found some way of averting the later disasters and final catastrophe, because Tito was still weak.

In *Grand Strategy,* John Ehrman has evaluated the British government's objectives regarding resistance in Europe: "The British Government—or rather the agent of the British Government in these matters, the Special Operations Executive (S.O.E.) —was always anxious to restrain the subversive movements in Europe from activities which would lead to their premature destruction. Their rôle, according to S.O.E., was rather to organize a common front, and secretly to build up a disciplined force whose operations could be connected at a later stage directly with those of the Allies. S.O.E.'s objects were thus always the same: to reconcile the racial or political groups on which resistance normally concentrated, and which were often hostile to each other, and to bring them effectively under the common authority of a British Command. The consequences for Yugoslavia were clearly stated in August, 1941 by the Minister then in charge of S.O.E., Dr. Hugh Dalton, in terms which held good for the Executive's policy over the next two years.

" 'The Yugoslavs [*i.e.,* the exiled Royal Yugoslav Government], the War Office and we are all agreed that the guerrilla and sabotage bands now active in Yugoslavia should show sufficient active resistance to cause constant embarrassment to the occupying forces, and prevent any reduction in their numbers. But they should keep their main organization underground and avoid any attempt at large scale risings or ambitious military operations, which could only result at present in severe repression and loss of our key men. They should now do all they can to prepare a widespread underground organization ready to strike hard later on, when we give the signal.'

"This was certainly not the policy of the Partisans."

The politicians' government collapsed when it most needed to close its ranks. In the early summer of 1943, the British chiefs of staff, under pressure from the Middle East command, proposed that "everything possible" be done "to promote a state of chaos and disruption in the satellite Balkan countries." R. Bruce Lockhart told me that he had been before the British chiefs of staff, who had asked him how "even the smallest forces resisting Germany in Europe could be stiffened." They had, in effect, revised Dalton's directive, and this was the factor that brought the British military authorities round to Tito's side from Mihailović's. But a firmly united Yugoslav government could have successfully defended the principle of continuing to abide by Dalton's directive on the grounds that there had already been too much bloodshed in Yugoslavia. If there had been no sympathy for this point of view from the British, then the Americans could have been approached for help. If that also failed, they could have threatened to resign, thus bringing their dispute with the Western Allies before a wider political forum and before public opinion. Mihailović, in consort with Croatian and Slovenian anti-Axis elements, could have advised the Yugoslav government that they would all be compelled to adopt a policy of collaboration with the German and Italian armies unless Tito ceased his attempts to carry out a Communist revolution. If Mihailović had done this, the government would have had a strong argument to present to the Allies. When the Greek government was confronted with a similar problem, the King threatened to abdicate and his government to resign. This produced the desired effect.

C. M. Woodhouse, chief of the British military mission to the Greek guerrillas, has strongly condemned the British decision in 1943 to step up guerrilla resistance in Greece and Yugoslavia. He believes that such activity should have been reduced, because by that time the Allies were certain of winning the war against Hitler. He admits that the resistance forces had made a valuable contribution while the Allies were still weak, but, as he wrote in his book *Apple of Discord,* "by August 1943 the Allies had passed to the offensive; numerical and material superiority made victory in the long run certain; the value of the guerrilla campaigns ceased to bear any proportion to the disasters which they brought upon the civil population, and the political troubles which they laid up for the future."

It must have been clear to the Great Serb faction in the cabinet that the dispute between Mihailović and the British government could not possibly end in victory for Mihailović, in either its military or its political aspect. Mihailović was tied up with representatives of an out-and-out Great Serb program, which was unacceptable to the British; this was another matter the Yugoslav government should have raised with them. A solution should have been sought that would have accommodated all of Yugo-slavia's political elements, including Tito's movement. In the autumn of 1944, Jančiković, who had been in Yugoslavia until the previous autumn, said to me, "Tito would have been content in the early summer of 1943 with two posts in the government; now he wants them all."

Mihailović was twelve months late in approaching Maček, twelve months late in consenting to be placed under the British Middle East command, and six months late in consenting to talks with Tito. Jovanović, Gavrilović, and Trifunović were twelve months late with their consent for British aid for Tito provided it was also given to Mihailović. Few nations in history have suf-fered such terrible consequences as a result of the various pro-crastinations of their political leaders. All of these shortcomings and procrastinations had their roots in our politicians' devious gambles and frustrated hopes. People in Yugoslavia and in the free world underestimated the Communist threat, even after the Communists had grown in strength following the fall of Italy.

Many of the errors and shortcomings of the Yugoslav govern-ment could have been corrected if Churchill had succeeded in implementing his plan for an Anglo-American landing in Yugo-slavia, rather than in the south of France, in late June, 1944. Harold Macmillan sees Churchill's failure here as having sparked off "the partition of Europe, and the tragic divisions which were destined to dominate all political and strategic thinking for a generation. . . . Through all these years I have looked back on this decision of June 1944 as one of the sad turning-points of history."

The American military expert Hanson W. Baldwin wrote in 1950 that the Pentagon admitted that it had made a great mis-take in rejecting the plan for a landing in southern Europe, and that "many of the great military figures of the war admit freely that the British were right and we were wrong." Philip Mosely has given us an excellent account of the tragic consequences of that mistake: "Between 1941 and 1947 American hopes for a democratic and liberal future for the one hundred million people of East Central Europe rose and fell. Hopes were high so long as American opinion failed to realize that in East Central Europe Soviet aims and American aspirations ran directly counter to each other. Here two separate wars were being waged, but Washington failed during the war to assure power positions from which it could achieve its hopes after the war. . . . By the end of 1946 . . . the American Government had a heap of broken Soviet promises to point to as a reminder that hope, divorced from power, is not a policy."

On May 8, the day of the armistice with Germany, Churchill wrote to King Peter: "I cannot conceal from Your Majesty that events so far have disappointed my best hopes and that there is much which is happening in Yugoslavia that I regret but am unable to prevent." And after the victory thanksgiving service at St. Paul's Cathedral, he told him personally, "I am sorry, deeply sorry." On another occasion, he said to King Peter, "I did not betray Your Majesty. I was betrayed."

It is said that at the San Francisco United Nations conference in the spring of 1945, Eden asked Šubašić: "When are you going to proclaim Yugoslavia a Russian province?" On June 5, Edvard Kardelj suggested to the Soviet ambassador, Ivan Sadchikov, that Moscow should consider Yugoslavia "one of the future Soviet republics." This was said to appease Stalin's anger at Tito's May 28 speech in Ljubljana, in which he had spoken out sharply against the policy of spheres of influence among the Big Three. He believed that Stalin's failure to back him when he was driven from Trieste by the British and Americans was the result of the Churchill-Stalin agreement of October 9, 1944. Tito, however, continued to serve as a most obedient tool of Soviet foreign policy. The social and economic system constructed by the Yugoslav Communists, including the army, the internal administration and secret police, the judiciary, and the educational system, was built entirely on the Soviet model. The whole of Yugoslavia's economy came under the oppressive thumb of the Soviet experts.

In August, 1946, American planes were fired on over Yugoslavia. The Greek rebellion broke out in September; British destroyers were damaged by mines in Corfu Channel; Archbishop Stepinac and some prominent Yugoslav political leaders were imprisoned. These events, as well as the United Nations Balkan Commission's findings against Yugoslavia as chief abettor of the rebellion in Greece, raised tension between the Western powers and Tito to a very high level. In 1947, Tito's regime decided that its citizens must break off all contacts with the Western world. Many were sentenced to long prison terms, which was meant to show that people could expect no help from the West.

Tito's ill-prepared and overambitious Five-Year Plan, modeled on Stalin's first Five-Year Plan, was launched in May, 1947. This was just what Stalin needed to settle Tito still more firmly in the Soviet embrace. In July, 1947, Stalin agreed to supply Tito with $135,000,000 worth of capital equipment for the first year of his Five-Year Plan. In 1948, Stalin asked Tito to send a member of the Politburo, possibly Djilas, to Moscow for discussions on Albania amd other current issues. Djilas was accompanied by the chief of staff, Koča Popović. They arrived in Moscow early in January, 1948. A month later, after preliminary talks with Stalin, Djilas and Popović were joined by Kardelj and Vladimir Bakarić. A Bulgarian delegation, led by Georgi Dimitrov, also arrived. In a meeting on February 10, Stalin demanded that a Yugoslav-Bulgarian federation be proclaimed immediately, and that the new state "annex" Albania. Tito's delegates rejected this, maintaining that a decision on such a proposal could be made only by the Central Committee of the Yugoslav Communist party, and the conference moved into stormy seas. Tito was quite right in suspecting that Stalin was trying to present him with a Trojan horse—and this at a time when relations between them on such issues as Greece, the control of the Yugoslav army, and the Yugoslav economy, were becoming increasingly strained. On March 1, 1948, the Central Committee of the Yugoslav Communist party rejected the proposal to join with Bulgaria.

From then on, Stalin began to step up his pressure in an attempt to curb Tito's disobedience. This led to an exchange of letters between Tito-Kardelj and Stalin-Molotov, and between the Central Committees of the two countries' Communist parties. Tito ignored a letter from the fraternal Communist parties announcing their agreement with the criticism made by the Soviet Communist party. He refused to attend the Cominform meeting in Bucharest, or to send delegates to it. Under the circumstances, Stalin had no choice but to carry out the threat implicit in his correspondence with Tito. The Cominform's excommunication and denunciation of Tito as a traitor was announced to the world on June 28, 1948.

According to Stalin, every Communist had to serve him "unreservedly, unhesitatingly, and unconditionally." Tito, by refusing to do this any longer, set the stage for the first conflict between two Communist states, thus showing that the Communist world is no more immune than the capitalist world from "inherent contradictions." Hamilton Fish Armstrong has related that Nikolai Bukharin told him in Paris in April, 1936, that national rivalry between Communist states was an impossibility. This basic Communist belief received a shattering blow with Tito's defiance of Stalin in 1948. The Soviet-Yugoslav dispute has continued, under Stalin's successors, up to the present day, and no one can predict with any degree of certainty what the final outcome will be.

In February, 1943, a long message from Stalin in reply to one of Tito's desperate appeals for help had ended thus: "You are doing a great thing which our Soviet land and all freedom-loving peoples will never forget." Who could have predicted that five years later this pledge would be rushed aside to make way for years of hostility between Yugoslavia and Soviet Communist parties? Who could have predicted that Djilas would write that to Stalin "will fall the glory of being the greatest criminal in history"? Djilas told me in Cairo in 1944 that Yugoslavia would have Russia as the great protector of her security in the future— and only five years later he was fulminating against Russia as the chief enemy of Yugoslavia's security.

Indeed, Djilas was destined, in his books *The New Class* and *The Unperfect Society,* to write a complete exposure of the enormity of the Marxist-Leninist-Stalinist system, giving the clearest evidence that human errors are, indeed, "the greatest curse on the human race."

BIBLIOGRAPHY

ARCHIVE AND MANUSCRIPT SOURCES

I Documenti diplomatici italiani, 1923–25 and 1939–43. Files of the Italian government.

Documents on British Foreign Policy, 1919–1939. Files of the British Foreign Office.

Documents on German Foreign Policy, 1918–1945. Files of the German Foreign Office.

Foreign Office Archives, Public Record Office, London.

Foreign Relations of the United States, 1941–45. Files of the United States Department of State.

Istorijski arhiv Komunističke partije Jugoslavije. Historical archives of the Communist party of Yugoslavia.

Jukić, Ilija. Diaries.

Mohorovičić, J. "The Origins of the Republic of Yugoslavia." Unpublished manuscript in family archives, New York.

Trials of the Major War Criminals Before the Nuremberg Military Tribunals.

Zbornik dokumenata i podataka o narodnooslobidilačkom ratu jugoslavenskih naroda. Collection of documents and facts about the Yugoslav National Liberation war.

GENERAL WORKS

Alexander, Harold. *Memoirs 1940–1945*. London, 1962.

Alfieri, Dino. *Dictators Face to Face*. Translated by David Moore. London and New York, 1954.

Andjelić, L. *Grad na Tari*. Titograd, 1966.

Anfuso, Filippo. *Roma-Berlino—Salo*. Milan, 1950.

Armstrong, Hamilton Fish. *Tito and Goliath*. London and New York, 1951.

Avakumović, I. *Mihailović prema nemačkim dokumentima.* London.
Badoglio, Pietro. *Italy in the Second World War.* London, 1948.
Bastianini, Giuseppe. *Nomini, cose, fatti* . . . Milan, 1953.
Boban, Ljubo. *Sporazum Cvetković-Maček.* Belgrade, 1965.
Borkenau, Franz. *European Communism.* London and New York, 1953.
Brugère, Raymond. *Veni, vidi, Vichy.* Paris, 1944.
Bryant, Arthur. *Triumph in the West.* London and Garden City, N.Y., 1959.
Butcher, Harry C. *My Three Years with Eisenhower.* London and New York, 1946.
Butler, J. R. M. *Grand Strategy.* Vol. 2. London, 1957.
Byrnes, James F. *Speaking Frankly.* London and New York, 1947.
The Četniks. Allied Force Headquarters, 1944.
Channon, Henry. *The Diaries of Sir Henry Channon.* London, 1967.
Churchill, Winston S. *The Second World War.* 6 vols. London and Boston, 1948–53. Vol. 1, *The Gathering Storm,* 1948. Vol. 2, *Their Finest Hour,* 1949. Vol. 3, *The Grand Alliance,* 1950. Vol. 4, *The Hinge of Fate,* 1950. Vol. 5, *Closing the Ring,* 1951. Vol. 6, *Triumph and Tragedy,* 1953.
Ciano, Galeazzo. *The Ciano Diaries, 1939–1943.* Edited by Hugh Wilson. New York, 1946.
———. *Ciano's Diplomatic Papers.* Edited by Malcolm Muggeridge. London, 1948.
———. *Ciano's Hidden Diary, 1937–1938.* New York, 1953.
———. *L'Europa verso la catastrofe.* Rome, 1948.
Clark, Mark. *Calculated Risk.* London, 1951; New York, 1950.
———. *From the Danube to the Yalu.* New York, 1954.
Clissold, Stephen. *Whirlwind.* London and New York, 1949.
Cowles, Virginia. *Winston Churchill.* London and New York, 1953.
Dalton, Hugh. *Fateful Years: Memoirs, 1931–1945.* London, 1957.
Deakin, F. W. *The Brutal Friendship.* London and New York, 1962.
———. *The Embattled Mountain.* London and New York, 1971.
Dedijer, Vladimir. *The Beloved Land.* London and New York, 1961.
———. *Dnevnik.* 4 vols. Belgrade, 1945–46.
———. *Izgubljena bitka J. V. Staljina.* Belgrade, 1969; (as *The Battle Stalin Lost*) New York, 1971.
———. *Josip Broz Tito.* Belgrade, 1953.
———. *Tito Speaks.* London, 1953; (as *Tito*) New York, 1953.
De Guingand, Francis. *Operation Victory.* London and New York, 1947.
Djilas, Milovan. *Conversations with Stalin.* New York, 1962.
———. *The New Class.* New York, 1957.
———. *The Unperfect Society: Beyond the New Class.* New York, 1969.
Donosti, Mario. *Mussolini e l'Europa.* Rome, 1945.
Dulles, Allen. *The Secret Surrender.* London, 1967; New York, 1966.

Eden, Anthony. *The Reckoning*. London and Boston, 1965.
Ehrman, John. *Grand Strategy*. Vols. 5 and 6. London, 1956.
Eisenhower, Dwight D. *Crusade in Europe*. London and Garden City, N.Y., 1948.
Falls, Cyril. *The Second World War*. London, 1948; New York, 1950.
Feis, Herbert. *Churchill-Roosevelt-Stalin*. London and Princeton, N.J., 1957.
Fotitch, Constantin. *The War We Lost*. New York, 1948.
Fricke, Gert. *Kroatien, 1941–1944*. Freiburg, 1972.
Fuller, J. F. C. *The Second World War*. London, 1948; New York, 1949.
Gafenco, Gregoire. *Derniers jours de l'Europe*. Geneva, 1947.
Grandi, Dino. *Dino Grandi raconta*. Rome, 1945.
Graziani, Rodolfo. *Ho difeso la patria*. Milan, 1947.
Harding, John. *Mediterranean Strategy, 1939–1945*. Cambridge, Eng., 1960.
Harvey, Oliver. *The Diplomatic Diaries of Oliver Harvey*. Edited by John Harvey. London, 1970.
Hassell, Ulrich von. *The Von Hassell Diaries, 1938–1944*. London, 1948; Garden City, N.Y., 1947.
Henderson, Nevile. *Water Under the Bridges*. London, 1945.
Hoptner, J. B. *Yugoslavia in Crisis, 1934–1941*. New York, 1962.
Howard, M. *The Mediterranean Strategy in the Second World War*. London, 1968.
Hull, Cordell. *Memoirs*. London and New York, 1948.
Jugoslawien. Cologne, 1954.
Kallay, Nicholas. *Hungarian Premier*. New York, 1954.
Karapandžić, B. *Gradjanski rat u Srbiji*. Munich, 1958.
Kennan, George F. *Memoirs, 1925–1950*. London and Boston, 1967.
Kennedy, John. *The Business of War*. London, 1957; New York, 1958.
Kimche, Jon. *Spying for Peace*. London and New York, 1961.
Kiszling, General R. *Die Kroaten*. Graz and Frankfurt, 1954.
Knatchbull-Hugessen, Hughe. *Diplomat in Peace and War*. London, 1949.
Knežević, Radoje, ed. *Knjiga o Draži*. 2 vols. Windsor, Ont., 1956.
Lawrence, Christie. *Irregular Adventure*. London and New York, 1947.
Leahy, William D. *I Was There*. London and New York, 1950.
Leverkuehn, Paul. *German Military Intelligence*. London and New York, 1954.
Maček, Vladko. *In the Struggle for Freedom*. Translated by Elizabeth and Stjepan Gazi. New York, 1957.
Maclean, Fitzroy. *Disputed Barricade*. London, 1957; (as *Heretic*) New York, 1957.
———. *Eastern Approaches*. London, 1950; (as *Escape to Adventure*) Boston, 1950.

Macmillan, Harold. *The Blast of War*. London and New York, 1967.

McNeill, William Hardy. *America, Britain and Russia: Their Co-operation and Conflict, 1941–1946*. London and New York, 1953.

Martinović, Bajica. *Milan Nedić*. Chicago, 1956.

Matloff, Maurice. *Strategic Planning for Coalition Warfare, 1943–1944*. Washington, D.C., 1959.

Mladenović, M. *Lažni idoli i varljivi ideali*. London, 1965.

Montgomery, J. H. *Hungary*. New York, 1946.

Moran, Lord (Sir Charles Wilson). *Churchill: The Struggle for Survival, 1940–1965*. London and Boston, 1966.

Murphy, Robert. *Diplomat Among Warriors*. Garden City, N.Y., 1964.

The National Liberation Movement of Yugoslavia. Middle East Headquarters, 1944.

Papagos, Alexander. *The German Attack on Greece*. London, 1946.

Peter II, King of Yugoslavia. *A King's Heritage*. London, 1955; New York, 1954.

Phillips, William. *Ventures in Diplomacy*. London, 1955; Boston, 1952.

Pijade, Moša. *La Fable de l'aide soviétique à l'insurrection yougoslave*. Paris, 1950; (as *About the Legend That the Yugoslav Uprising Owed Its Existence to Soviet Assistance*) London, 1950.

Plenča, Dušan. *Medjunarodni odnosi Jugoslavije u toku drugog svjetskog rata*. Belgrade, 1962.

Rendel, George W. *The Sword and the Olive*. London, 1957.

Ristić, Dragiša N. *Yugoslavia's Revolution of 1941*. University Park, Pa., 1966.

Roatta, Mario. *Otto milioni di baionette*. Milan, 1946.

Roberts, Walter R. *Tito, Mihailović and the Allies, 1941–1945*. New Brunswick, N.J., 1973.

Rootham, Jasper. *Miss Fire*. London, 1946.

Royal Institute of International Affairs. *The Soviet-Yugoslav Dispute*. London, 1950.

Schellenberg, Walter. *The Schellenberg Memoirs*. Translated by Louis Hagen. London, 1956; (as *The Labyrinth*) New York, 1956.

Schmidt, Paul. *Hitler's Interpreter*. London and New York, 1951.

Schmidt-Richberg, Erich. *Der Endkampf auf dem Balkan*. Heidelberg, 1955.

Sforza, Count Carlo. *L'Italia dal 1914 al 1944*. Milan, 1944.

Sherwood, Robert E. *The White House Papers of Harry L. Hopkins*. London, 1949; (as *Roosevelt and Hopkins*) New York, 1948.

Stakić, Vladimir. *Moji razgovori sa Musolinijem*. Munich, 1967.

Stalin, Joseph. *Stalin's Correspondence with Churchill, Attlee, Roosevelt and Truman, 1941–1945*. New York, 1958.

Starhemberg, Prince (Ernst Rüdiger). *Between Hitler and Mussolini*. London and New York, 1942.

Thayer, Charles W. *Hands Across the Caviar*. London, 1953; Philadelphia, 1952.

Tippelkirch, Kurt von. *Geschichte des zweiten Weltkrieges*. Bonn, 1959.

Thompson, George M. *Vote of Censure*. London and New York, 1968.

Toland, John. *The Last 100 Days*. London and New York, 1966.

Topalović, Živko. *Borba za budućnost Jugoslavije*. London, 1967.

Toscano, Mario. *Una mancata intesa italo-sovietica nel 1940 e 1941*. Florence, 1952.

————. *Le Origini del Patto d'Acciaio*. Florence, 1948.

————. *Pagine di storia contemporanea*. Edited by A. Guffre. Milan, 1963.

The Trial of Dragoljub-Draža Mihailović. Belgrade, 1946.

Ulam, Adam. *Titoism and the Cominform*. Cambridge, Mass., 1952.

United States Department of State. *Background, Yugoslavia: Titoism and U.S. Foreign Policy*. Washington, D.C., 1952.

Ustanak naroda Jugoslavije 1941. Belgrade.

Vrančić, Dr. Vjekoslav. *Hochverrat. Die zweite italienische Armee in Dalmatien*. Zagreb, 1943.

Wheeler-Bennett, John W. *King George VI: His Life and Reign*. London and New York, 1952.

Wilson, Henry Maitland. *Eight Years Overseas*. London, 1950.

Winant, John G. *A Letter from Grosvenor Square*. London and Boston, 1947.

Woodhouse, C. M. *Apple of Discord*. London, 1948.

Woodward, Llewellyn. *British Foreign Policy in the Second World War*. London, 1962.

Zanussi, G. *Guerra e catastrofe d'Italia*. Rome, 1945.

NEWSPAPERS AND PERIODICALS

Demokratije, Belgrade

The Digest, London

Drina, Valencia, Spain

Epoca, Milan

Le Figaro, Paris

The Geographical Journal, London

Glas Kanadskih Srba, Windsor, Ontario

Hrvatska Revija, Buenos Aires

Hrvatski Glas, Winnipeg, Manitoba

International Affairs, London

Journal of Central European Affairs, Boulder, Colorado

The Listener, London

The Manchester Guardian

Naša Reč, London

The New York Herald Tribune, European edition

The New York Times

The New York Times Magazine

News Review, London

Njegoš, Chicago

The Observer, London
Politika, Belgrade
Le Populaire, Paris
Poruka, London
The Review of Politics, Notre Dame, Indiana
The Saturday Evening Post, Philadelphia
Schriftenreihe der Vierteljahrshefte für Zeitgeschichte, Stuttgart

The Spectator, London
The Sunday Pictorial, London
The Sunday Times Weekly Review, London
Time and Tide, London
The Times, London
The Times Literary Supplement, London
The XIX Century, London
Yugoslavia, London

Alsop, Stewart. "Cloak and Dagger." The New York Herald Tribune, European edition, 4 May 1948.

Brosat, Ladislas Hory-Martin. "Der kroatische Ustasha-Staat 1941–1944." Schriftenreihe der Vierteljahrshefte für Zeitgeschichte, no. 8, 1965.

Cvetković, D. Reply to Radoje Knežević's article concerning Prince Paul, Hitler, and Salonika. International Affairs, October 1951.

Djonović, J. "Telegrami Draže Mihailovića." Njegoš, June 1960.

"The Eastern Question Again." Time and Tide, 29 December 1945.

"German Hopes and Fears." The Digest, 5 March 1945.

"Horthy's Posthumous Self-Slaughter." The Times Literary Supplement, 12 November 1964.

Knežević, Radoje. "Prince Paul, Hitler and Salonika." International Affairs, January 1951.

———. "Slobodan Jovanović." Poruka, January–March 1959.

Kvaternik, Eugen. "Ustaška emigracija u Italiji i 10.iv.1941." Hrvatska Revija, September 1952.

Lippmann, Walter. "The Cruelty of Ignorance." The New York Herald Tribune, European edition, 1 June 1949.

Luburić, Max. "Bitka na Lievče Polju." Drina, February 1955.

Marković, D. "U Vrhovnom Štabu pred veliku ofanzivu." Politika, May 1955.

Mosely, Philip. "Hopes and Failures: American Policy Toward East Central Europe, 1941–1947." The Review of Politics, October 1955.

"Other American Comment." The New York Herald Tribune, European edition, 13 April 1950.

Popović, V. B. "Trojni Pakt i martovski dogadjaji 1941." Politika, 23 February 1961 et seq. (42 articles).

Pundeff, M. "Two Documents on Soviet-Bulgarian Relations." Journal of Central European Affairs, January 1956.

Reale, E. "Avec Jacques Duclos au banc des accusés." Le Figaro, 30 April 1958.

"Resistance Must Hasten Allied Split." The Digest, 27 March 1945.

Sommers, M. "Why Russia Got the Drop on Us." *The Saturday Evening Post*, 8 February 1947.

Toscano, Mario. "Aperti gli archivi segreti." *Epoca*, 27 June 1954.

Woodhouse, C. M. "Prolegomena to a Study of Resistance." *The XIX Century*, February 1949.

Zec, N. "Neprijateljske represalije posle ustanka 1941 u Crnoj Gori." *Njegoš*, June 1960.

Zečević, V. "Od Podgorice do Gradiške." *Njegoš*.

INDEX

Stevenson, R. C. (*cont.*)
237–40, 242, 246, 266, 269, 270,
285, 286
Stojadinović, Milan, 16, 22, 24, 55, 79,
85
Šubašić, Ivan, 90–91, 163, 168, 204,
231–42, 246, 247, 249–51, 253–
56, 264–72, 274, 281, 285–87, 295
Sulzberger, C. L., 145, 146, 285
Šumenković, Ilija, 37, 210, 267
Šutej, Juraj, 90, 91, 111–14, 139–40,
144, 148–50, 155, 180, 187–88,
190–91, 194–97, 199, 200, 202,
204, 205, 231, 272, 281, 285
Szegedin Committee, 30

Teheran agreement (1943), 212–13,
244, 248
Teleki, Paul, 30, 67–68
Terzić, Velimir, 226
Thayer, Charles W., 259
Thompson, George, 88
Tildy, Zoltan, 68
Tito (Josip Broz), 95, 96, 99, 104–
06, 108, 109, 114, 117–24, 128,
138, 140, 142, 146, 149–59, 163,
166, 167, 169, 173–80, 202–03,
205, 207–10, 212–15, 217–19,
221–27, 229–33, 235–44, 246–
47, 249–60, 264–66, 268–74, 277,
280, 284–90, 292–97
Tobruk, 38
Todorović, Boško, 125
Todorović, Žarko, 125
Todt, Fritz, 175
Todt Organization, 175
Toland, John, 275–76
Tolbukhin, Marshal Fyodor, 252
Tomašić, Lujo, 228, 229, 231, 278
Topalović, Živko, 152, 237, 239, 241
Transylvania, 21
Travnik, 76, 277
Trevor-Roper, Hugh, 7–8
Trieste, 227, 258, 279, 280, 288–89,
295
Trifunović, Miloš, 133, 144, 169, 179,
186–88, 192, 195, 197, 198, 202,
294

Tripartite Pact, 25, 27, 29, 31–32, 43–
45, 47–48, 50–54, 57–60, 62, 78,
83–85, 140, 144
Truman, Harry S., 285, 286, 289
Tupanjanin, Miloš, 60
Turkey, 20, 26, 27, 31–33, 36, 39–42,
46, 48, 65, 70, 164, 165, 167, 212
Turks, 9–11

United Nations, 131, 171, 295
Urija, 5–6
Ustashi, 4–5, 7, 13, 90, 93, 94, 96–
104, 111, 113, 114, 124–27, 141,
142, 144–45, 148, 150, 151, 162,
163, 229–30, 236, 249, 275, 277–81,
283, 284, 291
Užice, 108, 109
Užička Požega, 108

Valona, 63
Vasić, Dragiša, 129, 155, 279
Vauhnik, Vladimir, 128–29
Veesenmayer, Edmund, 75
Velebit, Vladimir, 174–76, 222, 240,
264
Venizelos, Eleutherios, 22
Victor Emmanuel, king of Italy, 76
Vilder, Većeslav, 141, 149, 169, 192,
195–97, 202, 205
Vis, 209, 236, 237, 254, 256, 258
Vlaić, Božidar, 169, 192, 195, 196,
205
Vojvodina, 10
Vokić, A., 250, 278
Volkov (assistant Soviet minister),
206
Vrhunec (Slovenian economist), 128,
129
Vrnjačka Banja, 70
Vukčević, Alexander, 72
Vukmanović-Tempo, Svetozar, 278
Vyshinsky, Andrei, 34

Warlimont, Walter, 158, 177
Wavell, Archibald, 36–39
Weizsäcker, Ernst von, 175
Welles, Sumner, 57, 132
Wilmot, Chester, 254

314